A TROUBLED SEE

*In respectful memory of Hugh Mullan and Noel Fitzpatrick
and my brother priests and bishops who endeavoured to serve their people
faithfully during the thirty years of conflict in Northern Ireland.*

A Troubled See

Memoirs of a Derry Bishop

EDWARD DALY

FOUR COURTS PRESS

Set in 10.5 pt on 14 pt Janson Text for
FOUR COURTS PRESS LTD
7 Malpas Street, Dublin 8, Ireland
www.fourcourtspress.ie
and in North America for
FOUR COURTS PRESS
c/o ISBS, 920 N.E. 58th Avenue, Suite 300, Portland, OR 97213.

A catalogue record for this title
is available from the British Library.

ISBN 978-1-84682-312-1

Printed in England
by CPI Group (UK) Ltd, Croydon.

Contents

Illustrations

Preface

This month marks the fifty-fourth anniversary of my ordination to the priesthood. It has all passed so quickly. There were many times during my life, when I looked forward to the benchmark of fifty years; there were other times when I thought that I would never reach it, because of health and other reasons. I have much to thank God for. After surviving thirty years of almost continuous conflict, I have lived to see the peace process develop in Northern Ireland. I have experienced crises in my physical health – a moderate stroke and several other serious illnesses necessitating major surgery.

There was also another type of conflict; a conflict within, periods when my spiritual health was not as it should have been. There were occasions when I was critical of the Church and the value of my priesthood was challenged; times, particularly during the past decade or more, when, like many others, I was painfully demoralised and humiliated by the many dimensions of the clerical child sexual abuse scandals. However, on the whole, I have greatly enjoyed the past fifty-four years. It has been a great privilege and a wonderful experience to have served as a Catholic priest for more than five decades. I have had the opportunity to meet and serve remarkable people, and to witness and experience some extraordinary events. I have also had the opportunity to travel and to preach and to speak and meet with people in different parts of the world and become more conscious of the world-wide family that is the Catholic Church. I have had great friends, colleagues as priests and bishops. Most of all I have been sustained by the prayers and friendship of many lay people, men and women, to whom it has been my privilege to minister.

The Church and priesthood into which I was ordained in 1957 have been transformed. The society here in Ireland in which I now carry out that ministry has changed out of all recognition. The Second Vatican Council brought about many changes and challenges to the Church. The growing influences of secularism and materialism in Western society have had a significant impact. We live in a hugely different world than that in which I began my priesthood.

The Catholic Church in Ireland is less dominant and much more defensive now than it was in the 1950s. There are not as many people attending Mass or affiliated as regular members. However, it is, in many ways, a much healthier Church than it was. I feel that the Church is at its best when it is in a minority in the society in which it finds itself, when it is powerless rather than powerful. For this reason, I was always glad that I served for almost all of my life in Northern Ireland where the Catholic community is a minority community, a community often under pressure. There is a core here, a leaven of believers, who are wonderful.

Ireland has been transformed in the last half-century. The Republic of Ireland has gone almost full circle from economic depression to boom and back again. In the last decade, the people of the Republic of Ireland experienced unprecedented prosperity, the emigration exodus all but dried up, and there was almost full employment and huge numbers of immigrants were flooding into Ireland. Now the situation has been almost completely reversed.

Here in Northern Ireland, the changes have been different in nature and in pace. We have never experienced an economic boom. The conflict that engulfed our society here has ended and we are struggling painfully to reconcile past differences and catch up on the economic and social developments that took place in the rest of the island and in the rest of Europe whilst we were busily engaged in fruitless war. Political dialogue has now thankfully taken precedence over violent confrontation. The peace process has taken root.

Like Gaul, my fifty years of ministry was divided into three parts. There were seventeen years of parish ministry as a curate in Castlederg and Derry, almost twenty years of ministry as a bishop and seventeen years of ministry in the Foyle Hospice, where I still serve as chaplain. The three ministries were contrasting and quite different from one another. It made for a very interesting and challenging life. The only certainty about Catholic priesthood is that one is never quite sure of what lies ahead.

I have already written about my years of parish ministry.* I worked for a short period with RTÉ in Dublin in late 1973 and early 1974, and in February 1974 I was appointed as Bishop of Derry.

I have tried to describe in this book some of my experiences as a Catholic bishop in Northern Ireland during a period of conflict in the 1970s, 1980s and early 1990s. I have written only about matters in which I had a significant and direct involvement. What I write is subjective, about events and situations as I saw them. However, I accept that other people may have perceived things differently. I have learned that it is unreliable to depend too much on memory. Much of the writing is based on written archive material. I believe that it is better and more reliable to refer to contemporary recorded sources.

I dedicate this book to my brother priests and bishops who endeavoured to serve their people faithfully during thirty years of conflict in Northern Ireland. Particularly remembered are Father Hugh Mullan and Father Noel Fitzpatrick. Both were priests of the diocese of Down and Connor. Hugh Mullan was shot dead on 9 August 1971. Noel Fitzpatrick was shot dead on 9 July 1972. Both were shot dead by the British Army. Both lost their lives while endeavouring to minister to wounded people in Belfast during gun battles. Many other priests had terrifying experiences, fortuitous escapes and suffered considerable intimidation in the course of their duty. Their work should not be forgotten. This book is a tribute to them.

After I retired as bishop in late 1993, I was hugely blessed to experience a new ministry in the Foyle Hospice in Derry, where I still serve as chaplain. The Foyle Hospice provides ongoing palliative care for patients with cancer and other life-limiting illnesses, while supporting their families and loved ones. Hospice ministry is hugely fulfilling and challenging. There is an opportunity to meet with people of all ages and backgrounds at an extremely difficult and

---

* Edward Daly, *Mister, Are You a Priest?* (Four Courts Press, Dublin, 2000).

defining time in their lives. There is an opportunity to share a spiritual journey with each patient, in a deeply personal way, day by day. There is an opportunity to see at close-up the Lord at work in 'those who labour and are overburdened'. A hospice is such a tranquil place, a place of peace, dignity and quiet. It is a unique perspective from which to view life and faith and has had an immeasurable impact on me. I have never felt more fulfilled as a priest.

When a person is elderly, as I now am, there is the tendency to look back at one's life and to review that life critically. People nearing the end of their life feel the need to talk or write about their hopes and joys, disappointments and sorrows. For much of our lives, we are so busy dealing with day-to-day issues that there is little time to reflect and look at the bigger picture. In retirement, there is more time to read, to reflect and to pray. There is also time to stand back a little and write down and express views that, perhaps, should have been written or said years earlier when there was neither enough time to think about them or enough courage to write about them. For someone like me, there is also time and space to look at the Church that I dearly love and address various issues. I have tried to do that in this book. I hope that it is written in a constructive spirit of friendship and charity. I thank God for an interesting life and a fascinating journey.

I am an enthusiastic and very happy priest. I have to admit, however, that I was a somewhat reluctant bishop.

March 2011

CHAPTER I

Becoming a Bishop

The second phase of my priestly ministry began on Sunday, 31 March 1974.

I had never before been present at the ordination of a bishop. In the years prior to the Second Vatican Council, this ceremony was called an episcopal consecration. Subsequent to the Council, the liturgy of the ceremony underwent a considerable review, as did the understanding of the ministry of bishops. As a result, the ceremony came to be described, more accurately, as an episcopal ordination. Just a year before my episcopal ordination, in the spring of 1973, the Holy See issued a Directory on the Pastoral Ministry of Bishops. This Directory addressed the various contemporary needs of the Church in the wake of the Council and suggested ways in which bishops should respond to them. When I was in Rome preparing for my episcopal ordination, I was given an English translation of this document by Archbishop Benelli.* This document was helpful as I tried to comprehend what my new responsibilities were and as I grappled initially with the exercise of my ministry as a bishop.

My episcopal ordination took place in St Eugene's Cathedral in Derry. I had just turned forty and I became the youngest bishop in Ireland and one of the youngest bishops in Europe at the time. The principal celebrant was Cardinal William Conway, Archbishop of Armagh. The Papal Nuncio to Ireland, Archbishop Gaetano Alibrandi, and my predecessor, Bishop Neil Farren, assisted him. Bishops from various parts of Ireland joined them. Lay men and women, chosen by ballot from every parish in the diocese, formed

---

* Archbishop Benelli was Sostituto (Deputy) Secretary of State, in the Holy See at that time in 1974. In 1977, he was appointed as Archbishop of Florence. In the same year, he was created Cardinal.

the main body of the congregation. Almost all the priests of the diocese were present as were many religious sisters and brothers. Bishop Cuthbert Peacocke, Church of Ireland Bishop of Derry and Raphoe, was there with his wife, along with representatives of the other Christian Churches. Most of my classmates from the Irish College in Rome were present. My mother and family and a large number of relatives, including my nephews and nieces, took part. Friends and classmates from my home town of Belleek attended. Former parishioners from Castlederg and colleagues from RTÉ were there, as well as people whom I served in the Bogside in St Eugene's parish. John Hume and his wife, Pat, and public representatives from local government, the Northern Ireland Assembly and Dáil Éireann, joined the newly elected SDLP Mayor of Derry, Dr Raymond McClean, in the congregation. Three choirs, St Eugene's Cathedral Choir, the Foyle Singers and the Colmcille Ladies Choir sang various parts of the Mass. The congregation represented all the aspects and interests of my life.

The Bogside had been cleaned up. There were flags and bunting everywhere. To my embarrassment, there were even banners and flags carrying my picture hanging from some windows. The Provisional IRA and the British Army observed an unofficial truce for the day. There were no visible patrols. Large crowds of local people had assembled in the cathedral grounds before the ceremony began. It was a cold, dry and crisp sunny day.

The morning was spent greeting my mother and family and relatives who had travelled to Derry for the occasion. I joined the visiting bishops for lunch in Bishop's House. I had met only a few of the Irish bishops prior to this occasion. They were, without exception, extremely kind and encouraging. I left the lunch after the main course to have a little while alone before the ceremony. I spent this time in the oratory in Bishop's House. Then I prepared for the ceremony. I walked out of Bishop's House and I was overwhelmed by the crowds in the cathedral grounds who greeted me. I do not recall being nervous at this stage. I was certainly excited. The warmth of the love and support that surrounded me buoyed me up.

St Eugene's Cathedral, which has been the scene of so many happy and sad experiences in my life, was a beautiful setting. The century-old Gothic cathedral, opened in 1873, looked magnificent. It was just the fifth occasion that an episcopal ordination had taken place there. A fisherman from Greencastle and a shirt factory worker from Derry City were among those taking part in the Offertory Procession. Father Bernard Kielt, whom I had already appointed as my Vicar General, preached an eloquent homily. I still remember one striking phrase from that homily that caused a chuckle from the congregation. He urged me memorably to use my crosier 'more as a weapon of defence rather than as a weapon of attack'. Cardinal Conway spoke a few words of support and encouragement. Towards the end of the ceremony I addressed the congregation for a short time, welcoming and thanking all those who were there and asking the prayers of everyone for me in the ministry on which I was embarking. After the ceremony, I emerged into the sunlight to be greeted by huge crowds of people who had assembled outside. It was a humbling experience and not a little daunting. It was the moment when the full realisation dawned of the expectations that people had placed in me. Until then, I had not been nervous. At that moment, I became very fearful and apprehensive of what might lie ahead.

I subsequently joined the guests for a buffet reception in St Columb's College. This was a mammoth affair of organisation. Then, in the late evening, about ten o'clock, when most of my family and the more prominent guests had left, I decided to set off on foot on an unplanned visit around the Bogside, the district that I had in my pastoral care when I served as curate. It was a spur-of-the-moment decision. Some of my former classmates from the Irish College in Rome had expressed a wish to visit the Bogside area and I invited them to accompany me. Meeting all the old familiar faces and friends once again was the occasion for many tears and laughs and stories. I walked around Glenfada Park, Abbey Park and the three different levels of the famous and familiar multi-storey Rossville Flats, Garvan Place, Mura Place and Donagh Place and the other streets and areas where so many momentous events had occurred, events that changed and shaped my priestly ministry and my life. I visited many of the homes of the elderly and housebound whom I had visited and attended during the previous twelve years and enjoyed endless cups of tea. Crowds of young people followed me around the area and joined in the atmosphere of celebration. It was 2 a.m. when we got back to St Eugene's.

During the following week, I walked around most of the residential streets and estates in the parishes of Derry City, meeting the people and visiting the sick and housebound. On each of the evenings, I celebrated Mass in the parish church of the area I was visiting. I began in St Eugene's on Monday evening, the Long Tower on Tuesday, Creggan on Wednesday and Pennyburn on Thursday. On Friday, I returned to visit Castlederg in County Tyrone where I had served as a curate. The weather was splendid for all of that week, which added to the enjoyment of these visits. It took some time to become accustomed to the enthusiasm of the people's welcome. People grabbed my hand; many wished to kiss the episcopal ring, a practice that I found somewhat embarrassing. Much as I would try to withdraw my hand, they would persist. By the end of the first week, the fingers around the unaccustomed ring were a mass of blisters and raw flesh!

In my first Mass in St Eugene's Cathedral, I set out my position as regards violence and my response to it. In the course of my homily on that Monday evening, I said

> After any event in the North of Ireland in recent years, the media has often approached bishops and others for an 'instant comment' or condemnation. It is a pity that condemnation has to be predominant. How much more positive a bishop would feel if he could, in most statements, compliment people on their Christian beliefs and practice. There is also the dilemma in which a bishop finds himself when called upon to comment. This is the fact that he has more responsibility to guide his own flock than to guide others. Not all acts of an unchristian kind have been perpetrated here in Derry by people who were baptised in the Catholic faith … not all acts of an unchristian nature have been perpetrated by Derry people … but far too many of them could be classed in this category. Does one comment on every incident or just a chosen few? It is my hope that, in my episcopate, incidents that demand condemnation will decrease rapidly and soon disappear. I think, by now,

everyone is familiar with the Church's stand regarding the use of violence to achieve political objectives. That is how I stand. I deplore the use of violence of any kind by anyone. Too many people have suffered, too many have been bereaved, and too many have been imprisoned. Surely it must be clear to everyone by now that violence creates far more problems than it can ever hope to solve.*

In practice, over the years, this policy proved to be even more difficult to implement than I had anticipated.

In the course of that week, I preached and celebrated Mass in the other three Catholic churches on the west bank of the city, setting out my pastoral priorities and my understanding of my role to the people. I have particular affection for the Long Tower church in Derry. It is dedicated to St Columba, the patron saint of Derry. The Long Tower is a huge and beautiful church, full of symbolism and significance; it resonates with the monastic past and the long and colourful history of a great city. The heart of Catholic Derry beats there. The Long Tower welcome was particularly warm. And then there was Creggan, the most populous parish in the diocese at that time with a teeming population of young people. The funeral of the Bloody Sunday victims, etched indelibly on the city's memory and my own memory, had taken place there in St Mary's church. The community in Creggan had already suffered greatly in the conflict and was to suffer more in subsequent years. Again I was warmly received by huge crowds of people. Whilst the experience was most affirming, I was quite overcome and not a little frightened by the welcome I received everywhere. People's expectations were so high. I felt more and more inadequate.

On the following evening, I visited Pennyburn – embracing a whole new developing area of the city – hundreds of houses were being built in the Carnhill and Shantallow areas of the parish – green field sites – and it was quite clear that one of the immediate challenges would be providing pastoral care for the hundreds of families who were moving to those new areas of the city. I walked

---

* Derry Diocesan Archive.

around most of those areas during my visit to Pennyburn parish, then under the dynamic pastoral care of my friend and former fellow curate, Father Tony Mulvey.

On the Friday night in Castlederg, I sympathised with people there who had lost their homes and businesses as a result of IRA bombing. When I was a curate there in the late 1950s, Castlederg had been a rather sleepy and relaxed place. There were sectarian tensions under the surface but they were held in check, to a large extent. In the intervening years, more people had come to live in the town and a lot of new houses had been built. In the early 1970s, sectarianism had raised its ugly head, and, by 1974, Castlederg had sadly become a polarised and much less happy and carefree place. However, it was wonderful to meet so many old friends once again. These people had taught me so much about priesthood in the years immediately after my ordination.

I also went to my home town of Belleek and celebrated Mass and met the people among whom I had grown up. This visit provided an opportunity to recall my childhood, my parents and family, my wonderful neighbours and my early education and formation. St Patrick's church in Belleek was where I was baptised, received my First Holy Communion, was confirmed and ordained to the priesthood – a very special place for me.

During my first week as bishop, I experienced a honeymoon period. There were scarcely any bombs or shootings during that week in the city or diocese. Everything was very positive. All was love and smiles and laughter.

But like all honeymoons, this did not last for long.

The Provisional IRA and the British Army got back to their normal activities, and suddenly, I found myself back living and ministering in the real world. This was to be my world for most of the next twenty years.

CHAPTER 2

Finding My Bearings

A bishop in the modern Catholic Church is expected to have a multitude of abilities. He is expected to be a prayerful, learned man with good judgment. He is expected to be a leader and to have considerable management skills, both in people management and in administration. He is expected to be a pastoral leader for his people and his clergy. His primary mission is to preach the Gospel to his people. He is expected to be a good communicator, able to express himself effectively and convincingly in all the different aspects of media – newspapers, radio and television. To all these skills there must be added in latter years an understanding of the internet and all the associated information and communication technologies. He must be able to delegate. A person with all of those skills and qualities is extremely rare. There are no advertisements in the newspaper for the position. When a priest is appointed as bishop, in the normal course of events, he has little preparation. He may have been teaching, ministering in a parish or engaged in some form of administration – and suddenly he is expected to have all the requisite skills in a matter of weeks. Few people who are appointed as bishop have an inkling that such an appointment is coming. Few priests, in full possession of their senses, would actively seek appointment as bishop in the Church today! A bishop's responsibility is particularly difficult – even more difficult now than it was thirty-seven years ago in a less turbulent Church and world in 1974.

Thinking back on my appointment, I often wondered if there were priests who refused to accept appointment as bishops. I am sure there were. I have heard rumours of such refusals, but I was never given substantial evidence that anyone refused. My own experience was that the appointee is given very little time to make up his mind about such a radical life-changing appointment – a few short minutes! There is no apprenticeship. You have to hit the ground running. I had six years to make my decision to accept ordination as a priest – just a few minutes to make up my mind about accepting appointment as a bishop. I recall that despite being shattered by the request to accept the appointment, I simply accepted it on the basis of obedience. It did not enter my mind that it could have been refused! I presume that most priests who are asked to accept appointment as bishop act in a similar manner – on the principle that a priest, by virtue of his ordination, does what he is asked to do by his superiors.

Then there were the challenges about understanding precisely one's responsibility as a bishop. I had never, previously, considered myself as a likely bishop, and had not given a moment's thought to such a responsibility. Suddenly, I had to embark on the steepest of learning curves and place huge dependence on the prayers, understanding and support of my colleagues in the priesthood and the people whom I was destined to serve. I am sure that every newly appointed bishop undergoes similar experiences. I have been told that the Holy See now organises an induction course for newly appointed bishops. That is a positive development, although I wonder how a satisfactory training package can be devised for bishops for so many different social, pastoral, cultural and political situations in various parts of the world.

During my first weeks as bishop, I began to get a vague understanding of what my new responsibilities as Bishop of Derry would involve. Apart from what I had read in the Pastoral Directory given me by Archbishop Benelli, I had little idea of what those responsibilities entailed. Cardinal Conway gave me a general overview for a few hours during a meeting in Armagh on the Sunday after my appointment was announced in February 1974. There was no formal handover or exchange of information or briefing with my predecessor. Bishop Neil Farren left Bishop's House just a few days before my episcopal ordination and wished me well. He was almost 80 years old, exhausted after thirty-five years in office, bewildered and worn out by the conflict and mayhem that had engulfed the North over the previous four or five years. His first five years as bishop were served during the Second World War, a very difficult time in Derry. It is no wonder that he was exhausted. He assured me that he would be available to me if I thought he could be of any assistance. He made such advice available to me on a number of occasions and he gave me regular encouragement and affirmation until his death in May 1980. I picked up advice on my general responsibilities informally from Church documents and Canon Law and from other bishops and priests and what I perceived myself to be my duty. In fact, there was no shortage of advice from a few priests and some members of the laity. One of the first letters that I received a few days before my episcopal ordination came from a diocesan priest who was less than impressed with my appointment. He was very critical and urged me not to get delusions of grandeur or to get above myself. I respected his sincerity. It is always healthy for a bishop or anyone in a leadership position to be told what people truly believe rather than what they think he wants to hear. This correspondent and I subsequently became reasonably good friends and, for years afterwards, he provided a reliable sounding board for me. However, almost all of the many messages I received in those early weeks were positive. They came from both lay people and priests and offered warm support. People appreciated just how much I needed their prayers and understanding.

I perceived my first responsibility to be that of preaching God's Word and the teaching of the Church – to proclaim and explain this teaching to those in my pastoral care to the best of my ability – to apply God's Word and the teaching of the Church to the situations in which people found themselves at that time. I also had responsibility to delegate this authority to parish level through the diocesan clergy. I am neither a learned theologian nor a very gifted preacher, but I have never preached without careful preparation. My months in RTÉ immediately before my episcopal ordination taught me techniques about communication and presentation that I have found useful throughout my life. During my episcopacy, I have used those techniques to the best of my ability. I have a full copy, either a hard copy or electronic copy, of every sermon that I have preached since 1974.

I believed that I had two major responsibilities – the spiritual welfare and leadership of the lay people of the diocese and the spiritual and physical welfare of the priests and religious who served in the diocese. I always perceived myself as a servant rather than a ruler, serving the people and priests of the Derry diocese.

There were other responsibilities that were unfamiliar territory for me. I had some previous experience of administration in a minor capacity, but nothing of this magnitude. The appointment of clergy, the care of retired and sick priests, the choice of students to study for the diocesan priesthood, the management of diocesan finances and properties were among these responsibilities. Within a month, I became aware that the diocese had no significant reserve funds or investments and was being run on a shoestring, largely financed by current income. The late Archbishop Dermot Ryan of Dublin gave me a very good piece of advice on the day of my episcopal ordination. He advised me to find some lay person who was a skilled administrator and appoint him/her as my personal assistant or secretary. I took his advice and ultimately Colette Hynes, secretary in a local school, was appointed to this position. She remained in that position for all of the twenty years I served as bishop and I owe her a huge debt. She was a superb administrator. In the United States and some other places, there is a huge administrative structure with a large staff that runs each diocese. It is known as a chancery and in the larger cities occupies a whole street block and has a large staff – a little like the civil service in a government: politicians come and go but the civil servants are there forever – bishops come and go and may decide on policies but the day-to-day administration is largely carried out by the chancery staff. This does not happen in most dioceses in Ireland, as far as I know. It was certainly not the situation in Derry; the bishop was the sole administrator. In addition to Colette Hynes, I had a housekeeper who looked after the domestic chores and acted as receptionist. During most of my twenty years, I appointed a priest to act as diocesan secretary: his main responsibilities were to plan, prepare and act as master of ceremonies of all the liturgies I took part in around the diocese; he accompanied me and drove me to various ceremonies and engagements around the diocese. He also helped the priests in St Eugene's parish. Our 'chancery' consisted of three people, Colette Hynes who served as administrator/personal secretary; Maggie Doherty, who was housekeeper, cook, cleaner, laundress and receptionist and, finally the priest, diocesan secretary, who covered the responsibilities listed above. We got on very well. We were a good and efficient team, and we all lived or worked out of Bishop's House, which was, in fact, an apartment attached to the priests' house at St Eugene's Cathedral. I lived in the apartment. There was not even a guestroom. The facilities were very restricted, basic and limited and very draughty and cold in winter! The living conditions were Spartan. I was amused when people addressed letters to 'The Bishop's Palace'! Some palace!

In 1974, the bishop was, by virtue of office, a member of many bodies – among them various diocesan committees and Boards of Governors for five large schools around the diocese. These entailed many meetings. Unfortunately, I have a profound aversion to meetings! Countless individuals and groups sought appointments and asked to meet me about various issues. There was voluminous correspondence. I wrote hundreds and hundreds of personal letters a year during my years as bishop, answering all personal letters by myself. Initially, I wrote letters and homilies on a little Olivetti portable typewriter, then on an electric typewriter, and then, thanks to advances in technology, from about 1980 onwards I wrote everything on a computer. The computer was a godsend. Because of my almost illegible handwriting, I had to type everything. I owe a huge debt to Bill Gates!

Derry, because of the political conflict, was the focus of much media attention during my time as bishop. I believed and still believe that anyone in the business of proclaiming God's word should look upon the media as a necessary and beneficial tool in this mission. Therefore, as far as possible, whilst serving as bishop, I made myself available to the media. I cultivated and built up relationships with people in the ever-developing local print and broadcast media during those years and facilitated them as far as possible. We respected one another and could talk on and off the record about various issues. We had a meal together from time to time when we spoke candidly. I can say that my confidence in them was never betrayed. Irish and British national media and international journalists and broadcasters from all over the world were also facilitated. Many young reporters cut their journalistic teeth in places like

Derry and some of them subsequently became celebrated journalists covering stories all over the world. I had first met and had been interviewed by many of these people on the streets of the Bogside during the previous few years. I came to know many of these men and women very well and I am still in contact with some of them socially after all these years. Occasionally, special writers for various publications would come to Derry. One of these was the novelist, Graham Greene, in the summer of 1976. He was preparing an article for a weekend supplement for some Fleet Street newspaper. To the best of my knowledge, the article was never published. Generally speaking, I always felt that I got fair treatment in the media, although there were times when I was frustrated and infuriated by what was printed or broadcast about the Church. It is extremely difficult to give a comprehensive and coherent comment or explain a fluid and charged situation effectively to the media, without being seen to be partial or partisan. The borderline between religion and politics is also very blurred at times in Ireland, more, perhaps, than in other parts of the world. Misunderstandings and misperceptions are unavoidable. It is also challenging and difficult to explain a faith-motivated response to a journalist who is a committed unbeliever or someone who has an axe to grind about religious faith and particularly about Catholicism. Some such people are also evangelists of a kind who like everyone to dance to their own tune. Somebody once said that there is nobody more dogmatic than a liberal in full flight!

To further complicate matters, the diocese of Derry straddles the border between the Republic of Ireland and Northern Ireland. In 1974, about one fifth of the diocesan population lived in County Donegal, in the Republic. There were two different educational administrations, two different civil legislations, two different currencies, two different health services, two different social security and pension schemes and two different tax regimes among other things to cope with. There were also two very different governments – Stormont with its various short-lived Assemblies and its Direct Rule ministers from Westminster and Dublin with its sovereign government. All of these things were completely new to me. Before my appointment as bishop, they did not intrude on my life all that much.

Over those first weeks and months, I gradually became more and more aware of my diocesan responsibilities. What I had not been immediately aware of were the national responsibilities that I had to accept as a member of the Irish Episcopal Conference. I was about to be introduced to a whole range of other responsibilities that I had never anticipated.

The Irish Episcopal Conference (IEC) is the body or association of Catholic Bishops in Ireland. Some people continue to write about 'the Hierarchy', especially when they have some negative comment about the Church, which is more often than not. The term 'Hierarchy' disappeared with the Second Vatican Council and the Catholic Bishops' corporate body here in Ireland has been formally known as the Irish Episcopal Conference (IEC) since the 1960s. The IEC is an all-Ireland body; it incorporates all the Catholic Bishops in Ireland, North and South.

There is also a regional body of bishops covering the metropolitan area of Armagh, consisting of nine dioceses. Several times a year, or when subjects of mutual interest had to be discussed, the bishops of the dioceses that made up Northern Ireland came together. This group was known as 'the Northern Bishops'.

These groupings and associations – diocesan, national and regional – generated a huge number of meetings and much travel.

CHAPTER 3

People, Priests and Parishes

It was parish pastoral ministry that attracted me to priesthood in the first place. I loved pastoral ministry and I still love it after experiencing it for a large part of my service in priesthood. I was initially concerned that my duties as bishop might confine me to an office in Derry or the cathedral and that my time would be gobbled up in administration and meetings. To ensure that this would not be the case, I decided to embark on a plan of parish visitation that would enable me to get around the fifty-two parishes of the diocese in a systematic manner. This programme would enable me to work more closely with the laity and clergy in each parish of the diocese and help me to get to know and listen to the people throughout the diocese.

Until my appointment as bishop, I served as a priest in two parishes, Castlederg in West Tyrone and in St Eugene's Cathedral parish in Derry City. I was not very familiar with the parishes in other areas of the diocese such as Inishowen in County Donegal and most of County Derry, especially South Derry. In fact, there were a number of parishes where I had never been in my life. Three months after my appointment as bishop, I began this programme of visitation to the parishes of the diocese. I began the programme on a lovely summer weekend in June 1974 in the parish of Cappagh in County Tyrone, an extensive parish that comprises part of the town of Omagh and much of the area surrounding the town. I lived in each parish for three or four days, Sunday to Wednesday, usually staying overnight with the parish priest in the parochial house. I celebrated Mass and preached in each of the churches in the parish – in many cases it was the first time in many years that the diocesan bishop had celebrated Mass in the outlying churches. I visited each classroom in each primary school, meeting the children and each teacher individually. I celebrated Mass in each second level school, and met the senior pupils and staff at separate meetings. I met all the parish groups, such as the parish council, St Vincent de Paul Society, Legion of Mary, Scouts, Guides, local sporting and community organisations. I visited the shop floors of factories and industries in the parish. I visited hospitals and homes for the elderly. I met the religious sisters and brothers in the parish and celebrated Mass in their houses. In many places, I met the clergy of other denominations who served in the area. I baptised the children who were due to be baptised that weekend and I introduced and officiated at a ceremony of the Blessing of the Graves in one of the parish cemeteries on the Sunday afternoon. I visited the sick and housebound in their own homes and had a Mass on one of the evenings during which I administered the Sacrament of the Sick. The visitation of the sick and elderly in their own homes brought me into virtually every townland and street in the diocese and up and down lanes and boreens and facilitated me in meeting tens of thousands of people, young and old, where they were living. It was a good experience. I managed to get around the entire diocese three times in sixteen years. Each cycle of parish visits took about five years to complete. I regard this as the highlight and the most important activity of my episcopal ministry. It enabled me to get to know the priests and people of the diocese and to meet them on their own ground, in their homes and places of work and recreation.

I met some wonderful people in the course of these visits and they made a lasting impact on me. These were people who served the needs of their parish – quietly beavering away without fuss or notice doing valuable work in their communities in an unselfish manner. Some worked with young people, others with the elderly or those living alone, and many worked with those who were deprived in some way. I met sons and daughters in isolated rural homes looking after elderly parents – women struggling to bring up children on their own – parents coping with a child or children with special needs, parents in difficult urban areas struggling to keep their children out of trouble – travellers in their encampments. I was hugely impressed by the work of the GAA in many rural areas, their care and leadership for youth and their consciousness of community and

sense of parish. There were still, in 1974, homes in some rural areas
of the diocese that had no electricity. And, in many parishes, there
were victims of the Northern conflict trying to cope with huge difficulties – death, injury, destruction, imprisonment, internment and
intimidation, loss of business or work. The visitation of the parishes
gave me a new and broader insight into the sheer magnitude and
extent of the suffering people had experienced as a result of our conflict. I had been familiar with the urban victims of the conflict – now
I had an opportunity to meet the rural victims, and there were many
such people. The conflict in the rural areas was different in nature
and, perhaps, more frightening than that in urban areas. On occasions, neighbour felt threatened by neighbour. Some people felt very
exposed and vulnerable.

The conflict regularly impinged on the pastoral visitation. In
many parts of the North, there were ubiquitous checkpoints at that
time, and they were quite daunting, especially if manned by the
Ulster Defence Regiment (UDR).* These checkpoints were set up
at random. Travelling home by car late at night after visitation or
Confirmation, a red light being waved on a country road generated
fear and apprehension. In the darkness, one could not see who was
behind the waving red light. As you approached, you peered anx-
iously and fearfully through the gloom at the shadowy figures manning the checkpoint. They could be the RUC, British Army or
UDR; they could be Loyalist or Republican paramilitaries. It could
mean an identity check or a vigorous body search or car search. It
could mean having your car hijacked. And in some cases, if you happened to be the wrong person in the wrong place at the wrong time,
it could mean being the victim of sectarian murder. Until the identity of the person or persons behind the red light became clear, there
were moments of considerable anxiety and intense fear. These were
frequent experiences – at times, one experienced such a checkpoint
on every single journey. My face was well known and I was not the
most popular of individuals among some of those mounting such
checkpoints. On more than one occasion, I was asked to get out of

---

* The Ulster Defence Regiment (UDR) became operational in 1970. The
  UDR replaced the Ulster Special Constabulary ('B-Specials'), and along
  with a separate police reserve, assisted the regular police and army.

the car and forced to undergo a rigorous roadside identity check and a heavy-handed body search. They always asked where I was going. When I was heading for home, I answered 'Derry'. Then I was asked whether I was going to Derry or Londonderry! The mention of the word 'Derry' seemed to fill some of these people, particularly the UDR, with furious anger. Young people told me of the humiliation and terror that they regularly experienced at such checkpoints. I can only imagine how terrified they must have been. I was fortunate in that I never ran into a roadblock manned by Loyalist paramilitaries. I was always more than a little scared and apprehensive whilst travelling at night. However, duties like pastoral visits and Confirmations had to be carried out and many of these entailed late-night travel. I seldom travelled alone on such journeys.

The bomb in the Dropping Well pub in the village of Ballykelly on the night of Monday, 7 December 1982 was one of the bloodiest events of the entire conflict in the North West. Seventeen people were murdered and many more were injured. Some of the victims were soldiers and some were civilians who lived locally. This atrocity was perpetrated by the INLA. I happened to be celebrating Mass in St Finlough's church in Ballykelly just a few hours earlier that evening in the course of parish visitation in Limavady parish. After Mass, I visited sick and elderly people in several homes in the village shortly before the bomb exploded. This dreadful event led to the abandonment of that visitation and I was on the scene of the bomb early the next morning, visited some of the victims' families and subsequently officiated at or attended several of the funerals in our own Church and those of other denominations.

There were frequent bombs and bomb scares and shootings experienced during the course of these visitations. These incidents may have caused diversions and delays and prolonged searches for me but for others, they meant death and destruction and loss of property. It became very difficult to estimate the time it took to complete a relatively simple journey.

On the liturgical front, the pastoral visitation concentrated the minds of priests to a significant extent. Many priests were 'in denial' about the Second Vatican Council and, whilst they had made some effort to reorder the parish church when Bishop Farren had come to officiate at Confirmation, little effort had been made with the other churches in the parish. There was a resultant frantic flurry of work in the weeks and days prior to my visitation. Among many other liturgical reforms, the Vatican Council had decreed that Mass should be celebrated with the celebrant facing the people. In the immediate weeks and days before visitation, altars were turned around and other adjustments were made – some of these were temporary enough to be reversed hours after my departure! Parish Councils were hastily created and all sorts of other bodies and committees came into being. It was easy to identify those bodies or constructions that were in place for some time and those that had been created for the occasion. Nobody was really fooling anybody!

I believed that I should endeavour to do everything possible to implement the various recommendations of the Council throughout the diocese. This would mean involving the laity to an unprecedented extent in the administration of the diocese and parishes, including the establishment of Parish Pastoral Councils and Diocesan Commissions – creating a whole new sense of Church. It also involved making the necessary adjustments to the design of churches and particularly the reorganisation of church sanctuaries. The use of the vernacular in the liturgy had been introduced in the early 1970s, and some church sanctuaries had been tastefully reorganised. It would be accurate to comment that some other beautiful church sanctuaries had been horribly vandalised, rather than reorganised. Apart from these alterations, few of the proposed reforms of Vatican II had been introduced in our diocese. They were radical changes and it was difficult for priests and people to accept them. The philosophy was 'If it's not broken, don't fix it!' Huge crowds were still attending Sunday Mass, attendance at the sacraments was good, there were more vocations to the diocesan priesthood than we could handle, and the Catholic Church in the Derry diocese appeared to be in the very best of health. When I was appointed as bishop, the diocese was able to afford more than twenty priests in full-time teaching and, at the same time, staff every parish generously. Morale amongst the priests was generally high after recovering from the trauma caused by the large number of defections in the early 1970s. Whilst there was political turmoil all around us, the

Church, internally, was experiencing relative tranquillity. The voice of the laity was seldom raised above conversation level.

Various diocesan commissions were set up under my direction, dealing with Liturgy, Catechetics, Vocations, Youth and so on. These bodies, made up of laity, clergy and religious, carried out great work during the ensuing years. There was an excellent marriage education and counselling and support service, CMAC (Catholic Marriage Advisory Council), already in place when I was appointed. It was decided to establish centres for these bodies where they could have permanent meeting places and other resources. We called them pastoral centres. The first of these was set up in Bishop Street in Derry City in 1974. I understand it was the first such centre in Ireland. Subsequently, four other centres were established, one in each deanery of the diocese, in Maghera, Omagh, Strabane and Moville, in the following few years.

Whilst it was possible to do much at diocesan level, it proved much more difficult to implement similar changes and reforms at parish level. Some priests were enthusiastic. Others did not have the appetite for it. The laity, generally, did not show great interest, and prominent among the more vocal laity were those who were quite strongly opposed to changes of any kind. In such circumstances, the more timid priests were tempted to 'keep their heads down'. During the pontificate of Pope Paul VI, there was more enthusiasm and urgency to implement the reforms of Vatican II. However, within a few years of the advent of Pope John Paul II, it seemed to me that there was a notable change in attitude and a perceptible slowing down in implementing these reforms.

In general, the diocese had taken seriously the need to have the Parish Pastoral Councils suggested by the Vatican Council elected by the people. The first elections to Parish Councils around the diocese were satisfactory. The councils did good and valuable work, had considerable influence and were given good respect, although only about 15 per cent of the possible parish electorate bothered to vote. At the next election, a few years later in the late 1970s, there was a much bigger poll. One particular political grouping had obviously decided to get in on the act and to use their votes to good effect. A parish priest commented before he attended his first meeting of the newly elected parish council, that he feared that the majority of the members would be 'wearing balaclavas'! Some Parish Councils survived; many did not. A few Parish Councils did great work and were very successful. Others withered away. The 'balaclavas' were not the only reason for the non-survival of some Parish Councils. If truth be told, some of the clergy were not too enthusiastic about Parish Councils and there was a widespread misunderstanding of their true purpose on the part of both clergy and laity. There was in some cases a degree of mistrust between priests and people; in some cases, an individual or a group of individuals dominated and the others became disillusioned and discouraged. Some of the councils became 'talking shops' dominated by certain individuals. I must accept my share of the responsibility for that. The true role of the Parish Pastoral Council was not properly defined. On the positive side, the few Parish Councils that have survived since those years have made a significant contribution.

It is good that new efforts are now being made by the IEC to define the role of Parish Pastoral Councils and to give them new life. One of the main problems in the 1970s was that people or priests or bishops did not quite understand or agree on a particular role that such Councils might play. A new Formation Manual for Parish Pastoral Councils was launched early in 2011. It deals with the creation and sustaining of a Parish Pastoral Council. It outlines, in great detail, what needs to be done to form, enable and sustain a group of people who will work, with the clergy, to enhance the ministry of the parish. Such a council should always be seen as something positive and a blessing for a parish community rather than as threat to anyone involved.

But, to go back to the parish visitations, the first round of these in the 1974–7 period was extremely enjoyable. Visits to parishes offered a wonderful opportunity to get close to each individual priest in his own parish. For three or four days, we were together. I stayed overnight with them in their parochial houses, prayed the Divine Office with them morning and evening, celebrated Mass with them and shared meals with them. Some of them were initially distinctly uncomfortable and tense. Some were extremely relaxed. All of them, without exception, were extraordinarily kind and hospitable to me.

Some of them wished to talk to me about their life and their ministry. Others did not. I respected their wishes in these matters. I was keenly conscious that quite a number of the parish priests were ordained before I was born; some of them had been my teachers in St Columb's College in Derry. The visitation of the sick in their homes meant that the parish priest or curate drove me around the various areas of the parish. This provided memorable moments, some amusing, others terrifying, especially in the case of one elderly parish priest in a rural area who whizzed across every crossroads and there were many of them, calling 'Beep Beep' but never blew his horn or never slowed down! In the company of another not so elderly parish priest, we got completely lost late at night in the middle of a mountain area in his own parish – much to his embarrassment! We aimlessly and ultimately frantically went up and down bog roads in total darkness for more than an hour. He made me solemnly promise that I would not tell anyone about it! Another hilarious situation occurred in a city parish, when a family dutifully had the front door painted a new colour because 'the bishop was coming to visit'. The parish priest could not find the house because he could not find 'the usual white door'. However, in the main, I was filled with admiration for my colleagues in the priesthood. They were hard-working and committed and were great company.

Parish visitation offered a great opportunity to meet people and priests where they were, in their own place. There were two aspects of parish visitation that were particularly interesting. One of these was the period reserved for people in the parish who wished to see me privately. The second was the public parish meeting. All kinds of pastoral and personal problems came to light in the private meetings with individuals. For me, these confidential meetings were very instructive and provided me with a profound learning experience. A large number of callers came merely for a chat or to discuss some spiritual matter, or just to say 'Hello'. Others came with all kinds of amazing and agonising problems of long duration, problems that they felt unable to discuss with anyone before. And when the bishop was in their own parish, on their own ground, they felt able, for the first time, to discuss it. There was one lady who expressed the hurt about the public excommunication that a close relative had been subjected to thirty years earlier. She was formally and publicly excommunicated in the 1940s for marriage to someone who was not a Catholic. I always remembered that conversation, and I thought about it when demands were made, from time to time during our conflict, for excommunication for members of paramilitary groups. It was a most humbling experience for me. There were problems about mixed marriage and the children of mixed marriage. Some people in these situations in the North at that time suffered considerable pain, from both the Churches, their own families and the community. The subject of family planning in Church teaching was a very frequent and disquieting topic of discussion, especially in the 1970s. Those private meetings with people whilst I was on parish visitation gave me considerable grounds for thought and a further insight into the problems with which people had to cope.

The public meetings initially attracted only a smattering of people, but once people heard that these were serious meetings rather than mere window-dressing, the attendances grew. All manner of people were welcome at these meetings – members of the parish council, Church workers, members of lay apostolic bodies like St Vincent de Paul Society, Youth Workers, GAA and other sporting bodies, community workers of various kinds and so on. Often these meetings were heated and extremely frank. A few of the parish priests were concerned and anxious about such meetings – one parish priest even called it 'a supergrass meeting'! We discussed the needs of the parish and community – social needs, pastoral needs, economic needs. The pastoral care of young people was always high on the agenda. 'We have nothing here for young people' was a constant cry. These meetings provided me with an opportunity to discuss issues that could not be dealt with satisfactorily in the context of a sermon and also an occasion to hear feedback or criticism, positive or negative, from the participants. It was an opportunity to listen to people. I used it as a means to encourage people to take more active interest and real involvement in their parish and its life and to explain to them the responsibilities of laity to their parish and to the Church, especially in light of the Second Vatican Council. Appreciation of the ministry of their local priest was frequently expressed, as well as appeals not to transfer their parish priest or curate. I attended a parish meeting in each parish during the course of each visitation. It usually took place on the last evening of the visit. The agenda was open and the meetings lasted from one to three hours. I learnt much about the diocese from these meetings.

The teachers in the schools, especially the teachers in primary or national schools, made a profound impression on me. I managed to visit every primary teacher in the diocese and every primary classroom at least twice during my term of office. The importance of the work carried out by teachers can never be over-estimated. During all of my years as bishop, the North was convulsed in conflict. The schools were havens of tranquillity during all that time. The breakdown of social and family life was also developing apace. Teachers provided a point of reference and constancy for children whilst mayhem was going on all around. I was filled with admiration for them and the work that they did.

There are two villages in our diocese where all the Catholic and Protestant children have always attended the one primary school. These villages are Sion Mills in County Tyrone and Ballykelly in County Derry. Sion Mills primary school was established by the Herdman family who built and owned the huge Victorian spinning mill in the village. The mill is now, sadly, closed. The village was built in the nineteenth century around the mill and all the children traditionally went to the one school, the mill school. The school in Ballykelly had a third dimension. As well as local Protestant and Catholic children, children of British service personnel also attended this school in quite large numbers. There was a huge army base, barracks and married quarters in and around Ballykelly. From the Second World War to 1970, it was an RAF base and airfield. After 1970, it became a major base for the British Army. Whilst these schools were always integrated, there was never any hue and cry about them. I visited both schools on my visitation on several occasions. They were fine schools. The religious instruction in both was superb. However, I do not go along with the theory that integrated education would make a significant contribution to the solution of our political problems in the way that some people claim. It was interesting that, in the wider community of both these small villages, there existed similar political and sectarian problems to those that existed everywhere else in Northern Ireland. I am a firm believer in the value of faith schools. I am convinced that our education system will be the poorer if such schools disappear. As well as delivering an excellent quality of education, the truly Catholic school in the Catholic parish is a powerful influence for evangelisation and tolerance.

Whilst I consistently encouraged Catholic parents to send their children to a Catholic school if such was available and explained their responsibility in this regard, I always respected the rights and choices of parents who chose otherwise. I believed that parents should have their wishes respected as regards the education of their children. I felt very strongly about this. This led to my first and only major confrontation with a fellow bishop, the late Bishop William Philbin of the diocese of Down and Connor, in the mid-1970s. A group of Catholic parents in the North Down area, who styled themselves as All Children Together, had chosen to send their children to a State primary school. Bishop Philbin refused to administer Confirmation to them. I was shocked and deeply annoyed at his action. I cannot remember whether the parents contacted me or if I made the first contact. In any case, after several meetings with the parents, I offered to administer Confirmation to these children, provided they undertook a course of religious instruction to my satisfaction. I nominated someone to provide this instruction. Subsequently, for several years, I administered the Sacrament of Confirmation to all those children at various parish ceremonies in the Derry diocese. I did this, after careful consideration, because I believed that the very existence of Catholic schools was underpinned by the right of parents to choose a particular school for their children. I believed that the rights of these few parents to choose otherwise should therefore be respected. Before finalising the decision, I consulted the Papal Nuncio, Archbishop Gaetano Alibrandi, about my proposed action. He fully endorsed what I was about to do. This was a major controversy at the time and it led to painful exchanges with Bishop Philbin and his Vicar General, and a few rather fraught conversations. I believe that the denial of Confirmation to these children damaged the cause of Catholic schools at that time and gave a huge boost to those promoting integrated education. Whilst Bishop Philbin and I disagreed on this particular issue of policy, he was always gracious and courteous to me.

Confirmation provided an annual pastoral opportunity to visit the parishes and the people living there. There were usually more than 3,000 children to be confirmed in the diocese each year. This involved approximately fifty Confirmation ceremonies annually. During my years as bishop, I administered the Sacrament of Confirmation to more than 40,000 children. I enjoyed these ceremonies immensely. They provided further opportunities to visit most parishes of the diocese each year, and it was very pleasant to meet the children and their parents and sponsors. During many of these ceremonies, I used a form of homily where I conducted a dialogue with the children, based on the theme of the sacrament.

During these visits to parishes, I became aware from the comments of people and clergy that the boundaries and staffing of parishes needed review. Since the end of the Second World War, there had been much new building and development. Towns had grown in size and population. The population in some rural parishes had dwindled considerably. There was a significant movement of people from rural areas into towns. There had not been any radical review of parish boundaries for decades. I set up a Commission, with the rather unwieldy title, the Episcopal Commission for Diocesan Organisation (ECDO). ECDO looked at all the parishes and towns in the diocese, talked with clergy and laity, and made many recommendations about the staffing of parishes, parish boundaries and proposed amalgamation of some parishes and the establishment of new parishes or parish areas, especially in the city of Derry. I subsequently went to the parishes, convened meetings of the people and almost all of ECDO's recommendations were accepted and implemented. Several new parishes were created on ECDO's recommendation and other parish boundaries and staffing were modified and rationalised. The number of priests engaged in full-time teaching was significantly reduced; the number of priests in parish ministry increased.

As a result of visiting parishes, I also became aware of a huge disparity in the income that priests were expected to live on. Priests in some parishes had an adequate income. Others were living well below the poverty line; some depended primarily on parents and family members to help them with basic needs. Priests involved in teaching submitted their entire salary to the development of their school. In return, they were given a pittance for themselves. Another diocesan group was established to address this issue in liaison with the Diocesan Council of Priests. In late 1975, this group came up with an excellent scheme that established greater equity in the remuneration of clergy. A system of salaries and pensions was established that ensured that each priest had a reasonable and adequate living income and that no priest would have an inordinately large income. There was also a recognition of years served and responsibilities undertaken. This plan was reviewed annually and was implemented during the remainder of my time in office.

During my first round of visits to parishes of the diocese, a large number of people urged me to invite a religious order of priests to found a house in the diocese, a House of Prayer and Centre for Spirituality. The Diocesan Council of Priests, whose advice I greatly valued, also suggested that this issue be considered and were a great support. The Derry diocese had a long monastic tradition stretching from the Colmcille foundation in the sixth century until the Middle Ages and the Ulster Plantation. Since the Reformation and the coming of the English, there had not been the presence of a religious order of priests anywhere in the Derry diocese. During the late 1970s, with the assistance of the Diocesan Council of Priests, I began a lengthy consultation on introducing a religious order to the diocese. It was not the most opportune moment to establish a new house in the North. At that time, many religious orders were engaged in reducing the number of houses in Ireland and the conflict in the North was raging. A number of religious orders of priests gave consideration to the invitation. Various sites around the diocese were visited and assessed. Eventually, in 1982, the Discalced Carmelites (OCD) generously and courageously agreed to establish a house in Termonbacca on the outskirts of Derry City. They were introduced to the people and clergy of the diocese at a crowded Mass of Welcome in the Long Tower church on the Feast of St Columba on 9 June 1982. The presence and witness of the Carmelites have been a great and continued blessing to the city and the diocese ever since.

Being out and about in the parishes with priests and people was, by a long way, the most fulfilling and enjoyable dimension of my ministry as bishop. The Catholic Church at parish level can be, and has the potential to be, a magnificent power for good. That is where the Church is at its best. The community of the parish is very powerful and offers a common identity and focus to many disparate people. I spent many happy days and nights engaged in pastoral visitation and Confirmation.

But there were other dimensions to my life that were not so enjoyable.

CHAPTER 4

Coping with Conflict

The Northern conflict hung like an oppressive dark cloud over my twenty years as bishop. I am and I have always been an Irish Nationalist. I look forward to the day when the people of the island of Ireland will be united in some kind of agreed political structure, agreed by dialogue and mutual consent. These are my personal beliefs, but I was always conscious that there was a whole range of political views within the people of the diocese, and considered that it was prudent to keep my political views to myself and to keep them out of the public domain.

Samuel Devenney died on 16 July 1969. He was one of the very first people to die as a result of what has become known as the Northern Ireland conflict or 'The Troubles'. He was fatally injured when he was savagely beaten by RUC members in his own home near the cathedral in Derry on the afternoon of Saturday, 19 April 1969. I knew Sammy and his family very well. I was in his home in William Street minutes after he was beaten and attended his funeral in St Eugene's Cathedral.

Twenty-nine years later, on 19 August 1998, I attended the funeral of Breda Devine in St Mary's church, Aughabrack, County Tyrone. Breda was just 20 months old. She was one of the twenty-nine people who died as victims of the appalling Real IRA bombing in Omagh on another Saturday afternoon, 15 August 1998.

More than 3,590 people died during those twenty-nine years. Tens of thousands more were injured. A large number of those victims lived in various parishes in the Derry diocese.

When I was appointed bishop in 1974, I was conscious of the fact that many people in the North, especially in the Unionist community, and some in the Catholic community, erroneously perceived me as a Provisional IRA sympathiser. This perception was not confined to the North. I also found that it was a perception held by some people in the Republic of Ireland and abroad. This understanding was largely generated by the frequently shown film clip and photographs of Bloody Sunday. It was about the only thing that most people outside Derry knew of me. They were not aware of the fact that I was passionately and profoundly opposed to the use of violence by anyone in pursuit of political objectives here in the North. I had seen so much violence, destruction and human suffering at first hand over the previous four or five years that I could not feel otherwise. In addition to the natural human revulsion generated by many personal experiences, I was also convinced that a campaign of violence here could not be morally justified. I believed that there were other ways, peaceful non-violent ways, to pursue the legitimate political objective of Irish unity at that time. That is still my conviction. I believe that thirty years were stolen from all our lives and life itself was stolen from many people through an unjust and morally unjustifiable conflict in pursuit of a legitimate political objective.

Perhaps I could have made a cosy niche for myself if I had permitted myself to be used as a Republican icon. In the first few months after my appointment as bishop, I was invited to numerous functions, here in Ireland and in the US, on the basis of my perceived credentials. I declined them, lest acceptance would further compound the misunderstanding. I felt it imperative, at an early stage, to make my position quite clear. I was determined to be my own man and to avoid getting into any particular political camp and to keep my political views to myself, as far as possible. I was called to be a religious and moral leader, not a political leader. One of the problems with the North is that people constantly want to label everyone. They find it frustrating when an individual does not gently capitulate to one of their grotesque stereotypes and fit into the little box that they have designated for them; and if you are not 100 per cent with them, it is considered that you are against them.

My postbag was very revealing, especially after certain public statements. Most letters were reasonable and normal, critical or supportive, but about 10 per cent were anything but normal. There were letters, usually anonymous, from Belfast, Portadown or

Ballymena, some of them written in red or green ink, usually in capital letters with long passages underlined, and the Loyalist writers,
in particular, left little to the imagination. They frequently included
quotations from the Bible used in an abusive manner. These letters
contained apocalyptic warnings as to what would happen if I did not
change my 'Republican and Roman' ways. It was interesting that the
letters from Ballymena were very similar in language style and vit-
riol to those from the southern states, the Bible belt, in the United
States. I was amazed that there were quite a number of letters from
there. I was not aware that there were so many interested observers
of Northern Ireland in Alabama and South Carolina! There were
also some blood-curdling letters from Republican sympathisers,
especially from one extremely bitter man in west Belfast and a particularly venomous female in Dundalk; the United States was also
well represented among such sympathisers. Some of these letters
were signed, and some were anonymous. The Republicans did not
use scriptural quotations.

Anonymous phone calls, threatening and nasty, were a frequent
occurrence in the late 1970s and early 1980s. I was Press Officer for
the Irish Episcopal Conference for most of this time, so I was
obliged to be available to journalists on the telephone around the
clock, seven days a week. In the evenings after Colette, my secretary,
left for the day and at the weekends, I always answered the telephone
myself, if I was at home. As a result, in addition to legitimate callers,
I was, unfortunately, accessible to anonymous and usually unpleasant callers. There were some rather interesting callers. One evening,
I received a call from a fellow who claimed that he spoke for the
UDA. He told me that I was going to be 'got' by his organisation. I
asked him what he meant, and he said I was going to be shot for
being a Republican fellow-traveller. In a moment of whimsy, I asked
him when I was going to be shot. He paused for a moment, and then
he asked rather nervously 'Why do you want to know that, sir?' I
said that I would like to have a chance to put my affairs in order and
make my peace with God. He slammed down the phone. A few minutes later, the phone rang again and the newly courageous caller said
curtly 'It'll be next Wednesday, sir!' and quickly terminated the call.
He never called again. It was strange that the nastiest people always

addressed me as 'sir'! I always comforted myself that the person who really intended to murder or harm me would not ring me to notify me in advance. Nonetheless, many of these calls were chilling and frightening, especially late at night. Certain Republican sympathisers, if they wished to express disagreement or protest, had a practice of repeatedly ringing in the middle of the night, saying nothing and then hanging up – they did this for hours on end.

I began my episcopal ministry at a time of great fear and increasing tension. In late March 1974, a new Loyalist group, calling itself the Ulster Workers' Council (UWC), threatened widespread civil disruption in opposition to the Sunningdale Agreement. This agreement had been reached in December 1973 by the Irish and British Governments in consultation with representatives of the SDLP, Unionist and Alliance parties in the North at that time. The British Prime Minister, Edward Heath and the then Taoiseach, Liam Cosgrave both participated in the discussions that led to the Sunningdale Agreement. An election was held in February 1974, in which a new Northern Ireland Assembly was elected. In May 1974, the UWC called a general work stoppage to protest against the Sunningdale Agreement and the new Assembly. Loyalist paramilitaries backed this up with a series of multiple murders and bombings in Belfast, Dublin, Monaghan and elsewhere. Meanwhile, the Provisional IRA pursued its armed struggle relentlessly. Travelling at night became an even more terrifying experience. There were widespread power cuts, petrol was in short supply and there were frequent apocalyptic statements about 'doomsday scenarios' by many of the Loyalist leaders. Frequently there was no power available for Confirmation or other Church ceremonies – no light and no organ – they had to take place in candlelight. The BBC in Northern Ireland was extraordinarily partisan in its reporting of the UWC action. In the face of this pressure, Brian Faulkner, leader of the Northern Ireland Assembly, resigned on 28 May 1974. The Labour Government succumbed to the Loyalist threat; the Northern Ireland Assembly was prorogued on 30 May 1974 and, yet again, physical violence and the threat of physical violence were seen to be victorious. It was not the British Labour Government's finest hour. Violent confrontation once again overcame political dialogue.

In September 1974, I was called upon to officiate at my first funeral of a victim of violence since my appointment as Bishop of Derry. It was to be the first of many such funerals over the next twenty years. Judge Rory Conaghan was a member of a distinguished Derry family and a man of great intelligence, integrity and faith. He was a personal friend of mine and widely admired in both communities. He was murdered by a Provisional IRA gunman, posing as postman, at his home in Belfast on the morning of 16 September 1974. A Resident Magistrate, Robert McBirney, was murdered in Belfast on the same morning.

Rory Conaghan's funeral took place on 18 September in St Eugene's Cathedral. In my homily, I said:

> This Cathedral and this city have witnessed many scenes of grief in recent years. People have come to mourn young and old, to mourn those who were well known in life and those who only in death have been known outside their own families and their own streets. In every sad death that has come to this community in the last four years, we have all shared to some extent the sadness and the loss and the hopelessness of it all.
>
> The death we mourn today is not just the act of an individual but of an organisation. Before it took place, there was, in all probability a meeting, a discussion, a decision taken and a man designated to do the deed. Can any member of such an organisation feel free from the guilt of this crime?
>
> There are many divisions in our country, difference of religion, different ideals, and different brands of politics. But surely the murders of Judge Conaghan and Mr McBirney must bring home to us the fact that our country has now reached a state where it can afford only one division, the distinction between those who believe in such deeds and those who do not.
>
> Too many people who call themselves Christians offer passive support to organisations that, in their inner hearts, they know are directly opposed to the mind and teaching of Christ. Perhaps these deaths may help to unite all people in our community who are prepared to take a public stand for Christian

values. They cannot kill us all. The difference between Unionist and Nationalist, the difference between Conservative and
Labour, pales into insignificance when one is faced with this
kind of savagery where a man is sent to his death at breakfast
by a teenage gunman. It is a luxury to argue about union with
Britain or union with the rest of Ireland when this is taking
place in our community. It would be better to die confronting
evil than to live and condone it. The main requisite for the triumph of evil is that good men should do nothing.*

Whilst the UWC strike ended after the NI Assembly was prorogued, both Loyalist and Republican paramilitaries continued their
respective campaigns of bombing, shooting and murder relentlessly
culminating in the Guildford and Birmingham pub bombs in
November 1974, in which twenty-four people lost their lives.

During all this time, Bishop's House in Derry became a centre for
dealing with prisoner and security issues and all types of other matters
not strictly pastoral. After people were arrested, especially on Monday
mornings, the phones never stopped ringing from all over the diocese
– with allegations of ill treatment and damage to homes – with
requests to find out where a husband or son or daughter was being
held – what was he/she being charged with? Many of the raids on
homes in the early mornings were carried out with excessive violence.
Residents were terrified, humiliated and enraged. Many of the callers
were extremely angry. Colette dealt with many of these issues and followed them up with the RUC, Army and NIO. As well as calling my
office, people in such situations called the offices of political parties
and elected local representatives as well as local newspapers. Bomb
warnings were received at many parochial houses: 'Listen carefully –
there is a bomb in such and such a place and it is to go off at such and
such a time – this is the codeword'. These were particularly frightening. Many forget the huge emotional toll that this took on the people
who answered such calls. Often such messages were garbled, hurried
and vague. Threats and abuse from one side or another after various
episcopal or Church statements were a regular feature of life. There
was criticism for saying anything and there was criticism for saying

* Derry Diocesan Archive.

nothing. These came usually in the forms of anonymous letters or phone calls but sometimes individuals and, on occasions, groups arrived at my door to deliver such abuse personally.

In early December 1974, there were talks between clergy from the Protestant Churches and members of the Provisional IRA in Feakle, County Clare and a temporary ceasefire was called by the latter on 20 December. This ceasefire extended until 17 January 1975, but it was renewed on 9 February to facilitate negotiations with the British Government. By agreement with the British Government, incident centres were set up. These centres were staffed by Sinn Féin members and were supposed to liaise and negotiate with the Government and security authorities. Such centres were set up in Derry and Strabane. There was a distinct sense of unreality at this time. People did not quite know what was going on. Despite these incident centres, the calls to Bishop's House on Troubles-related matters never stopped, day and night, for the next eighteen years.

On 4 April 1975, whilst the IRA ceasefire was still in place, I had a ninety-minute meeting with the then NI Secretary of State, Merlyn Rees, at Bishop's House in Derry. It was a quite heated meeting. In a subsequent press release, I outlined the four points made by me to Mr Rees:

- I expressed my hope once again that the evil of internment would be speedily terminated in the present situation. I also said that I felt the current pattern of phased releases had served to accentuate rather than ease the tension amongst internees and their families. I insisted that internment should be ended at once.
- I also expressed the serious concern in all communities about the continuing sectarian assassinations. These cowardly murders have brought fear and terror to whole communities. Many people are not satisfied that sufficient action is being taken to bring these murderers to justice.
- Anger at the court decision in the case of the murder of Patrick McElhone* by a member of the British Army was

---

* Patrick McElhone was murdered by a British soldier while working on his family farm outside Pomeroy in County Tyrone on 7 August 1974.

also expressed. The impression has grown in many parts of the Catholic community that members of the security forces can kill innocent and unarmed people with impunity.

- Fears of a new campaign of violence were expressed.*

I will always remember a casual remark of Merlyn Rees to me in the middle of a discussion on one occasion. In response to a suggestion he said 'But I have to think about what people in Leeds South will think of that'. Leeds South was his parliamentary constituency in England. I think that those few words illustrated the quandary in which Direct Rule ministers often found themselves – whether people in the North and their needs or the people in their own constituency and their needs had priority. I believe that the people of their parliamentary constituency always won this argument. Leeds South always took precedence over West Belfast, East Derry or Mid-Ulster.

A few days after the April 1975 meeting with Merlyn Rees, I was invited to another meeting.

A priest and a lay person, both now deceased, called with me to convey the invitation. I was told that this meeting would take place in the Midlands and that it was imperative that I should attend. Although not stated specifically, it was implied that the meeting would be with the leadership of the Provisional IRA. After receiving further details on the following morning, the meeting took place on a night in April 1975 in a religious house near Maynooth College. When I arrived at the venue, I found to my surprise that two other Irish Catholic bishops, Bishop Cahal Daly of the diocese of Ardagh and Clonmacnois and Bishop Patrick Lennon of the diocese of Kildare and Leighlin had also been invited to attend. They arrived before me, as I had difficulty locating the venue in the darkness and I was afraid to ask anyone. The other two bishops were in dioceses in the Republic of Ireland, although Cahal was from County Antrim and a frequent commentator and close and perceptive observer of Northern affairs. None of us was aware that the two others had been invited. The other people attending the meeting appeared to be

* Derry Diocesan Archive.

senior members of the command structure of the Provisional IRA. There were eight or nine people at the meeting. Whilst I had never met any of them before, most of them were known to me through their appearances in the media and newspaper photographs. Dáithí Ó Conaill, Seamus Twomey and J.B. O'Hagan were among those present. I also recognised an individual who had escaped from an Irish prison by helicopter a short time before the meeting. I was somewhat surprised that there was no one from Derry amongst them. I was also apprehensive that at any minute, Garda Special Branch officers would break down the door! In the event nothing unforeseen occurred. There was a discussion lasting several hours during which we considered the ceasefire, internment and the lack of response by the British Government to their earlier approaches. The discussions were intense but friendly. They had a series of proposals or demands, six in all, to put to the British Government. Whilst it is difficult to remember the precise details of those proposals all these years later, the notes of this meeting being mislaid, it is my recollection that they appeared reasonable at the time. The people we met regarded as of primary importance the setting up of communications between Sinn Féin and the security forces to deal with and avoid the spreading of false rumours, and the resultant danger of the ceasefire breaking down (incident centres were already in place in many parts of the North); they asked that people under threat be granted permits to carry arms for self-defence; they demanded an end to internment without trial; they asked that there be no restriction on freedom of movement and that people on the wanted list be allowed to return home without being harassed; they asked, in the event of a sustained ceasefire, that the army be gradually withdrawn to barracks. They were of the impression, despite several approaches through the Protestant churchmen and others, that their proposals were not being treated seriously by the British Government at the highest level. They were convinced that their proposals were being blocked by civil servants in the Northern Ireland Office and not getting through to Downing Street. They asked us to ensure that a document detailing these proposals and the summary of our discussion would be conveyed directly into the hands of the Prime Minister in London. They expressed criticism about the lack of support for them from Catholic bishops in Ireland. I always recall one throwaway remark at the end of the meeting, when one of them commented to me, as I shook hands with him when I was leaving the room, 'Isn't it a pity that the only bishop in Ireland who understands us is not even an Irishman?' It gave me much food for thought then and thereafter! We promised that we would do our best to see that their message and their views and concerns were transmitted directly to the British Prime Minister, at that time, Harold Wilson. Early the following morning, Cahal Daly and I travelled to Armagh, delivered the document and reported in detail to Cardinal William Conway on our meeting. He assured us that he would personally ensure that the document would be put into the hands of the British Prime Minister. Cardinal Conway, apparently, for some years, had good access to Downing Street.

To the best of my knowledge, there was no response from Downing Street. I did not pursue the issues further or discuss it later with the Cardinal or my episcopal colleagues. Perhaps, in hindsight, I ought to have followed it up. However, I am confident that Cardinal Conway pushed the matter as far as he could.

In August 1975, the IRA ceasefire effectively ended. Another opportunity had been lost. From September 1975 until October 1994, the various military campaigns went on virtually unabated, with disastrous results for many individuals, families and communities.

Internment was brought to an end in December 1975 by Merlyn Rees. Internment had lasted for four-and-a-half years and it was a disaster. However, interrogation procedures and prison issues were to remain controversial for the duration of the Northern conflict. Among the methods being used by the RUC were what were known as the five techniques: wall-standing, hooding, subjection to white noise, deprivation of sleep, and deprivation of food and drink. In 1978, the European Court of Human Rights (ECHR) trial, *Ireland v. the United Kingdom*, ruled that the five techniques 'did not occasion suffering of the particular intensity and cruelty implied by the word torture ... [but] amounted to a practice of inhuman and degrading treatment', in breach of the European Convention on Human Rights. In February 1977, the UK Attorney General gave an unqualified undertaking that 'the five techniques' would not in any circumstances be reintroduced as an aid to interrogation.

Merlyn Rees introduced a 'criminalisation' procedure for paramilitary prisoners; they were to be treated as common criminals. This proved to be the launchpad for further, even more deadly, protests. In 1976, the blanket strike began in Long Kesh Prison, the dirt strike followed and, eventually, the hunger strikes began in 1980. The British authorities never fully appreciated the importance and influence of prisoners in Irish Republican popular culture. They were to learn this rather quickly and painfully in the following years.

When I set out on my episcopal ministry, I believed that the people and the priests in the diocese should be aware of where I was and what I was doing each day. I noticed that bishops in England published their daily engagements in advance in *The Universe* newspaper. As far as I knew, none of the Irish bishops did this. So I decided to publish my public engagements in the local newspapers each week. After discussion with the relevant editors, I sent the list of my engagements to the local media each week and they kindly published them. A few weeks after I began this practice, I was visited by a friendly and concerned RUC officer who told me that the RUC considered that such publication endangered my personal security and thought that I should review the situation. Such danger had never occurred to me. When the Provisional IRA contacted me on the same matter a few days later and made the same recommendation, I decided that it was best to cease such publication. These people obviously knew something that I did not know!

Around the same time, this same friendly RUC officer warned me that the RUC Special Branch were taking considerable interest in me and closely observing my activities, the people with whom I associated, the places I visited, what I said, etc. He suspected that they might be monitoring my phone calls. He suggested that I be more circumspect. Shortly afterwards, on 17 May 1974, I had a message, in writing, from an officer in the local Provisional IRA, informing me of the same matter, and adding that the Special Branch had given me the code name 'Halo'! I was fascinated by their joint concern!

My relationship with the RUC and British Army, throughout my period of office, was fraught. There were individuals in both organisations with whom I was friendly and whom I greatly respected and I think that the respect was mutual. However, I had little respect for the organisations, as such. Perhaps these attitudes were formed in the early 1970s and the many painful and shocking experiences on the streets during those years. After my appointment as bishop, I did try to be as open as possible and to leave the past behind. But, again and again, new events occurred that alienated me further. I was constantly being approached by people whose son or daughter was arrested or killed or injured and asked to make representations on their behalf to the security forces – largely to get some information about how their family member was, or where he or she was or the circumstances in which he or she was killed or injured. In almost every situation, I met with a brick wall. All kinds of excuses were proffered. They often claimed that this was because of intelligence material that they could not disclose. Complaints, serious and substantiated complaints, about the behaviour of individual soldiers or police officers, were met with the same reaction. Members of the RUC and British Army and especially members of the UDR frequently mistreated people in a cruel and gratuitous manner. They also murdered and seriously injured and maltreated people. They seemed to be above and beyond the law and were able to do as they wished with complete impunity.

The local commanders of the RUC and British Army made a point of keeping in touch with me and there were fairly regular meetings with them. Many of these meetings were constructive, positive and pleasant – some of them were unpleasant and negative. The local Army commander in the area was a Brigadier. Army brigadiers usually served an eighteen-month tour of duty here – they were just about getting the feel and sense of the place when they were transferred elsewhere. I was invited to dinner in the Brigadier's house on many occasions. Up until the mid-1980s, the British Army intelligence was so accurate that the invitations to various Army functions were sent to 'Bishop & Mrs Daly'! During my years as bishop, I accepted such invitations on just two occasions. Unfortunately, 'Mrs Daly' was never able to attend! The dinners were very formal and rather stiff affairs. The guests were usually served by scarlet-jacketed white-gloved squaddies. The topics of discussions at these dinners during the earlier years were often banal. I recall one such occasion, when the conflict was at its height and there were bombings and shootings almost daily but among the fevered topics of discussion at the dinner was the possibility of setting up a croquet pitch near one corner of the helicopter landing pad in Ebrington Barracks, the Army headquarters at that time! I also have to admit that I had some apprehension that I might be seen going to the Brigadier's home in the Waterside by some IRA member or sympathiser. Indeed, on one of the two occasions that I was present at such a dinner, the Provisional IRA let it be known on the following day that they were aware of my attendance at the Brigadier's house on the previous evening.

There were occasions when the discussions were more useful and constructive. Senior Army officers, including the brigadiers, regularly called with me in Bishop's House at St Eugene's. Some of these officers were anxious to learn about the local people and their social, historical and political background. A number of the officers in the early years were veterans of service in Cyprus and Aden, and they simply presumed that the situation here was similar and behaved accordingly. Many of them were excited to be in a situation which was 'active', with real bullets being fired at them. Such experiences 'sharpened everyone up', they would suggest. On the whole, I found that the senior Army officers had a very superficial and stereotypical understanding of the Catholic community and, until the late 1980s, largely went along with the assumption that virtually everyone in our community was an enemy. Their local social contacts seemed to be largely with the upper class, the old ruling class in the Unionist and Protestant community and their view and judgment of the local situation were, perhaps, unduly influenced by that. It was very difficult, with a few exceptions, to move them from that position. It could be argued that, in the 1970s and early 1980s, other Nationalists, including myself, failed as a result of our reluctance to engage socially with such senior officers and to better and more accurately and comprehensively advise them of the realities in the Catholic/Nationalist/Republican communities. That is a fair argument. In the late 1980s, however, there was a distinct change in attitude. Conversation with

Army officers, at that stage, revealed a deeper and more realistic understanding of the Nationalist community. In those later years, I got the impression that there appeared to be fewer of the public school types among the senior officers and more people with backgrounds in comprehensive schools or in middle- or working-class communities. Such people had a greater understanding of people in places like the Bogside and Creggan. One thing that was consistent in the senior Army officers, whom I met over the years, was their regard for the military ability of the Provisional IRA. One very senior officer said to me, 'Whether you hate them or not, they are damn good militarily at the dreadful things they do', or something to that effect.

From things that were said on unguarded occasions during the conversations of those years, I had deep suspicions that there was contact at high levels between the IRA and the British Army at various times throughout the conflict.

I was very impressed by the officers' pride in their various regiments. I knew very little about the regiments in the British Army. The only regiments that I and most of Derry people knew of were the Parachute Regiment and the Anglian Regiment – and that was for the wrong reasons! But the senior army officers seemed to think that everyone was aware of the different regiments that came from time to time. They thought that people would be wildly excited that such and such a regiment would be coming to take up duty in Derry in a few months time. They seemed to be under the impression that the people in the Creggan looked forward with great and breathless anticipation to the arrival of the Royal Fusiliers or the Black Watch or some such regiment! Possibly the IRA kept note of such events. But most civilians among whom I lived only knew them as soldiers or as 'the Army' or as 'the Brits'. We did not distinguish one regiment from another with two notable exceptions. They all wore the same battle dress or uniform. I suppose that it was similar to an outsider's perception of the various religious orders in the Church. To those outside our Church, they were all merely known as clergy or nuns or 'papishes', not members of any specific order.

One of my abiding memories is a phone call received one morning in the mid-1970s from an officer with a wonderfully posh public school accent. I cannot remember his rank, but he was a senior officer. He asked to see me urgently. I asked him to call that afternoon. He was straight out of central casting – the archetypal toff – a real-life Colonel Blimp. He told me excitedly that he had a wonderful idea to help bring the people of the Bogside and the Army closer together. He went on to explain to me at great length about the Blues and Royals and their band. He was quite aghast when I told him that I had never heard of the Blues and Royals! They were guardsmen, the perplexed officer informed me somewhat indignantly. He said that the Blues and Royals had the most impressive and wonderful ceremonial military band in the British Army. His 'wonderful idea' was that the Blues and Royals mounted band in full dress uniform should ride on horseback through the Bogside on the afternoon of St Patrick's Day playing 'Irish jigs and other jolly Irish music'. He thought that this exercise would significantly improve relations between the Army and the local community. Initially, I thought that he was joking. Then I realised that he was deadly serious. He was most disappointed and deflated at my lack of enthusiasm for his 'wonderful idea'!

The various local RUC commanders who served during my twenty years as bishop were more aware of local sensitivities than the Army. There was no likelihood of the RUC Band being sent to play 'jigs or jolly Irish music' in the Bogside! Two of the commanders were especially friendly and open and positive; one was quite hostile and very aggressive; others were polite and correct. They did not host any dinners; at least I was not invited to any of them. I was invited to and attended lunch during the Christmas season on a few occasions in the Strand Road barracks in Derry in the late 1980s and early 1990s. I got the impression that, at times, relations were quite strained between the RUC and the Army. Unlike the Army, the senior RUC officers did not have mixed feelings about the Provisional IRA. There were none of them that had any time for the IRA. They utterly detested them, hated them, loathed them. They expressed frustration that, because of political constraints, they could not deal with them to their satisfaction. As mentioned earlier, I formally brought many complaints to their attention. They would promise to investigate these matters, but I can only recall very few occasions when they responded in anything like a satisfactory manner. Like the Army officers, they were courteous, on the whole. However, I never could feel completely relaxed in their company. As a police force, they were not of the community among whom I lived. They were more of a paramilitary force than a police service. It must be stated that policing in a situation of conflict is enormously difficult, complex and dangerous. As a force, the RUC suffered terribly at the hands of the Provisional IRA. The RUC families had a particularly difficult time. RUC officers were under attack and at peril in their private lives as well as on duty. During my years as bishop, I officiated at the funerals of several members of the RUC. In fact, the last funeral I officiated at before I suffered a stroke was that of Constable Michael Ferguson, a young RUC officer, cruelly and cowardly murdered in broad daylight on a busy street in the centre of Derry on a Saturday afternoon. He was murdered on 23 January 1993. His funeral took place in the Sacred Heart church in Omagh. In the homily at his funeral Mass, I said, among other things:

> Michael was a practising Catholic and regular church attender. It took a lot of courage for him to join the police. And let it be said clearly that we need a Police Service, the membership of which reflects all sections of this community. Mrs Ferguson can and should be very proud of her son.[*]

Both the Army and the RUC sought my public support, from time to time. Whilst I did offer them my full support in their impartial exercise of their duty, I never felt able to offer unqualified support to either force. I greatly regretted being unable to do that. Many of the rank-and-file individuals in both forces were people of great courage and integrity, but, because of some of the actions and activities of their organisations and their unwillingness to admit or face up to these activities, I simply could not bring myself to offer them the type of unconditional support that they sought. They had inflicted too much hurt on too many of my people. Although they mellowed somewhat in the early 1990s, the RUC was never able to throw off its shackles of being perceived as a Unionist paramilitary force and I

[*]   Derry Diocesan Archive.

CHAPTER 5

Meetings and Media

A hotel in Mulrany, the little village in County Mayo on the road from Westport to Achill Island, was the unlikely setting for my first formal meeting as a member of the Irish Episcopal Conference. As already explained, the Irish Episcopal Conference was the new collective title by which the Irish Catholic bishops were formally known after the Second Vatican Council. The meeting in Mulrany was a five-day special meeting that set out to reflect in detail on the documents of the Second Vatican Council and how they applied to Ireland and what steps ought to be taken by the bishops to implement them. All the serving bishops in Ireland attended. It was roughly ten years since the Council ended and a large number of bishops had been appointed in Ireland since then. About half of those in attendance at Mulrany had participated in the Second Vatican Council. The meeting took place in April 1974, a few weeks after my ordination as bishop.

As it was my first Episcopal Conference meeting, I was anxious to arrive in good time. I was not sure how long the journey would take; as a result, I was one of the first to arrive. But there was one earlier arrival and he was sitting in the reception area of the hotel. He was the formidable Bishop Michael Browne of Galway whom I had often heard of but had never met. He had been Bishop of Galway for thirty-seven years. He looked me up and down, with a degree of curiosity, as I lugged a suitcase and large briefcase up to the reception desk. He said in a loud voice 'Would you be the new Bishop of Derry?' When I told him that I was, he introduced himself and observed that he had preached at the episcopal consecration of my predecessor in October 1939. Then he enquired about Bishop Farren and voiced concern about the youthful age of

57

bishops nowadays. I thought that he was speaking in jest, but I was not certain!

The Mulrany meeting provided an excellent opportunity to meet my new episcopal colleagues over an extended period and it was an enlightening experience. Theologians, sociologists and other experts, lay and cleric, came and made presentations to us. Many of these were interesting, radical, illuminating and challenging. We discussed the organisation and structure of the Episcopal Conference, ecumenism, adult religious education, liturgy, re-training of the clergy, communications and media relations and the greater involvement of the laity in the life of the Church in the aftermath of the Second Vatican Council and so much more. All kinds of exciting possibilities were opened up. It was an extremely busy, stimulating and interesting week. There were remarkably few tensions between the older and younger bishops. Quite a number of my colleagues had been involved for many years in academic life, teaching in schools, or seminaries or universities, before being appointed as bishops. In Mulrany, I became keenly aware that my knowledge of theology was profoundly inadequate, although I reassured myself by the knowledge that I had more parish pastoral experience than many of my colleagues. I particularly enjoyed the chance to meet colleagues informally at meals and relaxing in the late evenings, in the bar or lounge. They were very good company and very welcoming. On one afternoon, I took a few hours to relax and enjoy some hill walking in nearby Achill with Cardinal Conway, Bishop Eamon Casey and a few others. There were many opportunities during that meeting to meet with and get to know the other bishops.

The problems of the North were discussed, but mainly informally. I noted that this matter was not as high on the agenda as I had anticipated. With a few exceptions, the bishops in the Republic were not as interested in the North as I had thought they might have been. Perhaps coming from my Northern background and experiencing at first hand the challenges of living and ministering in the North made me biased in this regard. The North was, and is, my consuming interest. Everyone had an opportunity to speak on the matters under discussion, and most did speak. In the plenary meetings, the bishops addressed one another, at that time, in what I thought was a rather formal and quaint manner, by the name of their diocese – Galway, Cork or Kerry. Outside the formal meetings, things were more relaxed.

Towards the end of the meeting, many decisions and recommendations were made. Among these was the decision to establish a Press and Information Office for the Catholic Church in Ireland. Amazingly, up until 1974, there was no such office. I was asked to oversee the implementation of this decision. I presume that I was invited to do this because of my fairly extensive experience with the international media during the previous few years in Derry and my work in RTÉ for some time prior to my appointment as bishop. I gladly accepted this commission. From my background in RTÉ, I was keenly aware that there was a great need for such an office and service to the media.

For some reason, I had anticipated heated debates. Whilst the discussions were animated on occasions and there were contrasting views voiced on several issues, these debates were seldom confrontational or fevered and everyone was courteous to everyone else. Cardinal Conway impressed me as an excellent chairman. He kept the meetings under firm control and did not permit people to waffle or stray from the point at issue.

It was, without doubt, the best and most stimulating Episcopal Conference meeting that I attended in the twenty years I served as a member of that body. None of the subsequent meetings had the same enthusiasm, interest and sheer excitement. This may be a very subjective view and it may be coloured by the fact that it was my first such meeting, but I believe that it is an accurate and objective observation. I have often looked at and studied the documents of that Mulrany meeting in the intervening years, and many of them are still as relevant and interesting as they were in 1974. Had the implementation of all the decisions been as enthusiastic as the discussions that determined them, I am convinced that the Irish Church would have benefited immensely. However, many of the decisions became lost in translation from aspiration to reality.

After the Mulrany meeting, I set about establishing the Press and Information Office. I consulted with national and local newspaper journalists and editors and the Religious Affairs Department and senior people in RTÉ whom I had come to know. There were four journalists at that time who reported on religious affairs for the national media – Joe Power (*Irish Independent*), John Cooney (*Irish Times*), T.P. O'Mahony (*Irish Press*) and Kevin O'Kelly (RTÉ). Veteran commentators like Louis McRedmond and Seán Mac Réamoinn were men who had reported for the national dailies on the Second Vatican Council and they were all, without exception, very helpful and enthusiastic. I formed a small group of people involved and experienced in media to assist me in the task of setting up the office. We determined the services that we would offer and the staff that we would require to deliver those services, and identified a suitable location for the Press and Information Office. Then we drew up an outline budget and submitted it to the IEC for approval. We subsequently advertised the post of Press and Information Officer. I was surprised at the number and the quality of the applicants. After much consideration and many interviews, Jim Cantwell was appointed to head the Office. The Catholic Press and Information Office in Booterstown Avenue in Dublin came into being in February 1975.

The Irish Episcopal Conference, at that time, had three scheduled plenary meetings each year. Each meeting was usually of three days' duration. Most of the meetings were held in St Patrick's College in Maynooth, the national seminary. I attended my first regular scheduled meeting of the IEC in June 1974. Prior to that meeting in the summer of 1974, I had never been through the gates of St Patrick's College, Maynooth. In the 1970s, each meeting began on the late afternoon of Monday and ended on the Wednesday evening. Although there were occasions when the meetings sprang into life and were interesting, the discussions and meetings were, in the main, repetitive, tedious and very lengthy. Some matters came up for discussion again and again and again. Journalists had campaigned for years to be admitted to the meetings. They did not realise how incredibly lucky they were to be excluded!

There was a widespread assumption that the Catholic Bishops Conference in the Republic of Ireland was a powerful, influential, superbly organised body that had an undue and unhelpful influence on political life. That may well have been the case in the earlier years of the State. However, it was not my impression from the inside during the years that I served as a member of the Conference between 1974 and 1993. The amendment of the Constitution of Ireland by referendum in December 1972 made a significant and positive difference that I welcomed. This removed from the Constitution a controversial reference to the 'special position' of the Roman Catholic Church. Before my time, in the 1950s and 1960s, there were, undoubtedly, a few very formidable and influential individual bishops who were also powerful national figures, but, in subsequent years, I considered the corporate body to be lacking in political clout. In my twenty years in the Conference, I was not aware of any ambition by the bishops to be anything more than Church leaders endeavouring to preach the Gospel and to offer moral leadership and guidance to the people in their pastoral care.

There were certainly some contributions to political debate in the South. The Irish Episcopal Conference, after lengthy discussion and undue hesitation, sent a delegation to the New Ireland Forum. The delegation attended the Forum on 9 February 1984. The New Ireland Forum consisted of a series of meetings in 1983–4 at which Irish Nationalist political parties discussed potential political developments which might alleviate conflict in Northern Ireland. The Forum was established by the then Taoiseach, Garret FitzGerald, and the hearings took place at Dublin Castle. Our delegation was made up of bishops, clergy and laity. Mary McAleese was a member of our delegation. I was also a member. The Forum was an interesting intellectual and political exercise. It was good for bishops and politicians to be able to articulate their views and have them challenged publicly and discussed on live TV. Unfortunately and unsurprisingly, Mrs Thatcher was not impressed by the conclusions of the New Ireland Forum.

I vaguely remember one other meeting in a Dublin hotel when I was part of a group of bishops who met some Dublin politicians. I cannot now remember who convened the meeting or what it was about nor can I find any note of the meeting. However, I have recently been reminded of this meeting when reading a tribute to the late Cardinal Cahal Daly by Bishop Joseph Duffy in *Seanchas Ard Mhacha* (2010). Bishop Duffy describes how, in a TV series in 2005, the Cardinal explained for the first time to the general public the facts behind what he called 'the monumental misunderstanding', which arose between the bishops and the FitzGerald Government over their meeting to discuss the Divorce Referendum of 1986. The ministers got the impression that the bishops were making a bizarre proposal to introduce the concept of Church nullity of marriage into State law, whereas, in an effort to be helpful, they were merely referring to a process of civil nullity which existed on the statute book but had become defunct. I am virtually certain that this was the meeting I attended in the Dublin hotel but I have no recollection of the details of it. I do remember, however, that there was some subsequent controversy.

Charles Haughey once invited me to meet him during the hunger strikes. I think he was Taoiseach at the time. I met him briefly in a hotel in Buncrana. As far as I recall, it was during a general election or a bye-election in that area of Donegal. I am sure that there were many other meetings involving Irish bishops and Dublin ministers from time to time, particularly involving education and social welfare. That would not be surprising.

There were very frequent meetings of the Northern Bishops with Secretaries of State in the North and with their Ministers about education, prisons, allegations of mistreatment, human rights issues and other matters of current and/or mutual concern.

My memory of the Irish Catholic bishops, when I served, is that they were 26 to 30 individuals who went back to their dioceses after their meetings in Maynooth and jealously guarded their independence and autonomy. Whilst there were seldom public differences or spats between bishops at meetings, there were different views and nuances freely expressed on various issues. I especially remember Bishop Peter Birch of Ossory and Bishop Connie Lucey of Cork and Ross in my early years; they often made interesting and original contributions to debates. The discussions were very civilised and courteous. Differences were kept within house.

I was particularly struck by the enormous gap between the Church in Dublin and the remainder of the country. This was very significant. In the 1970s and 1980s, Dublin was really a fifth province; its population was more than 25 per cent of that of the total island, and many times the population of any of the other twenty-five dioceses. There were many differences between North and South, East and West, urban and rural. It was difficult, at times, to establish common policies and even more difficult to have them implemented in each of the twenty-six dioceses of Ireland. Efforts to implement the reforms of the Vatican Council and the resolutions of the Mulrany Conference were made, with some success and quite a degree of failure.

No particular political grouping or party was favoured by the Conference. I can never recall a single occasion in twenty years when party politics, as such, were discussed. Senior Dublin politicians and one Belfast politician did address letters to the Conference from time to time on various issues, and endeavoured to suggest or influence policies or what might be said in statements by the Conference, as was their right as members of the Church and public representatives. The Church had a huge involvement in education. This was always the subject of considerable debate. It was the issue that was most frequently the basis for dialogue with government – but seldom a cause for serious friction within the Conference. Social issues, of course, were regularly on the agenda – after all, we tried to follow someone who taught us to love God and to love our neighbour. I believe that the Catholic Church in Ireland initiated many worthy social initiatives and care for various groups who had been neglected by others. There were, of course, very comprehensive and interesting meetings on the divorce and abortion referenda in the Republic during my time as bishop, but these were perceived by us as moral issues on which we had every right and even a duty to speak and articulate our views and the teaching of the Church and offer leadership to the members of our Church. Catholic bishops and other Church leaders do this in most democratic countries when such issues come up for debate or decision in the public forum. I believe that groups, such as bishops, would be failing in their responsibility if they did not make a contribution to the public debates on what they perceived as moral issues. In Ireland, such comment has often been misconstrued and represented as political interference and a power play by bishops and caused an outcry in sections of the national media. I do not accept that such allegations were justified.

Whether one agrees with it or not, the input of any Bishops Conference should be seen and respected as a legitimate contribution to the public debate – just as it is in other democratic countries. To consider it otherwise betrays immaturity at best and bias at worst. It is a sign of a healthy democracy that individuals and groups like Churches can make their voices heard and present their views on issues of concern and offer moral leadership to their people without fear or favour. It was my belief that any influence exercised by the bishops was moral and pastoral rather than political. The voice of religion should be heard.

Pope Benedict XVI spoke very powerfully about this issue in his address at Westminster Hall in London on 17 September 2010 during his State Visit to Britain, when he said:

> The inadequacy of pragmatic, short-term solutions to complex social and ethical problems has been illustrated all too clearly by the recent global financial crisis. There is widespread agreement that the lack of a solid ethical foundation for economic activity has contributed to the grave difficulties now being experienced by millions of people throughout the world. Just as 'every economic decision has a moral consequence' (*Caritas in Veritate*, 37), so too in the political field, the ethical dimension of policy has far-reaching consequences that no government can afford to ignore. A positive illustration of this is found in one of the British Parliament's particularly notable achievements – the abolition of the slave trade. The campaign that led to this landmark legislation was built upon firm ethical principles, rooted in the natural law, and it has made a contribution to civilisation of which this nation may be justly proud.
>
> The central question at issue, then, is this: where is the ethical foundation for political choices to be found? The Catholic tradition maintains that the objective norms governing right action are accessible to reason, prescinding from the content of revelation. According to this understanding, the role of religion in political debate is not so much to supply these norms, as if they could not be known by non-believers – still less to propose

concrete political solutions, which would lie altogether outside the competence of religion – but rather to help purify and shed light upon the application of reason to the discovery of objective moral principles. This 'corrective' role of religion vis-à-vis reason is not always welcomed, though, partly because distorted forms of religion, such as sectarianism and fundamentalism, can be seen to create serious social problems themselves. And in their turn, these distortions of religion arise when insufficient attention is given to the purifying and structuring role of reason within religion. It is a two-way process. Without the corrective supplied by religion, though, reason too can fall prey to distortions, as when it is manipulated by ideology, or applied in a partial way that fails to take full account of the dignity of the human person. Such misuse of reason, after all, was what gave rise to the slave trade in the first place and to many other social evils, not least the totalitarian ideologies of the twentieth century. This is why I would suggest that the world of reason and the world of faith – the world of secular rationality and the world of religious belief – need one another and should not be afraid to enter into a profound and ongoing dialogue, for the good of our civilisation.

Religion, in other words, is not a problem for legislators to solve, but a vital contributor to the national conversation. In this light, I cannot but voice my concern at the increasing marginalization of religion, particularly of Christianity, that is taking place in some quarters, even in nations which place a great emphasis on tolerance. There are those who would advocate that the voice of religion be silenced, or at least relegated to the purely private sphere. There are those who argue that the public celebration of festivals such as Christmas should be discouraged, in the questionable belief that it might somehow offend those of other religions or none. And there are those who argue – paradoxically with the intention of eliminating discrimination – that Christians in public roles should be required at times to act against their conscience. These are worrying signs of a failure to appreciate not only the rights of believers to freedom of conscience and freedom of religion, but also the legitimate role of religion in the public square. I would invite all of you, therefore, within your respective spheres of influence, to seek ways of promoting and encouraging dialogue between faith and reason at every level of national life.

The Pope's words could also be applied to Ireland.

There was correspondence from various individuals and groups at the Conference meetings. All received due consideration. In my latter years as bishop, various pressure groups emerged, particularly of the right-wing variety. They lobbied on particular issues that interested them.

One aspect of the Conference deliberations that particularly stands out in my memory is the formulation of statements. It is virtually impossible to formulate a statement that encompasses accurately the views of more than thirty people on an important subject on which there are deeply held views. The various nuances of such statements and the wordings on major issues took an inordinate amount of time and many drafts before acceptance. Drafts of statements that were excellent and strong initially, were sometimes analysed and filleted in the process of discussion until they were weak and flaccid. In some cases, I held the view that some of our finally published statements were anaemic as a result.

The informal aspects of the bishops' meetings were often the most useful. The chats and conversations with other bishops about initiatives or mutual problems in their respective dioceses were often very helpful and illuminating. These conversations took place at meals or during walks in the grounds of Maynooth during breaks in the meetings. It was always interesting to hear what other bishops and priests and laity in their diocese were doing about various issues. A bishop can experience great isolation in his own diocese. The interaction with colleagues was very helpful and informative. They were excellent and supportive colleagues. I also enjoyed the experience of celebrating Mass together with other bishops at meetings of the Conference. This was an integral part of each meeting – a time to reflect.

The bishops' regular meetings provided the normal conduit through which documents from various congregations and offices in the Holy See were communicated. A period at the beginning of each meeting was devoted to these documents. There were many such documents. Some of them were relevant, interesting and useful; many were not.

We would then go on to discuss various aspects of Church life and practice in Ireland. During my time in the Conference, at every meeting, there was always a short period given to discuss the situation in Northern Ireland. Third World issues, justice and peace issues, social welfare issues, liturgy, laity, pastoral care of emigrants, pastoral care of various marginalised groups, ecumenical matters, and reports from various national Church bodies featured regularly on the agenda. Current issues of interest were also discussed from time to time. Experts on various subjects addressed us occasionally. The Trustees of Maynooth College, the national seminary, met subsequent to the General Meeting.

I recall that the journeys home from episcopal meetings in Maynooth were among the more pleasant journeys of my life as bishop and the journeys, usually on Monday mornings, to attend the meetings were invariably among the most miserable. It was my impression that there were too many meetings at all levels in the Church in the post-Vatican II period and a lot of these meetings were pointless and wasteful of time and resources. For my first seven or eight years as bishop, I was required to attend the full Conference meetings, meetings of the Standing Committee as well as meetings of the various IEC Commissions, Justice and Peace, Social Welfare, Communications etc. I found myself driving the exhausting 300-mile round trip from Derry to Dublin or Maynooth on poor roads several times a month. These journeys were made more arduous during all of that time by a permanent British Army border checkpoint at Aughnacloy on the Monaghan/Tyrone border that often caused delays of sixty to ninety minutes – as well as other random checkpoints between Aughnacloy and Derry. Journeys were frequently interrupted by bombs or security scares and subsequent delays and diversions. The one-way journey often took four to five hours driving. Some of the meetings were a waste of time and energy. All this travelling was time consuming and exhausting and I felt that it was taking me away from the ministry that I perceived as my first priority as Bishop of Derry – to minister and preach the

Gospel to the people of the diocese. I always experienced a considerable tension between my national responsibilities and my diocesan responsibilities. Whilst I realise that bishops must undertake national and international duties and obligations in addition to their diocesan responsibilities, I found this to be extremely difficult. I never really adjusted to it. This is a criticism of myself rather than the structures. I am not a 'meeting person' and I was, in my younger days, perhaps too impetuous and impatient.

There were also meetings of the Northern Bishops on a regular basis. During my early years as bishop, Cardinal William Conway was my mentor. He was Archbishop of Armagh during those years. A superb chairman at a meeting, he had the gift of summarising a long and complex discussion in one concise minute for the record. He kept speakers focused on the subject and had little time for those who wandered into other areas. (Another excellent chairman whom I experienced was Robert Runcie, Anglican Bishop of St Albans in England. He was chairman of the Central Religious Advisory Committee (CRAC) to the BBC and the IBA.* I served on this committee in London for five or more years and it was a very good and stimulating experience. It was made up of many interesting people from politics, the media and Church life in Britain. Robert Runcie subsequently became Archbishop of Canterbury. He was also a good friend.) But back to the Northern Bishops ... we had three of four meetings every year during which many issues of particular interest to the North were discussed – education, acts of terrorism, discrimination, justice issues, intimidation by the RUC and Army, prisons/prisoners and other pastoral and social matters. These were usually much more interesting, more focused and much shorter than the meetings of the full Conference. These meetings usually took place in Armagh. I enjoyed these meetings and found them very helpful and relevant. Statements directed to the Northern Ireland Office from the Northern Bishops were usually constructively received and discussed. They did not receive the huffy reaction that similar statements from Maynooth often received in the environs of Leinster

---

* The IBA was the Independent Broadcasting Authority, which, at that time, acted as overseer of independent broadcasting, television and radio, in Britain.

House. Northern officials usually answered correspondence in a comprehensive and prompt manner, whilst Dublin officials often confined themselves to an acknowledgment and sometimes not even that. There was a striking contrast between the efficiency of the civil service, North and South.

I was greatly saddened by the death of Cardinal William Conway in April 1977. He was just 64 years old. He wrote to me and to all his episcopal colleagues a few weeks before he died. In this letter he said 'my prognosis is very bad' and asked for prayers. I suspected that he had been unwell but I had not, until then, realised the gravity of his illness. He was someone whom I greatly respected, and I consider that he led the Irish Church wisely in the challenging times after the Second Vatican Council. He had the added challenge of leading the Northern Church through the tumultuous early years of the conflict. He was always very cautious, weighing his words carefully. He did not speak until he had acquired a full understanding and grasp of any situation. When he did speak, people paid attention. His death, at such an early age and such a crucial time, was a great loss.

Tomás Ó Fiaich was Cardinal Conway's successor. He also died at a relatively young age. He was only 66 when he died suddenly in May 1990 while with his archdiocesan pilgrimage in Lourdes. He was Archbishop of Armagh from 1978 until he died. A great colleague, a great friend, a huge source of knowledge, he had a great zest for life. Life as a bishop in the North was much duller after he died. I will be referring to Cardinal Ó Fiaich in subsequent chapters.

CHAPTER 6

The Pope Comes to Ireland

The election of Pope John Paul II on 16 October 1978 was one of great events of my years as bishop. His election was a complete surprise. He was the first non-Italian Pope for centuries. 1978 was the year of three Popes. Pope Paul VI died on 6 August 1978. Albino Luciani, Archbishop of Venice, was elected as Pope John Paul I on 26 August. I was in Lourdes with our diocesan pilgrimage at the time of his election, and there were many pilgrims there from Venice and Rome and other parts of Italy. That night in Lourdes was a night of celebration for the thousands of pilgrims who were there. Tragically, within a month, John Paul I died. We all waited expectantly when the next Conclave began. Karol Wojtyla, Archbishop of Cracow, was elected as Pope and chose the name John Paul II. The Pope from Poland generated a huge surge of excitement and expectancy throughout the Church. He was 58 years old, full of energy and vigour, a wonderful linguist and a charismatic personality with great gifts of communication. He was from Eastern Europe, at that time still behind the Iron Curtain. He had lived through the Nazi and Communist totalitarian regimes. He was destined to be a primary force and influence in consigning the Iron Curtain to history. I had briefly met Cardinal Wojtyla at the International Eucharistic Congress in Philadelphia in the United States in 1976. He had preached at the Justice and Peace Mass that was celebrated in the Veterans Stadium on the Tuesday night of the Congress. He made a powerful impression on me. On a very personal note, I was fascinated by the fact that we shared an interest and involvement in theatre in our younger days. Suddenly, it became 'respectable' for a priest or bishop to have a background of being actively involved in artistic and theatrical pursuits!

There were rumours early in 1979 that the new Pope might visit Ireland. He had been invited to visit Knock to mark the centenary of the apparition there. A reigning Pope had never visited Ireland. Monsignor James Horan was the dynamic Parish Priest of Knock and he had made no secret of the fact that he had personally invited the Holy Father there for the centenary celebration of the Knock apparitions in 1979. James Horan's invitation was supported by the Irish Episcopal Conference at the prompting of the Archbishop of Tuam, Joseph Cunnane. In December 1978, the bishops of Ireland sent a formal invitation to the Holy Father. Bishops were enthusiastic about the idea. However, many of us thought that a visit in the near future was most unlikely. But we underestimated both Pope John Paul's enthusiasm for travel and James Horan's powers of persuasion. For the man who could persuade a government to help him build an international airport on what one cynic described as 'a foggy, boggy mountain', persuading a Pope to come to Ireland was not an insurmountable challenge!

The IEC decided to send a small group of observers to Poland to observe the Papal Visit there in early June 1979. It was believed to be important to get some idea of the logistical planning and arrangements that would be required if such a visit were to take place in Ireland. In hindsight, this proved to be a very enlightened decision.

At the meeting of the Irish bishops in mid-June, it was established that a short visit to Ireland was being given serious consideration by the Holy See. There had been some speculation in the media. It was known that the Pope was to address the United Nations in New York in early October and that he hoped to combine this engagement with a pastoral visit to some other cities in the United States. The feasibility of an Irish visit, en route, was being examined. We were asked to treat this information as confidential. Summer holiday plans were put on hold.

There was another very significant event in 1979. On 26 May, Tomás Ó Fiaich, Archbishop of Armagh, was named as Cardinal. Whilst the announcement had been awaited and expected for some time, it was the occasion of considerable rejoicing and satisfaction especially among the Catholic community in the North. The deaths of the two Popes in 1978 had possibly brought about a delay in the conferring of the Red Hat. But rumours abounded about other more sinister reasons for the delay. Some sections of the British media were strident in their criticism of Tomás Ó Fiaich, especially relating to his stand on prison issues and his interest in the Irish language and culture. There was considerable speculation that the British Government, concerned about the Archbishop's nationalism, had been lobbying the Holy See against his appointment as Cardinal. Some went so far as to allege that Cardinal Basil Hume of Westminster was actively involved in this lobbying. In fact, the rumours were so strong that Cardinal Hume felt obliged to issue a public statement dismissing and rubbishing these allegations. I have to say that I never found any evidence to substantiate these rumours. I did not ever believe that Cardinal Hume would have involved himself in such activities. In any case, it was my belief that, in the mid- and late 1970s, the Holy See no longer gave much weight to, or paid undue attention to, British lobbying on Irish issues. To my mind, the presence of Archbishop Benelli in the Secretariat of State brought an end to that malign influence with regard to Irish affairs, an influence that had been quite powerful in the earlier part of the twentieth century. The diplomatic activities of the Irish Government, the submissions of the Irish Episcopal Conference and the presence of a very active Papal Nuncio in Ireland, Gaetano Alibrandi, filtered through Archbishop Benelli, a former Papal diplomat in Ireland, were the major influences on shaping the Holy See's view of Irish issues in the late 1970s.

I was present at the ceremony in Rome when Cardinal Ó Fiaich received the Red Hat from the Pope on 30 June 1979. The ceremony was much less formal than when Cardinal D'Alton received his Red Hat more than twenty-five years earlier when I was a student in Rome. On 2 July, I joined the new Cardinal and his family and a big group of clergy and laity from Armagh for an audience with the Holy Father. It was my first time to meet the new Pope since his election – and he was hugely impressive and inspiring. There was a new excitement abroad in Rome. Much of the free time during those days in Rome was spent seeking appointments with everyone of influence we could meet, lobbying and looking for support for the Papal Visit to Ireland. A small group of Irish journalists travelled to Rome covering the consistory. Naturally, they were extremely interested in the possibilities of a Papal Visit. The new Cardinal repeatedly told them that we would know within days. I returned home on 3 July. Cardinal Ó Fiaich returned a few days later – and we still did not know whether there would be a Papal Visit or not! There was no commitment, one way or the other.

There was considerable anxiety at this stage. Bishops were aware of the huge preparations that would be required. It was virtually certain that the Holy Father would come. The possible date for a visit was thought to be late September or early October and, in the second week of July, we still did not know for certain whether or not there would be a visit and nothing was planned. It was decided to convene a meeting of the Standing Committee of the Irish Episcopal Conference in Dublin on Wednesday, 11 July. This was to be a very significant meeting. Father Michael Smith, secretary to the IEC and later to be Bishop of Meath, at the request of Cardinal Ó Fiaich, prepared a memorandum for that meeting. He had been one of those who went to Poland to observe the Papal Visit there. In this memorandum, he outlined the new Pope's understanding of Papal Visits as a stage to speak to the world on various themes. He pointed out that preparations for a Papal Visit had begun in Poland in 1965 in preparation for Pope Paul VI's hoped-for visit. The blueprint was there and work began as soon as Pope John Paul II was elected. Father Smith urged preliminary thinking and planning to begin immediately and made detailed recommendations about the model of organisation and other matters. The possible liturgies were discussed, as well as a potential itinerary, accommodation, travel and stewarding. A great deal of emphasis was given to the importance of pastoral preparation in every diocese and parish of the country. This template formed the basis of the entire subsequent organisation. Michael Smith's memorandum was a most accomplished piece of work.

Bishops were told that they could forget about summer holidays for that year. It was anticipated that there would be an announcement within days. It was thought that the visit would be of three days duration and the wise money was on the last days of September.

The long-awaited news came to me via a phone call from Cardinal Ó Fiaich in mid-afternoon on Friday, 20 July. The Holy

Father was coming on a pastoral visit to Ireland from Saturday, 29 September to Monday, 1 October. It was official. The Cardinal asked me, as Press Officer, to liaise with the Press Office in Dublin and arrange a press conference to announce the visit the following morning at 11 a.m., to coincide with a similar announcement in Rome. The Cardinal was excited and beside himself with joy. The press conference was arranged for Booterstown in Dublin. Even the press corps was excited in anticipation of the visit. One of the most frequently asked questions was 'Would the Holy Father visit the North?' We just did not know at that stage. All that was known, for certain, was that he would visit Dublin and Knock. The Irish Government, the Irish people and Irish media and most of the British media welcomed the announcement with enthusiasm. The only dissenting note came from a predictable quarter, in the person of Ian Paisley who threatened 'very serious trouble'* if the Pope attempted to visit the North. Whilst we were, of course, hoping that the Holy Father would visit the North during his visit, there were a lot of hurdles to be overcome before such a visit could be a reality. These were primarily political and diplomatic hurdles. We left the nitty-gritty of such negotiations to the Vatican's Secretariat of State and the Foreign Office and Northern Ireland Office in London. We had too many other things on our minds at that stage.

There was an extraordinary general meeting of the IEC on Tuesday, 24 July in Maynooth. Various committees were set up. I was asked to be a member of Committee of Bishops with overall responsibility to make all the decisions and arrangements necessary to prepare and organise the visit. The other members of this committee were the Cardinal and the three Archbishops, and the Bishops of Meath, Galway, Kilmore and Limerick. A National Committee and secretariat was established. This Committee, chaired by Bishop Francis McKiernan of Kilmore, was made up of a number of bishops and priests, Mr Joe Malone of Bord Fáilte, and Assistant Commissioner Eamonn O'Doherty of the Gardaí, Colonel Daly of the Irish Army, Mr Dowd of the Taoiseach's Office, Reg Ryan from Derry, Mother Jordana representing women religious,

---

* *Belfast News Letter*, 23 July 1979.

Maureen Groarke from Dublin and Jim Cantwell, Director of the Catholic Press & Information Office in Dublin. Father Michael Smith (now Bishop of Meath) and Father Seán Brady (now Cardinal Archbishop of Armagh) were joint secretaries. This National Committee, effectively, was the group that organised the visit. They accomplished a mammoth task and did incredible work in the space of sixty days. Liaison with the Irish Government, the Gardaí and the Army was arranged. We would need the whole-hearted cooperation of everyone, if the visit was to be a success. It was decided that a programme of pastoral preparation should be prepared for every parish in the country. The itinerary was again discussed, and the Committee of Bishops was asked to draw up a detailed itinerary and timetable for presentation to the Holy Father. Aer Lingus and Bord Fáilte had already come in and had been most helpful. It was also decided that a National Collection would take place early in September to cover the costs of the visit. We had no idea what the cost would be, although we realised that it would be significant.

The following weeks were filled with meetings and discussions and travel. The cooperation was quite magnificent. Gradually, an itinerary developed. It was hoped that a visit to the North would be included – a site in Armagh City, the playing fields of St Patrick's College, was identified and negotiations went on quietly in the background between the British and Vatican diplomats. If a visit to Armagh was not possible or feasible, Drogheda was chosen as a fall-back venue. It was felt that at some stage, the Holy Father should visit and speak in some location in the archdiocese of Armagh, the Primatial See and the See of Patrick. The main difficulty, however, was with a location much further south. The clergy and people of Cork, as the second city, were very keen that the Holy Father should visit there. There was unanimous support in the organising committees for a visit to Cork. But there were several insuperable difficulties about it. The Pope would be spending little more than fifty hours in Ireland. Dublin, as the capital city, and Knock, for which the initial invitation was forwarded, had to be on the itinerary. The Holy Father was to arrive on Saturday morning and had to be in Boston at 5 p.m. local time on Monday. The only airports in the Republic that could accommodate a Boeing 747 departing for a transatlantic flight, at that time, were Dublin and Shannon. All kinds of permutations and combinations were tried, but Cork could not be fitted in. The first day of the visit, Saturday, would be spent in Dublin and a visit to the Armagh archdiocese – Armagh or Drogheda. The Holy Father had asked for an opportunity to meet young people. Galway was decided upon as the venue for this meeting, because it could easily be accessed from all parts of the country and it had an excellent site, Galway racecourse at Ballybrit. Knock, of course, had to be visited. Galway and Knock were decided upon as the primary sites for the Sunday. The Holy Father also wished to speak to priests, seminarians and religious. It was decided that this should take place in Maynooth. Sunday or Saturday would not be feasible for this because of the weekend parish commitments of priests, so it was decided that this should take place on the Monday morning. The only possibility of a visit to Munster would be if it were to take place somewhere convenient to Shannon airport and the Pope's departure for Boston. Limerick was the location that was finally agreed upon. Everyone was disappointed that Cork could not be fitted into the itinerary, but perhaps on the next occasion of a Papal Visit to Ireland, Cork and Derry will figure on the itinerary!

Towards the end of July, Margaret Thatcher, the British Prime Minister, indicated to Gerry Fitt MP that she would have no objection to the Holy Father visiting the North. A few days later, very significantly, a group of Protestant clergymen expressed support for such a visit. The sensitive diplomatic and security negotiations continued in the background. The signs were favourable. Just one northern location was ever considered, the city of Armagh.

My main work during these weeks of preparation was focused on arrangements for the media. I headed up the national committee to plan services for the media at the various sites during the visit. Many of the leading figures in press and public relations in Ireland offered their services to us voluntarily. Their assistance was gratefully accepted and was hugely effective and valuable. There was an incredible media interest from all over the world. The Holy Father had previously visited Mexico and Poland. This would be his first visit to a western European country and he would be preaching and speaking in English on such a visit for the very first time. As it was the immediate prelude to a visit to the United States, there was considerable interest from there. On the day that the visit was announced, the Director General of RTÉ, Mr George Waters, wrote to me seeking cooperation in what he described as 'the biggest single programme and engineering operation ever undertaken by RTÉ'. He offered the assistance of senior executives to advise us on a confidential basis. This offer was also gratefully accepted. The Irish Government, which was incredibly helpful and generous, offered Dublin Castle as a possible national media centre for the operation. The media centre had been set up for European summit meetings. Jim Cantwell, the Press Officer, and I inspected facilities there on Thursday, 2 August, accompanied by other specialists in media organisations. It was immediately decided to accept this superb and generous offer. We set up liaison with Aer Lingus and Aer Rianta, the Airports Authority. We also set about preparing a media centre at each of the main venues for the papal ceremonies. By mid-August, these venues were determined as the Phoenix Park in Dublin, Drogheda or Armagh, Galway, Knock, Maynooth and Limerick. In early August, it was estimated that more than 1,000 journalists and media personnel would be involved. By then, 600 had sought accreditation. We were conscious that in planning the layout of each site it was important to include facilities for the visual media. These would have to be incorporated in the design and be coordinated at national level. RTÉ was hoping to cover every moment of the visit on live television. Telephone lines and telex machines would have to be installed at the various locations.

August 1979 was a blur of meetings for everyone concerned in organising the Papal Visit. On a few occasions, I left Derry at 4.30 in the morning and drove to Knock for a meeting at 8 a.m. and on to Galway and then on to Limerick for other site meetings and back for an evening meeting in Dublin. There were problems of one kind or another, but they were all eventually ironed out amicably and satisfactorily. The site at Knock presented particularly difficult and complex challenges. Most of the other sites consisted of open ground and could be planned and laid out from scratch. The Phoenix Park in Dublin, a huge set of open fields on a hillside outside Drogheda, racecourses in Galway and Limerick, were the suggested sites. In Knock, however, a main trunk road ran right through the centre of the site and there were many buildings and structures and the planning had to take place around these. Passage and access of emergency services had to be considered. This, allied to the strong personality of Monsignor Horan, led to some 'interesting' meetings. The press could not get enough stories about the visit, and the international interest grew and grew. Every new little nugget of information was gobbled up. The detailed plans for the week of pastoral preparation in each diocese and parish went on. People and priests were very enthusiastic. There was a wonderful spirit of cooperation throughout the country. Gradually, as the days passed on, the details about the visit and the itinerary became clearer. Cardinal Ó Fiaich, Archbishop Dermot Ryan of Dublin, Father Michael Smith and I were appointed by the Committee of Bishops to go to Rome to present and discuss the planned itinerary and other arrangements with the Holy Father and other senior Vatican officials at the end of August. The Holy Father would have the final say in these matters.

I travelled to Lourdes with the Derry Diocesan Pilgrimage on the night of Thursday, 23 August 1979. After spending a few days in Lourdes with the pilgrims, I flew from there to Rome on the evening of Sunday, 26 August. I joined the Cardinal and Archbishop Dermot Ryan in the Irish College there late on Sunday night. The Cardinal was in high spirits. He had just been told, in confidence, by Vatican officials that the visit to Armagh had been cleared both by the Holy See and by Britain. I was so excited that I found it difficult to sleep on that Sunday night. The approved itinerary was to be formally announced in Rome at 11 a.m. on the following Wednesday, 29 August.

There were various meetings on aspects of the visit with Vatican officials on the Monday morning. On Monday afternoon, we had a crucial meeting with Archbishop Paul Marcinkus. I was never quite sure of his precise position in relation to the visit, but he seemed to have responsibility for the Holy Father's security. Marcinkus was an American, from Chicago. He was tall, burly and imposing – but he was a very pleasant and capable individual. He had just returned from the United States, where he had been finalising arrangements for the Papal Visit there. The meeting took place in a reception room in the Irish College in Rome. Archbishop Marcinkus told us at the beginning of the meeting that we would be told formally the following day that the visit to Armagh had been cleared and approved on all sides. There would be simultaneous announcements in Rome, London and Dublin. We went through the details of the itinerary, the security and other arrangements with him in considerable detail. We were about two hours into the meeting when there was a knock on the door. Monsignor Eamonn Marron, Rector of the Irish College, entered and told us the terrible news that Lord Louis Mountbatten and members of his family had been murdered by a Provisional IRA bomb in Mullaghmore in County Sligo. They had apparently been engaged in a fishing trip and a bomb had been detonated in their boat. This had just been reported on an Italian news bulletin. Shock, sadness, silence and disgust transformed the atmosphere. We were all immediately aware that this development could have a potentially significant and damaging impact on plans for the Papal Visit, especially the visit to Armagh. The earlier elation evaporated. An hour later, Monsignor Marron called again to tell us that a large number of British soldiers had been murdered by an IRA bomb near Warrenpoint. We all experienced deep gloom and sadness. It is very difficult when one is abroad to assess precisely the full impact of any event at home. It was particularly difficult at that time of limited communication. However, we were quickly aware that these dreadful events would have a considerable impact on Armagh as a venue and, even, perhaps, on the very visit itself.

The following morning, many of the Rome newspapers led with the two stories of the outrageous and obscene slaughter and bloodshed in Mullaghmore and Warrenpoint. The Pope, in a statement, described the murders as 'an insult to human dignity'. On that same morning, we met with Cardinal Agostino Casaroli, the Vatican Secretary of State. Like us, he was deeply affected by the previous day's tragic and shameful events. He said, because of the fact that the Holy Father's Irish itinerary was to be announced the following day, it was his view that the visit to Armagh should not go ahead. Drogheda would now replace Armagh on the itinerary. We were deeply disappointed but not surprised in the circumstances. We discussed other aspects of the visit with him and we also discussed the general situation in Northern Ireland. Casaroli was a hugely impressive individual, the architect of *Ostpolitik* – the reaching out of the Church to Eastern Europe.

Later that day, Tuesday, 29 August, we met the Holy Father at his summer residence in Castel Gandolfo. We spent several memorable hours with him. He was accompanied by his secretaries, Father John Magee and Father Stanislaw Dziwisz. We had a lengthy meeting and dinner together. He was obviously looking forward to his visit to Ireland. He expressed his great shock and sadness at the Mountbatten and Warrenpoint murders. He was deeply upset about the atrocities. During the meeting, we discussed his forthcoming visit in detail and the various venues and possible topics for his various homilies and addresses. I was fascinated by the Pope's meticulous preparation. He discussed each venue and sought out any historical background or connotation. We talked with him about the Eucharistic Congress in the Phoenix Park in 1932 and the Eucharistic theme of the homily that he planned to preach there. Cardinal Ó Fiaich had visited the Drogheda and Armagh sites just before departing for Rome. He was able to point out that, from the speaking position on the podium in Drogheda, the Hill of Slane was clearly visible. At the Holy Father's request, panoramic photographs taken from the speaking position in Drogheda were subsequently prepared and sent to Rome – and the Hill of Slane was clearly pinpointed. In his address at Drogheda the Holy Father said, pointing towards the Hill of Slane:

> Not far from this spot on the Hill of Slane, it is said that he (St Patrick) lit, for the first time in Ireland, the paschal fire so that the light of Christ might shine forth on all of Ireland and unite all its people in the love of the one Jesus Christ. It gives me great joy to stand here today, within sight of Slane, and to proclaim the same Jesus, the Incarnate Word of God.*

The Holy Father was also deeply interested in the travels of the Irish monks in Europe and in his homeland. Cardinal Ó Fiaich was one of the great authorities on this aspect of Irish history and was only too

* *The Pope in Ireland: Addresses and Homilies* (Veritas, Dublin, 1979).

happy to discuss this. In passing, the Holy Father expressed an interest in visiting Clonmacnois, the site of the great monastery on the Shannon. Subsequently, this was incorporated into the itinerary, as it was close to the flight path from Dublin to Galway on the Sunday morning of the visit. Throughout the discussion, the Pope was very relaxed and informal. It was a truly unforgettable evening.

On the following day, Wednesday, 29 August, the full itinerary was announced at press conferences in Rome. The Holy Father would visit Dublin, Drogheda, Clonmacnois, Galway, Knock, Maynooth and Limerick. Cardinal Ó Fiaich said

> With Archbishop Dermot Ryan of Dublin, Bishop Edward Daly of Derry and Father Michael Smith, Secretary of the National Committee for the Papal Visit, I have spent the last two days in Rome finalising plans for the Holy Father's pastoral visit to Ireland.
>
> During these days we have had a two-hour Audience with the Holy Father at Castel Gandolfo. We have also had meetings with Cardinal Casaroli and officials of the Secretariat of State, with officials of the Sacred Congregation for Divine Worship, and with officials of the Vatican Press Office.
>
> The terrible events of recent days cast a heavy shadow over all our meetings and discussions.
>
> We welcome this afternoon's statement by the Holy See, and are grateful for the generous time the Holy Father has made available to our people.
>
> We have had personal experience of the deep grief of the Holy Father at the recent murders in our country. We share this grief and heartbreak. We would appeal for calm in Ireland in the period leading up to the Holy Father's arrival. We would ask that the pastoral preparation for this visit be undertaken with a new intensity and urgency.*

After we got back from Rome, the atmosphere in Ireland had changed significantly. Security had become the priority and now it dominated all the plans and preparations. The Gardaí were most

---

* Derry Diocesan Archive.

helpful in this, but insisted that security would be very tight and strictly enforced. Anyone getting anywhere close to the Holy Father would have to have individual security clearance and an identity badge denoting this. The already huge international press and media interest had also increased substantially and the Media Committee, like all the other committees, was at full stretch. By the first week of September, 2,000 applications for press accreditation had already been received. The Public Relations Institute of Ireland gave wonderful support in this area. More staff had to be recruited for the Press Office. There was a remarkable spirit of good will. Everyone pulled together and nothing was perceived as an insuperable problem. On the various sites around the country, the planning and design were completed and the construction of the massive altars and podiums was already under way. An advance party from Rome, led by Archbishop Marcinkus, visited the various sites in early September and made a number of suggestions.

People who were thought to be Loyalist paramilitaries were sighted in Knock one afternoon in mid-September. It was considered unlikely that they were there on a Marian pilgrimage from Sandy Row! This caused a significant security flap. There were other rumours that the Provisional IRA would exploit the situation for a major publicity stunt. However, there were no real security scares in the period of preparation or during the visit itself.

A Pastoral Letter from the Archbishops and Bishops of Ireland was published on the first Sunday of September. It was entitled *Ireland Awaits Pope John Paul II*. It was a rallying call to the faithful, inviting them to prepare for, participate in and enjoy this momentous occasion.

> This is an event unique in our history. For each one of us it is an event unique in our life-time. We must all be involved in the prayers and spiritual preparation and the material organisation required for the visit.

The Media Committee held a press briefing in the Montrose Hotel in Dublin on Thursday, 20 September. We announced the arrangements for press coverage there, introducing the directors of the nine press centres and one in reserve. Michael Dennehy headed the team at the National Press Centre in Dublin Castle. This was many years before email or the internet. It is difficult now to believe that fax had not yet been introduced into Europe at that time in 1979. We had a few fax machines presented to us by a Japanese company that manufactured them, but few journalists, apart from the big American networks and the Japanese had fax facilities to receive messages at the other end! The telephone, telex and wire photo terminals were the means by which reports were transmitted. Each of the nine centres was equipped with approximately 100 telephones, 30 telex machines and 10 wire photo terminals. Dark room facilities were provided at each centre. By 20 September, 2,400 journalists had sought accreditation and most of these had been processed for security clearance. RTÉ had decided to give live television coverage to every public event of the visit.

Every parish in the country was mobilised and the pastoral preparation was under way. There was an air of high excitement and great expectancy everywhere. Whilst people from the various regions were advised to go to one venue or another, people were making their own plans. Some decided to try to attend more than one venue. People turned out in great numbers to the various ceremonies held in each parish during the period of pastoral preparation. People were sighted in churches who had not been seen there for a long time.

Saturday, 29 September was a brilliant, sunny warm day. The Aer Lingus Boeing carrying the Holy Father arrived in Dublin Airport right on time, having flown over the multitudes assembled in the Phoenix Park. The Taoiseach, Jack Lynch, and members of the Government, as well as all the Irish bishops were there on the tarmac to greet the visitor. And thus began three wonderful days.

I was fortunate enough to attend most of the ceremonies during the visit. I was fascinated by the manner in which the Holy Father had woven the ideas we had discussed in Castel Gandolfo into his various addresses and homilies. The Phoenix Park was a superb setting and the sight of the assembled congregation of more than a million people was quite breathtaking. The liturgy and music were worthy of the occasion and the Holy Father's powerful homily on the Eucharist and his ability to communicate effectively with such a huge assembly completed the wonder of the occasion. All the weeks of painstaking and laborious planning suddenly seemed so worth-while. The music and singing were superb. Everything seemed to work very well. There were no security scares. The visit was off to a great start.

With some other bishops, I then flew by helicopter to the site at Drogheda. After take-off, we had an aerial view of the huge congregation of more than a million people in the Phoenix Park. The view was even more spectacular and breathtaking from the air and one got a greater sense of the sheer magnitude of the crowd. In a matter of minutes, as we approached Drogheda from the south, crossing the Boyne, we could see in the distance the assembled multitudes waiting on the Holy Father. They were assembled in fields on a hillside to the east of the main Dublin/Belfast road at Killineer, a few miles north of Drogheda. This was a particularly moving experience, in light of all that had gone on in previous weeks. As soon as I got to the platform, I looked out over the crowds stretching to the west and tried to identify the Hill of Slane, discussed in our meeting in Castel Gandolfo. I wondered if the Pope would mention it. The people were expectant and excited and happy. It was estimated that a quarter-of-a-million people were there. There was no palpable tension. There had been some fears that there might be some kind of disruption, protest or security threat at the Drogheda ceremony. There was no visible security but I was certain that it was in place. The only note of sadness was that this event should really have taken place in Armagh, within the Six Counties.

The Holy Father arrived, accompanied by Cardinal Ó Fiaich. He was given an ecstatic reception. I will always remember Cardinal Ó Fiaich during those days. He never stopped smiling. He was happy and radiant, beaming all over. John Hume fittingly read one of the scriptural readings. I had looked forward to the Holy Father's address in Drogheda. I knew that his theme would be peace and reconciliation. I wondered how he would address the particular complexities of our situation. There was huge worldwide media interest in the Drogheda address. As far as the media were concerned, this was *the* important address of his Irish visit. The event was transmitted live to a huge television audience around the world.

It was a powerful address. He first spoke about being in the episcopal see of Armagh, and then he spoke about St Patrick. He mentioned Slane and the lighting of the paschal fire by St Patrick. Gradually and powerfully, he developed his main theme. He quoted Pope Paul VI, who said 'True peace must be founded upon justice, upon a sense of the untouchable dignity of man, upon the recognition of an indelible and happy equality between men, upon the basic principle of human brotherhood'. And then he said 'Peace cannot be established by violence, peace can never flourish in a climate of terror, intimidation and death'.

He then spoke of reconciliation and applauded 'the efforts that had been made by countless men and women in Northern Ireland to walk the path of reconciliation and peace' and praised 'the spirit of Christian forgiveness shown by so many who have suffered in their persons or through their loved ones'.

Then he addressed individual constituencies:

Now I wish to speak to all men and women engaged in violence. I appeal to you, in language of passionate pleading. On my knees I beg you to turn away from the paths of violence and to return to the ways of peace. You may claim to seek justice. I, too, believe in justice and seek justice. But violence only delays the days of justice. Violence destroys the work of justice.

I appeal to young people who may have become caught up in organisations engaged in violence. I say to you, with all the love I have for you, with all the trust I have in young people: do not listen to voices which speak the language of hatred, revenge, retaliation. Do not follow any leaders who train you in the ways of inflicting death. Love life, respect life; in yourselves and in others.

Now I wish to speak to all people in positions of leadership, to all who can influence public opinion, to all members of political parties and to all who support them ... Never think you are betraying your own community by seeking to understand and respect and accept those of a different tradition. You will serve your own community best by working for reconciliation with the others.

To all who bear political responsibility for the affairs of Ireland, I want to speak with the same urgency and intensity with which I have spoken to the men of violence. Do not cause or condone or tolerate conditions which give excuse or pretext to men of violence. Those who resort to violence always claim that only violence brings about change. They claim that political action cannot achieve justice. You politicians must prove them to be wrong. You must show that there is a peaceful, political way to justice.*

It was a powerful address, delivered with striking clarity, conviction and sincerity. John Paul had the actor's skill of projecting himself and his voice to his audience. His words were listened to with great attention and he was interrupted on many occasions by clamorous applause. The points were very well made. I did not like the use of the term 'men of violence' because it was used in the parlance of that time as a pejorative term to describe only the violence of paramilitaries, primarily Republican paramilitaries. But that is merely a personal quibble. Sadly, whilst the address was very well received by the mass of the people, the response from those to whom it was specifically addressed was very disappointing. Eventually, a whole decade later, in the early 1990s, the various parties concerned began to address the issues highlighted by the Holy Father. It was a huge tragedy that there was not the required response at the time. Hundreds of lives could have been saved and much of the subsequent suffering could have been averted. I am convinced that the address offered the Provisional IRA a golden opportunity to get out of the conflict situation with some honour and they chose to ignore it. Had they made some significant gesture at that time of international worldwide attention, it could have borne much fruit. Their beleaguered community in the North could have had the sympathy of many people around the world. Many hundreds of people who subsequently lost their lives or liberty would have lived.

Later on the Saturday evening, the Pope met and addressed various groups, including the leaders of other Christian Churches and religious groups in Ireland. I had the privilege of accompanying the

* *The Pope in Ireland: Addresses and Homilies* (Veritas, Dublin, 1979).

Holy Father when he gave an audience to members of the media very late on the Saturday night. Hundreds of journalists had patiently waited for hours in a hall in Cabra. They gave the Holy Father a tumultuous welcome when he appeared on the balcony of the hall and addressed them.

On Sunday, the Holy Father visited Clonmacnois as a salute to the early Irish missionaries to the Continent and especially to Poland. Then there was the Mass for the Youth in Galway. An estimated quarter-of-a-million young people created a unique atmosphere despite the drizzle that fell throughout that Sunday. It was the first time that I had witnessed at first hand Pope John Paul II in the presence of young people. I simply don't know and can't analyse the chemistry that took place on such occasions. I witnessed it on a few subsequent occasions. Whatever the language, whatever the situation, however large or small the crowd, he seemed to be able to communicate in a remarkable manner with young people. It was a wonderful gift, fascinating to behold.

The Pope continued his journey in the afternoon by celebrating Mass in Knock, the primary reason for his visit. Among those he met in Knock were the sick and people with disabilities. He preached a powerful homily about Mary, the Mother of Christ, a homily that was obviously much influenced by his Polish background. I was very happy and pleased for Monsignor Horan on that day. He was the man who had invited the Holy Father, who had always thought that a visit was possible, and on that day, he saw his dream realised. On the down side, there were many tens of thousands of people who came to Knock and who were unable to see the Pope. His arrival was later than scheduled – the weather and the approach of darkness restricted his tour of the site in the Popemobile after the celebration of Mass – and the site itself astride a main road with many buildings made things extraordinarily difficult. My own sister and her family were among the thousands who had travelled through the night and waited from early morning but saw nothing of the Holy Father, except the helicopter flying overhead. They heard his voice dimly in the distance. That was a great pity. As mentioned earlier, the site in Knock presented huge challenges.

On the Monday morning, the Holy Father went to Maynooth and addressed priests, religious and seminarians. This was the only major event I missed during the Papal Visit – bad weather and poor visibility ruled out our helicopter flight. I made my way with some others to Shannon by Aer Lingus and on to Limerick for the final Mass of his visit. We flew from Dublin to Shannon on the aircraft that, later that day, would bring the Holy Father to the United States and had an opportunity to view the section of the aircraft prepared for the Pope's personal use. After the Mass in Limerick, the Pope left from Shannon Airport, in time for the Mass in Boston at 5 p.m., Boston time. Archbishop Marcinkus, who, during the planning stages, had frequently expressed concern about his punctual arrival in Boston, must have been pleased.

With the other bishops, I flew back to Dublin after the Holy Father's departure. There was a lot of relief and satisfaction that everything had gone so well. I went to Dublin Castle and all those involved in the media coverage were extremely happy. The Media Centre was crowded with hundreds of journalists from all over the world. Carried away by the occasion, I announced a free bar in the Media Centre that evening. After an hour, I had to 'review the situation' and briskly bring things back to normality! I had seriously under-estimated the thirst of journalists after three days' hard work!

There was a 'feel good' atmosphere throughout the country. There was a sense that Ireland had done itself proud, that the visit had been superbly organised and was relatively free of any major glitch. Despite incredible traffic congestion, huge crowds had travelled to see the Holy Father at various venues and the television coverage had been spectacular. RTÉ, who coordinated television coverage, had performed magnificently and were rewarded with huge viewing figures. The British television networks gave the visit saturation treatment. Newspapers gave the visit blanket coverage. The dynamism, personality and communication skills of the Pope had impressed even the most cynical. They were good days for Ireland and for the Church.

The Papal Visit to Ireland took place just over thirty years ago. There seems to be a collective amnesia about the positive aspects of that visit, about those few wonderful days. Understandably, but sadly, the distressing events and revelations within the Church in recent years have tended to overshadow those momentous days. The visit of Pope John Paul II to Ireland in 1979, however, should not be forgotten. The ability of the Irish people to organise an event of this magnitude in such a short period of time is something of which we can all be proud. Any event that attracted an attendance of virtually half of the population of the country over a forty-eight hour period is hugely significant, by any standards.

In the few years immediately after the Papal Visit, there was an increase in the numbers entering the seminary to study for the priesthood. The visit boosted my own morale as a priest and bishop and I think that it boosted the morale of many others. I was deeply disappointed that there was not a more positive response from Republican paramilitaries. It was my perception that, despite the pastoral follow-up to the visit, there was not any significant or notable increase in religious practice. Perhaps the Church did not exploit fully the pastoral opportunities and the goodwill that the visit generated.

It is difficult now to place oneself in the environment of the early 1980s. Perhaps the national euphoria in the wake of the Papal Visit lulled the Church, both clergy and people, into a false sense of well-being. The following twenty-five years were years of radical and unprecedented change in Ireland. The Celtic Tiger arrived on our shores. The Catholic Church and a substantial section of Irish society, particularly in the Republic, were found to be singing from different hymn sheets. Then the child sexual abuse issue emerged. All these elements are part of the explanation of why the 1979 Papal Visit is often unfairly characterised today by featuring an impromptu warm-up act in Galway rather than the congregation of a million people in the Phoenix Park.

Will there ever be another Papal Visit to Ireland? Security requirements and modern health and safety regulations could make such a visit almost prohibitively expensive. Two things are certain. If a Pope is ever to visit the island of Ireland again, the North and Cork will have to be on the itinerary and there will be no unscheduled warm-up acts.

CHAPTER 7

Prisons and Prisoners

I considered parish visitation to be one of the priorities of my epis-copal ministry. During the pastoral visits to parishes I went to see those who could not come to see me – the sick and those confined to their homes through age or disability. There was another group of people who could not come to meet me – those who were in prison.

My first visit to a prison was in the mid-1960s when a parishioner was serving a term in Crumlin Road Prison in Belfast for some mis-demeanour or other. I have to admit a sense of excitement and a twinge of curiosity when I was travelling there to visit a prison for the first time. Crumlin Road, designed by Sir Charles Lanyon and opened in the 1840s, was the archetypal Victorian prison, just like those portrayed on old black-and-white British films. There were just two prisons for adult prisoners in the North at that time, Crumlin Road in Belfast, and Armagh. I had very few opportunities at the time to visit prisons, because the Bogside district was relatively crime-free and I can scarcely recall anyone else from the area being sent to prison from my arrival there until the outbreak of conflict in 1968/9.

After the Battle of the Bogside in 1969 and the increasing street confrontations taking place, many young people found themselves in prison, being arrested during rioting. The sentence was usually six months – a long time in the life of a teenager. But imprisonment almost became a badge of honour at that time. In August 1971, internment – imprisonment without trial – was introduced, and the number of people in captivity, as well as the number of prisons esca-lated rapidly and considerably. There were now two new hastily built prisons or internment camps in the North – Long Kesh, outside Lisburn, and Magilligan on the estuary of the River Foyle about twenty-five miles from Derry. There was also a prison ship anchored in Belfast. It was called HMS *Maidstone*, a former submarine depot ship. Both the Long Kesh and Magilligan sites were military camps that were hastily converted into internment camps, and subsequently prisons. Internees were held in Magilligan as well as Long Kesh. There were also prisoners from Derry being held in prisons in the Republic – in Portlaoise and in Mountjoy Prison in Dublin. Gradually, I found myself visiting prisons and internment camps with increasing frequency during my latter days as a curate.

Prisons are not the type of place you can casually visit when you happen to be in the neighbourhood. Permission has to be sought in advance. Very intense searches have to be undergone by visitors. And, in the larger prisons, the access to the prisoner is usually painfully slow and involves long periods of waiting in the visiting area. I had great sympathy with the families of those in prison. It requires huge commitment to visit a prison a few times a month. Most families were exceedingly generous to any family member held in prison. Many of the internees and those imprisoned for offences related to the conflict refused to eat prison food. This resulted in their families bringing them food every week. I remember one family telling me that the only time they saw butcher meat in the home was when they purchased it to bring it to their son in prison.

As a bishop, I tried to visit all my diocesans in prison at least once a year. This involved considerable amounts of travel. The majority of those from our diocese who were imprisoned or interned were held in Long Kesh or Magilligan. Magilligan Prison, sited at the very mouth of the Foyle estuary, was and is the only prison in the Derry diocese. The historic Derry Gaol in Bishop Street in the city was closed in the 1950s. Visits to Long Kesh were complicated – it was a huge complex with a mixture of Second World War prison camp accommodation and subsequently H-Blocks. I was filled with enormous admiration for the prison chaplains and the work they carried out. Crumlin Road Prison was phased out early on in my ministry.

Then there was Armagh Prison. This was where female prisoners were held. This prison was commissioned by the Church of Ireland Archbishop of Armagh in the 1770s and could have been the set for a film based on a Dickens novel. Still in use 200 years later,

Armagh Prison was a most appalling place. It had a splendid façade, located at the end of a mall, a substantial green park, surrounded by elegant Georgian houses in the middle of Armagh city. You could just imagine in days gone by, gentlemen playing cricket in their whites, society women resplendent in long crinoline dresses walking and nannies wheeling their prams in the park, whilst nearby other women were held in the most dreadful and humiliating conditions. The conditions were still terrible in the 1970s and 1980s. I always found visiting women in prison to be a discomfiting experience. Somehow, it seemed incongruous that women should be imprisoned. The conditions and surroundings in Armagh Prison further accentuated that incongruity. It was a hideous place. Father Raymond Murray did wonderful work as chaplain there.

After my appointment as bishop, visiting people from the diocese in various prisons became an integral part of my pastoral ministry. It also became quite a challenging aspect of ministry. Most commentators writing about the conflict in the North agree that the prisons and prisoners formed a very significant and influential dimension of the conflict. At various times, there were people from the diocese in prisons all over the island of Ireland and in many parts of England.

I celebrated Mass for the prisoners in Magilligan Prison at least once each year during my term as bishop – usually on the Sunday before Christmas. On a few occasions, I celebrated Mass in Long Kesh and on one occasion in the female section of Durham Prison in England. Most of those I visited in prison were prisoners from the diocese. A visit often took up a considerable period of time. When there was a large number to visit, I was occasionally permitted to go on to the prison wings. When there were just one or two, I usually met them in the visiting area.

In my early years as bishop, visits to the internees were perhaps the most memorable. They were housed in groups of rather dilapidated Nissan Huts surrounded by coiled barbed wire and link fencing. Each of these enclosures was called a 'cage' by the prisoners and a 'compound' by the prison authorities. The prison officers remained outside and the prisoners seemed to control everything inside the wire. The setting was strikingly similar to the Second World War German prison camps that one sees portrayed in films.

It was quite clear that the internees were disciplined and self-sufficient. They covered a wide range of age groups, from teenagers to men who could have been their grandfathers. They cooked their own food, wore their own clothes and the command structure inside the compound or cage determined the daily timetable. Education was deemed important, especially, at that time, education in the Irish language. Despite their justified frustration about being locked up without charge or trial, morale always seemed to be high. There was great solidarity and mutual support for one another. There was, however, a palpable controlled and justifiable anger. None of them had been charged or tried for any offence; yet they were deprived of their freedom.

Many people have the doubtful distinction of being thrown into prison. I had the even more dubious distinction of being thrown out of prison, on two occasions, once by prisoners and once by the prison authorities! I had the first experience in Magilligan when I was there in the course of a pastoral visit to the parish of Limavady. It was in May 1975. The afternoon before the visit, an RUC officer was murdered on the city walls in Derry. I had criticised the murder in the strongest possible terms in a radio interview and some of the Provisional IRA members held in the prison had taken grave exception to what I said. I visited one or two compounds, but when I arrived at the compound where the IRA Commanding Officer in the camp was housed I was met by him at the gate accompanied by a few of his underlings and formally told that, in view of my comments on the previous day, I was not welcome or acceptable in that compound. I was asked to leave the compound immediately. The CO was from Derry City. I knew his family, especially his mother, very well. The confrontation was not angry but cold and military and formal. There was another young Derry man held in that compound whose mother had called with me a few days previously and asked me especially to talk to him about a delicate and pressing family matter. I asked the CO to come aside and, in broad terms, told him privately about this, without mentioning the individual's name. He was unmoved. I had to leave. I would not be permitted to speak to any of his men under any circumstances. I then departed and, ironically, as I passed a nearby Loyalist compound, was greeted warmly by some of the men there and we had a friendly discussion through the wire. I was fascinated by the fact that they were already aware that I had been refused entry to the Republican compound only a few moments earlier.

The second time that I was 'ejected' from a prison occurred in Portlaoise a few weeks later. I found myself travelling from Derry to Cork on a Saturday morning, and I decided, when I was passing, to visit several of my diocesans who were held in Portlaoise Prison. I was told that there had been a security scare earlier on that day and, because of this, I was refused permission to visit. I appealed to the authorities and even, by telephone, to the Department of Justice in Dublin to no avail. In an interview with RTÉ radio a short time later, I complained about this and my complaint gave rise to an amazing and lengthy letter from a senior civil servant in the Department of Justice. I have to admit that the authorities on that occasion were quite justified in their decision. I was wrong to complain and I have to admit that I was a little 'over the top' in my radio interview. I had not given the prison authorities adequate notice of my intention to visit. I was able to visit Portlaoise Prison without any difficulty on many subsequent occasions.

On most occasions, I was treated with correctness and courtesy by prison officers. On almost every occasion, I was permitted to be alone with the prisoner or prisoners – except in Limerick Prison. The authorities there insisted that I be accompanied by a male prison officer who sat beside me across the table from the prisoner throughout the visit. On my first visit there, I had a lengthy discussion with a female prisoner from Derry. The discussion became quite heated as we chatted about the political situation in the North and she took the opportunity, as was her right, to express criticism of some of the things I had said about the activities of the IRA. Whilst accompanying me back to the main gate of the prison, the prison officer remarked 'And I always thought that you were a Provo sympathiser!' I was only really frightened in a prison situation on one occasion. That was when I was locked in a small Portakabin on my own in Portlaoise with a prisoner who was obviously very disturbed and angry with the world in general. He got very irate and his eyes were full of aggression. However, to my relief, he gradually calmed down. On most occasions, visits were pleasant and prayerful and, on many occasions, interesting and challenging. Paradoxically, it was the only situation in which one could discuss and debate many of the most important moral issues of the conflict with those who were actively involved on the Republican side. In prison, people freely admitted they were in the IRA and were glad to discuss and argue the morality issues – outside nobody would admit to membership!

After my appointment as bishop, I began to get letters from people in prison. I responded to these and this became a large part of my week's work. Over the years, I received hundreds of letters from people in prison and replied to virtually all of them. Prisoners' letters dealt with all kinds of topics. Some were concerned at the injustice of their detention, or the injustice of their conviction. Others were concerned about family and domestic situations at home. There were some who took great exception to things I had said or the position of the Church on some issues related to the conflict. There were allegations of maltreatment in custody and complaints about prison food. Others were concerned about parole and early release. Many of the prisoners had been convicted by Diplock Courts* on very suspect evidence often elicited during interrogation in Castlereagh Interrogation Centre, outside Belfast. Many of the interrogation techniques used in Castlereagh were subsequently found to be grossly unjust and infringing the human rights of those being questioned. A lot of letters were received from people who were being held 'at the Secretary of State's pleasure' – SOSPs, as they were called. These were people who were found guilty by Diplock Court of offences committed when they were under-18 (minors) and sentenced to indeterminate periods. There were short letters and long letters – one prisoner who spent long periods in solitary confinement frequently sent me letters more than thirty pages long in close handwriting! He regularly discussed theology and scripture, politics and Irish history in some considerable detail. Then there were the 'comms' – these were letters written in tiny amazingly

---

* The Diplock Courts were a type of court established by the British Government in Northern Ireland in August 1973, in an attempt to overcome widespread alleged jury intimidation in trials related to the Troubles. The right to trial by jury was suspended for certain 'scheduled offences' and the court consisted of a single judge. The courts were eventually abolished in 2007.

legible print on a sheet of toilet paper folded over and over again and wrapped in cling film and smuggled out of prison in the various 'orifices' of the human anatomy. These were usually the most interesting of all items of prison correspondence because they were not seen by the censors!

Letters came from both Loyalist and Republican prisoners. I was surprised on the first occasion that I had a letter from a Loyalist prisoner. He had read something that I had written or said about prison issues. That began a long and interesting correspondence. This subsequently led to some of the Loyalist prisoners' families from Carrickfergus and Belfast coming to see me in my house in Derry about prison matters. There was an unusual atmosphere about that meeting between a 'Roman' bishop and hard-line Loyalist families in the heart of the Bogside in the mid-1970s. I always remember that they were scathing in their criticism of their political leaders. They felt that they had been abandoned by everyone, by their own clergy and politicians. I endeavoured to advise and assist them as best I could. The Republican prisoners' representatives on the outside seemed to be much better organised than the Loyalists' at that time. Both sets of prisoners had similar problems and issues. In some prisons, the prisoners were only given a limited amount of paper for writing. It was amazing the amount of information that could be fitted into such a restricted space. Responding to these letters was a time-consuming but very worthwhile activity. I usually did it late at night. Prisoners had all the time in the world to write letters. I did not have as much time. Responding to one letter from a prisoner could involve writing to the Northern Ireland Office, to the prisoner's solicitors and to the prisoner himself or herself. During my years as bishop, I wrote all my letters myself. I tried to acquire the technique of dictating letters for my secretary to type up, but I was never able to master this skill. As a result, every single letter was typed by myself on either a typewriter, or, in latter years, a word processor or computer. I wrote hundreds of letters a year to my many correspondents around the world. I found it easier to think when I was writing rather than dictating.

There was one prisoner with whom I had a very special involvement. He was a young Derry man who received thirty life sentences in the Old Bailey in 1976. He served in various prisons in England and subsequently in Long Kesh and Maghaberry here in the North. He was eventually released from prison in 1989. During much of his time in prison, I conducted a lengthy correspondence with him. He is and was a highly intelligent man and, like many others, he would never have been in prison had it not been for conflict that consumed us at that time. He used his time in prison to develop his mind and intelligence and pursued A Levels and subsequently several university degrees. Through him, I got a powerful insight into the motivation that drove young people to become involved in the IRA. He was an amazing young man who taught me a lot about the virtue of fortitude. His name was Shane Paul O'Doherty, a young man from St Eugene's parish in Derry.* Through him, I first met and got to know Paddy Hill and some other members of the Birmingham Six at Gartree Prison in the English Midlands in the late 1970s. Shane and Paddy convinced me of the innocence of those serving sentences for the Birmingham bombing and persuaded me to take part in the campaign to prove their innocence. (I will discuss the case of the Birmingham Six in a later chapter.) Shane was also one of just three or four of the hundreds of people I visited or corresponded with in prison who kept up contact with me after they re-emerged from that part of their life. He was moved from high-security prison to high-security prison around England with cruel frequency – he once memorably described a journey through Stratford-on-Avon in a prison van when he could only see the sky outside through the narrow windows near the roof of the vehicle as he mused on the wonders of Shakespeare's writing and plays!

Shane was the first prisoner I visited in an English prison – Wormwood Scrubs in London. Subsequent to that visit, I spent about a week each summer and a day or two each winter visiting prisoners in various high security prisons in England. This usually involved driving from Derry to Durham, via Larne and Stranraer, and on to the Midlands and other prisons located there and then down to London and prisons in the south. As a result, I got to know the English motorway network very well. After a few visits, I was

---

* Shane wrote a fascinating book on his experiences: Shane O'Doherty, *The Volunteer* (Fount, London, 1993).

allowed on to the wings to meet the prisoners. I usually found accommodation in religious houses or colleges, or in hotels or B&Bs. I had a number of relatives and many friends in England, who would have been glad to put me up, but I was always reluctant to stay with them lest they be suspected by the Special Branch or other security agencies of having Republican sympathies and suffer the consequences. There were a number of people in English prisons just because they inadvertently attracted attention to themselves by offering such hospitality to Irish people and relatives visiting prisons. The most notable example was, perhaps, Annie Maguire. She and her family were the victims of dreadful injustice. It is one of my great regrets that I did not arrange to meet Annie Maguire during some of my visits to Durham Prison, when I visited prisoners there from Derry and Donegal.

Visiting Wormwood Scrubs for the afternoon visiting period was particularly interesting. There was always a colourful bunch of people, mostly women and mostly Londoners, in the queue to get through security, awaiting the opening of the visiting period. These Cockney women had lots of comments, many of them unprintable, some hilariously funny, to make about the men whom they were going to visit and about the prison authorities. They were fascinated by the presence of 'a vicar' in the queue. The conversation was as colourful as the people. I remember once, many years ago, standing in a queue outside Wormwood Scrubs for the afternoon visiting period that begins at 2 p.m. Some of those in the queue insisted that 'you are a vicar and you should not have to stand in the queue'. They insisted that I go and present myself at the door. I was very reluctant to do this as I was enjoying the banter and the meetings with various interesting individuals, and besides, I do not particularly like 'pulling rank'. I tried to persuade them that I was happy to remain in the queue. In that particular queue there were two heavily bejewelled blonde ladies who had arrived at the prison in a chauffeur-driven Bentley. There were straight out of a 1940s George Raft black-and-white movie. They eventually prevailed on me to go to the main door and seek admission. I was brusquely refused admission and told to take my place in the queue like everyone else! The people outside were furious. One of the bejewelled ladies said in her Cockney accent, 'Although I am not a religious person, I am very upset about this'. I was not upset in the slightest. In fact, I was delighted to have another twenty minutes of chat and craic with the people in the queue!

I was normally afforded great courtesy and assistance from the prison authorities. During all those years, the only two prisons where I was subjected to a full body search, prior to a visit, were Portlaoise and Limerick. In both cases, I had to remove my coat and jacket and shoes and be subjected to a full body search before being admitted. I was treated with more suspicion in prisons in the Irish Republic than elsewhere. The authorities there obviously did not trust me. It is interesting to note that I never experienced such searches in any prison in the North or in England – even though one prisoner succeeded in escaping from Long Kesh dressed as a priest! I did not object to being searched. I just found it interesting that I was closely searched in one jurisdiction and not the other. I usually brought a plentiful supply of cigarettes with me during visits, but I would not dream of bringing anything else. The prison author-ities showed me respect and I wished to show them respect. I hasten to add that, during all those years, no prisoner ever asked me to smuggle anything into or out of prison for them. It was never even suggested.

Long Kesh was, by far, the best-known prison in the North. It was the scene of the most dramatic prison escape in 1983 and, of course, it was the scene of the hunger strikes in 1980 and 1981. Formerly a military base outside Lisburn, it came into use as a prison at the time of internment in 1971. It gradually became the biggest prison in the North. The first H-Blocks were built there – H-shaped buildings with four wings, the central crossbar in the H being the location of most of the prison officers' posts and controls. Each H-Block was a self-contained prison with walls and wire around the buildings and the surrounding exercise area. Despite all the efforts to the contrary, each wing housed and was controlled by a paramili-tary grouping, either Loyalist or Republican. The wings were noisy with the constant clanging of metal doors and shouting. The heat was always oppressive; a lot of the prisoners just seemed to wear football shorts and nothing else. The odour of stale perspiration and staler cooking predominated. At times, the tension was akin to a pressure cooker; at other times, it was relatively relaxed. Over the years, I had the opportunity to visit wings housing Loyalist and wings housing Republican prisoners. There was a striking contrast between the two. The Republican prisoners, in the main, seemed to be constantly engaged in study of various kinds, reading, learning languages, discussing politics and in the latter years after the hunger strikes doing A Levels and studying with the Open University and other universities. The Loyalist prisoners generally seemed to be engaged in more corporal and mundane activities, such as body building and weight lifting. There were exceptions, of course, in both situations. But generally, that was a true description of the contrasting situations. On one visit to a Loyalist compound, I was taken out by some of the prisoners into a small yard in one of the H-Blocks and I was shown around a very elaborate aviary there. There was a wide and impressive variety of exotic birds. The birds seemed to be very well cared for. As far as I could see, there were no carrier pigeons!

I spent most of my time visiting Republican prisoners. Apart from the one rejection in Magilligan in 1975, already mentioned, I was always welcomed with courtesy and warmth by prisoners. The dimension of courtesy and warmth reflected the political atmosphere outside, and what had been said in the recent past. Had I reason to be critical of the IRA in the previous few weeks, the atmosphere was on the cooler side; had I reason to be critical of the RUC, British Army or Government in the previous few weeks, the atmosphere was warmer and more welcoming. I always found it easier to relate to the prisoners from Derry City than to any of the others – perhaps because I knew many of them and their families. The intensity of some of the men frightened me. There was a clear sense that the war was being fought in the prisons as well as outside. It was much easier to relate to people when individual meetings took place. The group meetings were usually dominated by one or two of the hardest men and the others did not say anything. I found in meeting men individually that there was a much greater variety of views and a much more constructive and open discussion.

I was always struck by the morale of prisoners. Even in the most dire circumstances they seemed to be in good form. The late Father

Denis Faul once said to me that if prisoners are in good form, it is a sign that they are digging a tunnel and that progress is good! If, on the other hand, they are in bad form, it is a sign that a tunnel has recently been discovered by the authorities!

At one stage, I think in the mid-1980s after the hunger strikes, Long Kesh was renamed as The Maze. There seems to be a British penchant for renaming places or things when they gain unpleasant connotations. The local area is called The Maze and there is a nearby racecourse with the same name. But posterity will always know that prison outside Lisburn as Long Kesh which, I think, was the name of the original Second World War base on that site. There is a nuclear processing facility in England on the Irish Sea just across from County Down that was called Windscale for years. And then, when people began to get concerned about nuclear waste in the Irish Sea, the plant was renamed as Sellafield. Whether it was called Windscale or Sellafield, it was and still is an extremely suspect nuclear processing facility – just as Long Kesh or The Maze is, or was, the name of a notorious prison.

When speaking of those in prison, the families of prisoners have to be remembered. The families of most prisoners were extraordinarily devoted and loyal to their sons and daughters. They made regular visits, usually once a week. They brought them food and all kinds of other little permissible luxuries. They often left themselves and other members of their families in considerable need as a result. It should also be borne in mind that many of the people in prison spent ten years or longer there. Few families had cars of their own. Public transport did not cater for prisons in isolated areas. The families, therefore, depended on privately commissioned minibuses to take them to and from prison. A return journey to Long Kesh from Derry took many hours – most of a day. These distances were substantially magnified for those who had to travel to the Republic or England. There was a modicum of funding from Social Welfare and other funds were raised to assist such families, but, even with this assistance, many of the families were left in penury as a result of the imprisonment of a family member. Many of them made repeated visits to me and the local public representatives on various issues related to their sons and daughters. The families outside and particularly parents possibly suffered more anxiety and stress than the person imprisoned. In addition to all the other pressures, their homes were regularly raided by the Army and RUC. On some occasions, families of prisoners complained to me that they were experiencing undue pressure from the IRA and their representatives. Family members paid an inordinately high price for the activities of their sons and daughters, although, at the time, many of them were totally unaware of their clandestine activities.

CHAPTER 8

The Hunger Strikes

The hunger strikes in 1980 and 1981 were seminal events in the thirty-year history of the Northern conflict.

Internment, imprisonment without charge or trial, was brought to an end in December 1975 by Merlyn Rees, NI Secretary of State. Internment had lasted for four-and-a-half years. It was completely unjust, administered in a largely sectarian manner and it was a political and social disaster. However, interrogation procedures and prison issues were to remain controversial for the duration of the conflict. Merlyn Rees introduced a 'criminalisation' procedure for paramilitary prisoners as from 1 March 1976. All prisoners charged with politically related crimes committed after that date were placed on the same level as common criminals. They were convicted by non-jury Diplock Courts very often largely on the basis of evidence elicited by questionable means. This criminalisation procedure proved to be the launch pad for further, even more deadly, protests. Republican prisoners demanded that they should be given 'special category status' and treated as prisoners of war. In September 1976, the 'blanket strike' began in Long Kesh Prison, when a Republican prisoner protested at being treated as a common criminal by refusing to put on prison uniform. He had his own clothes taken from him. In his naked condition, he wrapped the blanket of his cell bed around him and remained in that garb day and night. Subsequently, other prisoners joined him in this protest. Because of their refusal to accept the prison rules, they lost all privileges regarding letters, parcels and visitors and lost all the remission to their sentences to which 'good conduct' normally would have entitled them. The men undertaking this protest were described as being 'on the blanket'. Violent confrontations frequently took place between prisoners and warders and cell furniture was broken up and used as weapons. Ultimately, the prisoners who refused to conform were deprived of beds, tables and chairs and were left with nothing in the cell but a thin foam rubber mattress on the floor.

In March 1978, the prisoners 'on the blanket' escalated their protest by refusing to clean out their cells, wash or go to the toilet. They smeared the walls and ceilings of their cells with their own excrement and the floors streamed with urine. The lasting memory of visits to Long Kesh during that protest was the horrendous stench. The cells were industrially cleaned by the prison authorities with power hoses from time to time and prisoners were moved to other cells. I have no idea how people lived or worked in those conditions. During my visits there to the wings, I was violently ill on several occasions. The revolting and foul smell seemed to permeate everything I wore, even days after the visit. Items of outer clothing, even after dry cleaning, were virtually unusable subsequently.

In 1980, after four years of unsuccessful protests appealing for special status, a status that would recognise them as political prisoners, prisoners of war rather than criminals, rumours began to circulate that a hunger strike was imminent.

Individually and jointly, Cardinal Tomás Ó Fiaich and I made several lengthy visits to the H-Blocks in Long Kesh Prison in the spring and summer months of 1980, meeting virtually all the protesting prisoners individually in their cells. These visits usually lasted from early morning until late in the evening. We also met with the prison authorities and visited some Loyalist prisoners, including some of their better-known leaders.

Those lengthy visits to Long Kesh are etched forever in my memory. Spending seven or eight hours at a time going around cells visiting young men in those conditions was unforgettable. It was a parallel universe. There were usually two men in each cell. Their hair was matted and they had long unkempt beards. They were thin and haggard and their eyes were sunken. They wore long blankets. There was no furniture in the cells. The stench was intense and all-pervasive. I simply do not know how people retained their sanity after spending such a long time in that environment. Yet I always found the prisoners in high spirits and imbued with a steely determination. Only a few of them talked about a hunger strike. However, Cardinal Ó Fiaich and I were both convinced that if they embarked upon that course, they would see it through. We also believed that if these men were to embark on their threatened hunger strike, it could have disastrous consequences for the community as a whole. We decided to approach the British Government jointly on behalf of the prisoners. We believed that they had a legitimate and arguable case and that both the Government and prisoners and society generally in the North would benefit from a less stringent and degrading prison regime. We reached this conclusion on the basis that were it not for the political circumstances that these young people found themselves in, most of them would never have seen the inside of a prison. Most of them came from stable family backgrounds. We also believed that these protests were undertaken on the prisoners' own initiative, rather than on bidding or orders from any group outside the prison. Equally, we believed that the protest in the prison was perceived by the prisoners as their continuing contribution to the struggle going on outside the prison. The issue was further complicated by the fact that a sustained paramilitary campaign was going on contemporaneously throughout the North. In the course of that campaign, many prison officers were murdered. Those who perpetrated these murders claimed that they were acting in support of the prisoners on protest. There was intense anger and hatred between the prisoners and prison staff. There were many allegations of assault. Intimate body searches were frequently carried out, often in a brutal and demeaning manner. There are few dignified methods where intimate strip searches are concerned. The searcher and the searched are dehumanised. Long Kesh was a loathsome, hateful place as well as a powder keg as the 1970s moved to the 1980s.

After our initial visits, the Cardinal and I sought an urgent meeting with Humphrey Atkins who was Secretary of State at that time. Margaret Thatcher was Prime Minister. Subsequently, during the summer months of 1980, we had five meetings with Atkins, three meetings with his senior officials of the Northern Ireland Office with responsibility for prisons and discussions with members of the Prison Board of Visitors who expressed support for our stance on the clothing issue. There were also meetings with parents and other relatives of prisoners on protest, as well as repeated visits to some of the prisoners. We formulated and argued for a new concept of prison work, arguing that education would be much more effective and productive than occupations of a penal or humiliating nature. We also insisted that prisoners should be allowed to wear their own clothes. Most of these meetings took place at Stormont Castle. One was held at another location in Belfast and one in Armagh. We were usually told to treat the meetings as strictly confidential. Yet, on almost every occasion, members of the media were there at the gates to meet us as we arrived at Stormont Castle or as we left! We discussed the situation in great detail. We consulted with prison chaplains and Father Denis Faul and other people interested in prisoners' welfare in preparation for these meetings. We informed ourselves of prison regimes in the Netherlands and other countries. We always insisted that any liberalisation of the prison regime should apply to all prisoners, paramilitary and otherwise. Cardinal Ó Fiaich, with his background in history, spoke on numerous occasions with uncanny accuracy about the possible long-term impact that a hunger strike would have on our community. We argued that nothing would be lost and much would be gained by permitting the prisoners to wear their own clothes, if they so wished. We insisted that the greatest penalty of imprisonment was loss of liberty and humiliation should not be superimposed on this. We repeatedly pointed out the importance of the provision of opportunities for education in this situation. Many of the prisoners whom we met were highly intelligent young people whose education had been disrupted by the conflict. We made the point that they could spend their time in prison constructively pursuing further and higher education, rather than being engaged in demeaning tasks or just wasting their time. Eventually, Atkins told us that he would make a decision on the matter and let us know that decision at an early date.

Many people, at that time in 1980, said to me 'Why are you getting involved in the prison issue? – the prisoners refused to keep the rules – the subsequent suffering of the prisoners is self-inflicted – prisoners should be left to stew in their own juice'. The Cardinal and

I believed that this was only half the truth and that the sufferings of relatives and the danger to the community demanded that a concerted effort be made to bring the situation to an end. We also felt that the prevalent philosophy of imprisonment was based more on humiliation and punishment than it ought to be, and that most of those in prison were there because of convictions in highly dubious courts of law. We felt that education and opportunities for education should have much greater priority in the prison regime. In one of our papers presented to the Northern Ireland Office, we made the following points among others:

1. Many of the deprivations imposed on the prisoners are not the result of their own actions, but are imposed by the prison authorities for non-conformity with rules. These deprivations now constitute a serious hazard to physical and mental health and are therefore gravely unjust. Whilst it is accepted that prison authorities are entitled to enforce discipline and to inflict penalties for non-observation of prison regulations, four years deprivation of everything that the normal man requires is a punishment far in excess of the crime of refusing to wear prison uniform.

2. The current situation is a source of grievance and alienation among many of the Catholic population. There are over 2,000 prisoners in Northern Ireland and the vast majority of these come from the half million strong Catholic community. This means that a very high proportion of Catholic working-class people have a relative in prison or at least know someone in prison and believe that he is being unjustly treated.

3. The ongoing situation in Long Kesh gains support and probably recruits for the IRA and is a useful rallying point for them among the Irish in the USA. At a time when the Catholic community have shown again their abhorrence of violence, it is tragic that this cause should be handed on a plate to the paramilitaries.

4. A solution to the prison deadlock must be found before things get worse in Long Kesh either through the sudden

death of one of the protesting prisoners or through a hunger strike among the protesters.*

5. Prison should be rehabilitative as well as punitive. It is hard to imagine anything more soul-destroying that the present monotonous existence of the prisoners with nothing to occupy their minds and hands when they could be engaged in all kinds of useful activities. On 30 July 1980, we sent a letter to the senior civil servant charged with prison administration. In this letter we detailed our proposals as regards alternatives to prison work, highlighting the importance of education, making use of the Open University etc.

6. Many of the prisoners were only teenagers when sentenced. They were sentenced by non-jury courts, the majority on the sole evidence of 'confessions' that they were forced to sign. Several of them were assaulted and ill-treated after arrest. Very many of them would never have been before the courts, were it not for the political motivation that lay behind their activities.

7. We are convinced that the situation, inside and outside the prison, could be transformed by the substantial changes we proposed in the regulations regarding prison dress and prison work.†

Early in October 1980, the Republican prisoners in Long Kesh announced that they were embarking on a hunger strike. Once again, the Cardinal and I got in touch with the Northern Ireland Office and pleaded with them that they give more urgent consideration and a response to our proposals and the prisoners' demands. They said they would be in touch.

I was in Omagh on parish pastoral visitation on Wednesday, 22 October 1980. I was actually visiting St Brigid's High School there, when I was summoned to the principal's office. Somebody wanted to

---

* Cardinal Ó Fiaich and I were convinced that one or more of the younger prisoners would die because of the conditions. Amazingly, that did not happen.

† Derry Diocesan Archive.

see me urgently. It emerged that the 'somebody' was a courier from the Northern Ireland Office with a hand-delivered message from the Secretary of State. Mr Atkins wanted me to come to London on the following day to meet him to advise me personally of an important announcement regarding the prison situation which was to be made on the following day (Thursday) afternoon. He stressed that this meeting should be treated with the greatest confidence. Cardinal Ó Fiaich, who was attending a Synod of Bishops in Rome at the time, received a similar message via the British Embassy in Rome. I contacted the Cardinal by phone and we both agreed to make arrangements to fly to London on the following day. We met at Heathrow airport, by arrangement, and went by taxi to Archbishop's House in Westminster to prepare for our meeting. We were buoyantly hopeful of a positive result to our discussions. We listened to the news at one o'clock on BBC radio. It was announced that a decision had been reached by the Cabinet on the issue of prison uniforms in the North. It was implied that the Government had made a major concession and would allow prisoners to wear their own clothes. As far as I can remember, it was also announced on the bulletin that we had arrived in London and would meet the Secretary of State during the afternoon. Our names were linked to the announcement. On the basis of that, we looked forward to the meeting with great optimism. We were convinced that our advice had been accepted and was about to be acted upon.

Our meeting was in the Northern Ireland Office in London in mid-afternoon. We met Humphrey Atkins and some of his senior officials. It was a strange, almost bizarre, meeting. Atkins started off with a lengthy rambling talk summarising the meetings we had had over the previous months. He and his officials were distinctly edgy. We were somewhat baffled by this. The reason became apparent about ten or fifteen minutes later. Atkins was playing for time until a document was ready. The document was brought into the meeting at this stage – obviously it was not ready until then. A copy was given to us. There were a few minutes silence as everyone read the document – both ourselves *and the people on the other side of the table!* The Cardinal and I read the document together. It consisted of four-and-a-half pages. We noted that the first document given to us was headed 'Final Version', although this document was subsequently replaced some time later by another without the mention of 'Final Version'. On reading it, we quickly realised that the 'concession' was not what we had anticipated. Before we made any comment, we were then told that it had been decided and agreed by the Cabinet that morning to allow the prisoners in Long Kesh to be issued with prison-issue civilian-type clothing. We were dismayed.

The two last paragraphs of the document read as follows:

8. There cannot be one regime for those who claim a political motive for their crimes and another for those who do not. All aspects of prisoners' living and working conditions with a common regieme (sic) will however continue to be kept under review, guided by a humane and responsive approach. In this context the Government has been considering for some time the requirement to wear prison uniform in Northern Ireland. Prisoners conforming with the rules may at present as a privilege wear their own clothing, subject to approval by the prison authorities, for visits and at evening and weekend association – though they do not always do so. Prison uniform is issued for use at other times. The Government have decided to abolish this prison uniform as such, and to substitute civilian-type clothing. Conforming prisoners will also still retain the privilege of retaining their own clothing for recreation and visits. This change will be introduced over the coming months as quickly as the necessary arrangements can be completed and it will apply to all male prisoners throughout the Northern Ireland prison service.

9. The Government's position on hunger strikes in prison generally was made clear in 1974 and has not changed. Where a prisoner refuses nourishment and is considered by a medical officer as capable of forming an unimpaired and rational judgment concerning the consequences of such a voluntary refusal, he or she shall not be fed artificially. The prisoner's capacity to form such a judgment will be confirmed by another independent consultant. The prisoner

will then be plainly and categorically warned that the consequent and inevitable deterioration in his health may be allowed to continue without medical intervention unless he specifically requests it. If therefore prisoners choose to try to starve themselves to death they may well die.*

We asked for clarification about what was quaintly described as 'civilian-type clothing'. We asked if this was to be chosen and supplied by the prison authorities. It was confirmed that this would be the case. We knew that this was not the type of concession the prisoners had demanded or would accept and it would not be sufficient to stop the hunger strike. We believed and we continued to insist that all prisoners, paramilitary and others, should, if they wished, be permitted to wear their own civilian clothing in prison, not clothing, of whatever style, that was prison issue. We could not believe that the Government could be so stupid as to make such a half-hearted concession, at this vital stage. We also believed that improved access to education and educational facilities would be in the best interests of everyone concerned, management and prisoners. We realised that all of our negotiations had come to nothing. We felt that we had been deceived and exploited by the British. We were both angry and disillusioned. There ensued an intense and heated discussion. During the discussion, we became more and more convinced that the decision we had been given at that meeting was not the decision proposed in the original submission from the NIO to the Cabinet that morning. We believed that we had won the argument and that we had persuaded and convinced the NIO officials of the validity of our argument. We believed that a proposal had been formulated by the NIO for presentation to the Cabinet and that this proposal suggested permitting the prisoners to wear their own clothes. We believed that Mrs Thatcher and her Cabinet had then decided to row back from this proposal on the morning of our meeting.† This,

---

* Derry Diocesan Archive.
† This view appears to be borne out in the British Government 1980 papers, released by the National Archives in London (PREM 19/282). There is a particularly interesting annotation, apparently in Mrs Thatcher's own handwriting, relating to the clothes issue on the draft of a proposed letter to Pope John Paul II.

we were convinced, was the reason for the late introduction of the 'final version' document in mid-meeting. I still believe that to be the case and I am convinced that if the British Government had conceded the clothing issue at that time, there would not have been the catastrophic hunger strike in 1981. So much death, suffering and misery could have been avoided.

The Cardinal and I travelled back to Heathrow Airport to catch our respective flights. The Cardinal went back to Rome and I went back to Derry. We were both disappointed and disheartened. Before we parted at Heathrow, we decided to continue our efforts at a higher level than the Northern Ireland Office.

Much of the following day was spent discussing the situation with various people, like Father Denis Faul, and on the telephone to Cardinal Ó Fiaich in Rome. I also discussed the issues with people close to the prisoners. We subsequently drafted and decided to issue a joint statement:

> In a last-minute effort to prevent next Monday's hunger strike in Long Kesh Prison we sought an urgent meeting with the Secretary of State for Northern Ireland to discover what decisions have been taken regarding our earlier proposals for substantial changes in the regulations regarding prison dress and prison work. Our proposals were not by any means revolutionary – in fact compulsory prison dress and work have already been abolished for prisoners in the Republic of Ireland and several European countries. More important still, we had reason to believe that a generous gesture in these two areas on the part of the authorities – made in the context of prison reform for all prisoners in Northern Ireland – would have produced in recent months the long awaited solution to the dreadful H–Block impasse that has now entered its fifth year.
>
> We believe that yesterday's announcement of the abolition of 'prison uniform as such' throughout Northern Ireland is a step in the right direction, but we are deeply disappointed that it stops short of what is demanded by the situation. Little enough is now required, we feel, to end the present critical situation. We therefore appeal once more both to the

Northern Ireland Office and to the prisoners to think again during the next few days of the awful consequences which a mass hunger strike could bring to the whole community.

We ask all Christians to pray fervently during the coming weekend for an end to the present deadlock. Even at this late stage we believe that this is possible if:

1. The Northern Ireland Office brings yesterday's change in prison rules to its logical conclusion by recognising a prisoner's own clothes among the 'civilian-type clothing' which he will henceforth be permitted to wear.

2. The relatives and friends of prisoners earnestly beseech them to call off the hunger strike to allow for the implementation of this far-reaching reform.*

My memory is that, after the London meeting, the Cardinal advised the Holy See of our experiences and subsequently there was correspondence between Mrs Thatcher and the Pope on the issue of the hunger strike. This seems to be borne out in the 1980 Government papers referred to earlier.†

I have often thought about these experiences since. I think the Cardinal and I were somewhat naïve in our dealings with the Northern Ireland Office. In hindsight, we let the British off the hook far too easily. We should have made a much greater public outcry about the way that we had been treated and about the manner in which we believed that the document was changed at the last moment. I believe that we were used and exploited by them. There is so much respect for confidentiality in the business of 'bishoping' that it often militates against us. We were also used, to some extent, by the prisoners and those who supported them. It is inevitable that if one endeavours to resolve a difficult and long-standing problem between two parties there will be some attempt at exploitation by both sides. However, I have no regrets about getting involved in what I regarded as a humanitarian issue. I felt that it was the Christian duty of Cardinal Ó Fiaich and myself to become so involved. We were right to do so. We came very close to success in

* Derry Diocesan Archive.
† See page 111.

reaching a solution that would have saved many lives. We did our very best, but it was not enough.

The first hunger strike began on 27 October, the Monday after our meeting in London. More than twenty prisoners were on hunger strike by mid-December and one of them had become seriously ill and was moved to hospital. This hunger strike ended after more than fifty days, a few days before Christmas, following a further impassioned appeal by Cardinal Ó Fiaich. The Cardinal appealed to the hunger strikers and to the Prime Minister, Margaret Thatcher. There was confusion after the hunger strike had ended. The prisoners claimed that they had received all their demands. The Government denied this. As in most such cases, it was difficult to ascertain the truth of the situation. But it soon became obvious that the problem in the prisons was far from resolution.

I had visited a prisoner from the County Derry area of the diocese in the late 1970s during an earlier hunger strike. He had undertaken the hunger strike on his own, about particular issues that had distressed him. I visited him both in prison and in Musgrave Park Hospital in Belfast during the course of his lengthy hunger strike. There was very little publicity about his protest and he eventually ended it. During this experience, witnessing the ravages that a hunger strike wreaked on the human body and mind, I came to the conclusion that nothing could justify such a protest. I was appalled at what I witnessed. The memory of his gaunt features and sunken staring eyes and halting speech haunted me for long afterwards and considerably influenced my attitude to hunger strike. I felt that I could not both defend the sacredness of human life and condone a hunger strike that was not just damaging to the health and life of the person or persons involved, but, potentially, extremely damaging to the whole community. Whilst the weapon of the hunger strike has an exalted place in the history of Irish republicanism, I thought then, and still think, that it is objectively wrong.

David Beresford, in the one of the most powerful books about the Long Kesh hunger strikes wrote:

> Hunger-striking, when taken to the death, has a sublime quality about it; in conjunction with terrorism it offers a consum-

mation of murder and self-sacrifice which in a sense can legit-
imise the violence which precedes and follows it. If after
killing – or sharing in a conspiracy to kill – for a cause one
shows oneself willing to die for the same cause, a value is
adduced which is higher than that of life itself. But the
obverse is also true; failure to die can discredit the cause. To
scream for mercy at the foot of the gallows – or nod at the
saline drip as kidneys and eyes collapse and the doctor warns
of irreversible damage – is to affirm that there is no higher
value than life and none more worthy of condemnation than
those who take it.*

I was greatly troubled by the 1980 hunger strikes, but, deep down, I
believed that they would not go the full distance. I was very upset
and angry with the manner in which the NIO and the British
Government had dealt with the situation.

The 1981 hunger strikes, however, were of a different order.
From the outset, I believed that, if the concessions were not granted,
this series of hunger strikes would go to the ultimate and, as Cardinal Ó Fiaich had predicted, they would tear the community apart.

Bobby Sands from Belfast went on hunger strike on 1 March
1981. I remember meeting him briefly on one of my earlier visits to
Long Kesh. It was exactly five years since special category status had
been ended. On the day that Bobby Sands began his hunger strike, I
publicly voiced my opposition to it and said that it was not morally
justified. It was the beginning of a new wave of hunger strikes.
Gradually, over the following weeks, several prisoners from the
Derry diocese joined the hunger strike. It was, without doubt, the
most difficult period of my episcopate.

In normal circumstances, I would have gone to visit the men on
hunger strike, especially those from my own diocese. I would have
pleaded with them to end their hunger strike. I would have tried to
explain to them that human life is too precious to endanger it in this
way. I would have assured them that I and others were continuing
our appeals and pressure on the Government to grant their legiti-

*   David Beresford, *Ten Men Dead* (Grafton Books, London, 1987).

mate demands for a more humane prison regime, as we were. But this time it was different. The prisoners had asked their families not to intervene in their hunger strike – not to agree or collude in any way to give them nourishment if they were to lose consciousness. I met many close family members of the hunger strikers while the hunger strike was taking place. Almost all of them asked me not to visit their sons if I planned to attempt to persuade them to end their hunger strike. In conscience I could not accede to such a condition. If I were to visit anyone on hunger strike, I would feel conscience bound to appeal to that person to end his hunger strike forthwith – just as I would ask anyone to do what they could to save and protect human life. It was a very difficult dilemma. I decided not to visit the 1981 hunger strikers because of the conditions imposed on such visits. Throughout the period of that hunger strike, I saw any members of the families of the hunger strikers in the diocese who wished to see me. There were a number of such meetings. The meetings were always courteous. I had huge sympathy for the families and especially the parents whom I came to respect. To be the parent of a hunger striker in such circumstances must have been particularly agonising.

I spoke to Cardinal Ó Fiaich almost every day during this period. Both of us were in the midst of the annual diocesan programme administering Confirmation to the children of our respective dioceses. We were out in the parishes speaking to people a few times a week. Whilst people were clearly divided on the issue of the hunger strikes, almost everyone was greatly concerned and apprehensive about the future. Sinn Féin was conducting a very powerful campaign on this hugely emotive issue. There were posters everywhere. There was huge international media interest. Journalists were constantly on the phone, calling at the house or 'doorstepping' me at Confirmations and other public ceremonies.

The Cardinal and I also spoke regularly with the chaplains in the prison. Nobody could ever speak highly enough of those who were engaged in this very difficult ministry. Father John Murphy and Father Tom Toner of the Down and Connor diocese gave a powerful witness at this time. Over the years of the conflict, few people did as much for so many as Father John Murphy. He ministered to the prisoners and the hunger strikers and their families on a daily basis. He was very dedicated. He was deservedly given special papal recognition for his work in 2003. For most of thirty years, he managed to carry out his work as prison chaplain quietly and with great integrity and won the respect of all sides involved. The late Father Denis Faul was also indefatigable in his efforts to resolve the growing crisis. Father Faul's work in highlighting injustice, ill-treatment, torture and prisoners' rights was heroic and outstanding throughout those difficult years. He and his colleague, Father Raymond Murray, were two of the most courageous figures among the clergy of those years. They consistently spoke and wrote fearlessly with great clarity and great integrity. Denis was a passionate advocate for justice and the sacredness of human life. He had little time for warriors.

Another Cardinal became involved in the hunger strike debate in April 1981. Thomas Kelly, from St Mary's parish in Creggan in Derry City, was to be ordained to the priesthood for the archdiocese of Westminster. The ordinand came to speak to me during the Christmas holiday in 1980 to discuss the ceremony of his ordination with me. He invited me to officiate at the ceremony. I suggested to him that perhaps I should invite his own archbishop, Cardinal Basil Hume of Westminster, to officiate at the ordination ceremony. Tom was very sympathetic to this suggestion and excited by it. So I wrote to Cardinal Hume and invited him to come to Derry to officiate at the ordination. I had great admiration for Cardinal Hume, the Benedictine priest who had taught in Ampleforth College before his appointment to Westminster. I had read many of his books and admired his spirituality and leadership of the Catholic Church in England. I had met him on a few occasions and had a lengthy conversation with him during the Papal Visit to Ireland in 1979. Initially, he was most reluctant to come to Derry. In January 1981, to my amazement, he wondered in a letter* if he would be a '*persona grata*' in Derry. I assured him confidently that he would be most welcome. He eventually decided to come to Derry and officiate at the ordination in Creggan on Sunday, 26 April. Although neither of us realised this when the arrangements were being made, this date proved to be about six weeks into the 1981 hunger strike. Flying

* Derry Diocesan Archive.

from Heathrow to Belfast on his way to Derry, he was courteously escorted by a rather stuffy, if naïve, airline official into a seat beside the Reverend Ian Paisley! The Cardinal was highly intrigued and amused by this seating arrangement; apart from a brief greeting, there was little conversation between the two normally eloquent gentlemen of the cloth.

The Cardinal preached at an early Sunday morning Mass in St Eugene's Cathedral. He was very warmly received by the people in St Eugene's Cathedral and in Creggan. He met many people during his short visit, including the city's Mayor, Mrs Marlene Jefferson, an Official Unionist, John Hume, Bishop James Mehaffey, Church of Ireland Bishop of Derry and Raphoe. He impressed everyone. Throughout his visit, he was subjected to intense pressure by a large corps of local and British media. A camera crew from NBC television in the United States was also present with other sections of the international media, here to cover the hunger strike. The Cardinal was repeatedly pressed for comment on the hunger strike and the issues surrounding the morality of hunger strike. He carefully avoided making any comment on this matter whilst he was in Derry. We discussed the associated moral issues privately on a number of occasions during his visit. He also took the opportunity to brief himself on the relevant issues with quite a number of local people. The day after his return to London, Cardinal Hume called me on the telephone and told me that he had written me a letter with his views on the hunger strike and he was releasing this letter to the media. He thanked me and the people of Derry for our hospitality and wrote:

> It was an important experience for me. I came away with several strong impressions. First of all I was struck by the fact that over here in England we can all too easily be persuaded by what is seen on television or read in the newspapers and conclude that Derry is a city of constant rioting and unrest. This clearly is not so, and there is another side. The people are warm and friendly, and, like most of us just want to live in peace and harmony. My meeting with the Mayor reinforced this impression. I came away confirmed in the view that it is the extremists on both sides who make the headlines and

often distort the reality. It is utterly tragic that young people can be too easily caught up in a crisis which is not of their creation, but which has arisen from the injustices and mistakes of the past. None of us can be exempted from blame.

How much we all need to remember the powerful words of Pope John Paul II at Drogheda in September 1979. He spoke of the urgency to find a political solution, and I recall his strong appeal to stop violence, since violence leads to violence, and inevitably to injustice and tragic bereavements.

We face some difficult days. The hunger strike is a form of violence, and surely cannot be condoned by the Church as being in accordance with God's Will for man. I still find it hard to accept that the chance for a solution offered by the Euro - pean Commission for Human Rights has been finally lost.*

Three weeks before the Cardinal's visit, on Tuesday, 7 April 1981, there was a particularly revolting murder in Derry. There was a census taking place in Northern Ireland in 1981, which the Provisional IRA stupidly decided to boycott for reasons best known to themselves. They instructed people not to participate in one of the most important social instruments for any country or area. Joanne Mathers was a young Protestant married woman of twenty-five with a two-and-a-half-year-old son. She was helping a resident of the Gobnascale area of Derry's Waterside to fill out his census form when a masked thug came in and deliberately shot her dead at point blank range. It was terrorism at its most obscene. I did not know Joanne Mathers but everyone that did know her spoke of her most highly. Although Republicans denied it, I believed and still believe that this appalling action was a planned and calculated event in the hunger strike campaign outside the prison, chillingly carried out by a member of the Provisional IRA under instructions from his local command. It was designed to terrorise the community and certainly contributed to my abhorrence of this whole strategy and I have to confess that it considerably diluted my personal sympathy for those on hunger strike and their supporters.

There was a protest outside my door on two occasions – on one

* Derry Diocesan Archive.

occasion, a group of women dressed in blankets paraded up and down between my door and the doors of the cathedral. It seemed to me to be a rather pointless exercise as I was speaking with people directly involved in the hunger strikes almost every day. After the media cameras had departed, they left the cathedral grounds and walked away. Like many other activities, I felt that it was carried out for the benefit of the media – yet another photo opportunity. These women protested outside my door; another woman, a mother of a young child, was cruelly slaughtered on the other side of the River Foyle by a cowardly assassin from an organisation whom the people outside my door supported. A blanket was placed over her body. After the ubiquitous cameras departed that scene, Joanne Mathers was unable to walk away.

The Irish Catholic Bishops' Commission for Justice and Peace was asked by the bishops to become involved in trying to resolve the impasse and they did very good work. Bishop Dermot O'Mahony, Father Oliver Crilly, Jerome Connolly and Hugh Logue were among those involved in these efforts. They had a protracted series of meetings with all the parties involved but the hunger strike still went on. This was an extremely able and skilled group that strove manfully and with great patience but they failed to resolve the situation.

There was also an intervention, at a very late stage, by the Holy Father, Pope John Paul II. His secretary, Father John Magee, was despatched to bring a message to the hunger strikers. The first that I heard of this visit was on a BBC news bulletin where it was announced that Father Magee had arrived in London on his way to visit the hunger strikers. As far as I remember, Cardinal Ó Fiaich first heard of it through this medium also. Although I always held Pope John Paul II in the utmost respect, I thought that this visit was ill-advised and ill-judged. It sent out a confusing signal to many people here, to members of the Catholic community and particularly to people in the Protestant/Unionist community. The intervention dismayed many people in the Catholic community, and it further inflamed the extreme sectarian paranoia amongst many Unionists. I do not think that the Holy Father should have intervened in this way, unless there was very good reason to believe that his intervention would succeed. Like all the efforts to resolve the impasse, it failed.

In the 1981 hunger strikes, ten of the hunger strikers died. Five of them were from the Derry diocese – Francis Hughes and Thomas McElwee from Bellaghy, Kevin Lynch from Dungiven, Patsy O'Hara and Michael Devine from Derry City. The sequence of deaths ended when a wonderfully courageous mother, assisted by Father Denis Faul, authorised the feeding of her unconscious dying son. The hunger strikes brought about an intensification of the para-military campaigns. The community divisions were further widened. The hunger strike issue caused intense debate within the Church as regards the morality of the action. There were divided views on the issue. A very significant and lasting product of the hunger strike was the tentative first and successful steps of Provisional Sinn Féin into the political arena. The 'Armalite and the Ballot Box' strategy, as Danny Morrison later described it, had begun. It took a long time, however, for the ballot box to become more important than the Armalite, although ultimately, it proved to be much more powerful.

Much has been written about the 1981 hunger strike. For that reason, I do not wish to dwell on it further. It brought about the death of ten young men in prison, and caused many more deaths and misery and fear outside. It caused terrible heartbreak in the families of those who died and similar anguish in many other families and in the wider community. Within a few months, the British had implemented all the main issues that Cardinal Ó Fiaich and I had proposed one year earlier – the basic demands of the prisoners. After those measures had been implemented, the prisons calmed down and were no longer the intense cauldrons that they had been. If only those measures had been adopted one year earlier!

I hope that there will never again be a hunger strike in Ireland.

CHAPTER 9

'The Politics of the Last Atrocity'

During the 1980s, the gap between the Provisional Republican Movement, Sinn Féin, their political representatives and the Catholic Church leadership in Derry, which was already wide, significantly widened. Three murders by the IRA were perpetrated in the space of a few days in April 1982, two of them within fifty metres of Bishop's House. There was also a spate of incidents in which families had their homes or vehicles taken over whilst ambushes were prepared.

The murders on 1 April 1982, right outside where I lived, had a particular impact on me and deepened even further my intense distaste for paramilitary activities. I was writing letters at my desk around midday when I heard a burst of gunfire just outside. I dashed out and was one of the very first on the scene. Two men, covered in blood, lay dead in the front seats of a car that had crashed to a halt in Creggan Street. I administered the Last Rites to them. The car and the passengers were riddled with bullets. There was blood and broken glass everywhere. Both victims were dressed in civilian clothing and were slumped in the front seats, open-mouthed and wide-eyed. High velocity bullets inflict terrible damage on a human body. I learned later that they were soldiers, signalmen travelling from Rosemount Barracks, a short distance away up the hill. It was a shocking and distressing sight. They were the victims of a Provisional IRA ambush. It had been nine years since I had last seen victims in the immediate aftermath of shooting. I was sick with revulsion, appalled and extremely angry.

To respond to these and other recent events, I issued a Pastoral Letter to be read at all Masses in Derry City on the following Sunday, 4 April 1982. It contained the following paragraphs:

After an interval of relative calm, murder has returned to the streets of our city. In the last week, there have been three foul and callous murders, one of the victims being a man coming from his place of worship last Sunday in the company of his two young sons. It does not matter whether the victim is a soldier, a police officer or civilian; it does not matter what his religious or political viewpoint might be; the taking of human life as it has been taken in Derry this week is murder. It cannot be called by any other name. All those who claim to follow Christ have a responsibility to do everything they can to prevent these murders taking place.

In recent weeks, a succession of decent families in Catholic areas of the city have been held hostage in their own homes whilst ambushes were prepared. These families were terrorised and terrified, parents were humiliated in their own homes before their own children by people and organisations who dare to describe themselves as 'defenders of the community'. These people or organisations do not defend this community. They have persecuted, terrified and demoralised the community. The vast majority of the Catholic community wants nothing to do with them. They fundamentally disagree with and reject their evil and sinful activities. The members of the Catholic community here are amongst their most vulnerable victims.*

The Pastoral then went on to state:

All those who believe in the sacredness of human life have a Christian obligation and responsibility to make known anything that they may have seen or heard that might have any connection with a murder whoever the perpetrator or victim might be.†

The Republican Movement was furious and responded with an angry public statement and I was inundated with abusive letters and

* Derry Diocesan Archive.
† Derry Diocesan Archive.

phone calls. From that moment onwards, virtually all communications between the Republican Movement in Derry and me ceased for many years.

One of the factors that added to the increasing tension between the Republican Movement and the clergy was the fact that priests and bishops were obliged to officiate at a continuous succession of funerals of victims of the violence. These were, in the main, funerals of innocent civilians; but there were also funerals of IRA and INLA members, funerals of Catholic RUC and UDR personnel. These funerals, especially when the deceased were members of the Provisional IRA or INLA, were often occasions of elaborate paramilitary displays attended by a huge security presence and an intense and intrusive media contingent. Funerals were exploited by paramilitaries for propaganda purposes to further the armed struggle. It was immensely challenging for the local priest to cope with all this. Every word uttered in a homily was parsed and analysed. Sentences were often quoted completely out of context and received extensive media coverage. In his homily and in his ministry, the priest, in addition to his usual funeral duties, had to confront this panoply of paramilitaries, security and media. The whole affair often more resembled a circus or political rally than a religious liturgical ceremony. In the midst of this, the priest had to endeavour to comfort the bereaved and to address the morality or immorality of the circumstances of the death of the deceased. It was a daunting task and many priests carried it out with great courage. When the circus moved off to the next sensation or funeral, the priest in the parish was left alone with a grief-stricken and sometimes angry family and people to pick up the pieces and to cope with the criticism. The burden and pressure that paramilitary funerals imposed on priests during those years cannot be over-emphasised.

The British authorities from time to time picked up words critical of the IRA spoken or written by a bishop or priest and circulated them. A short excerpt from one of my homilies, taken completely out of context, was once distributed in handouts by the British Army through letter boxes in Republican areas of West Belfast! Needless to say, it was not a passage that was critical of the Army! Many of the handouts were subsequently posted to Bishop's House by angry recipients, with comments expressing their anger. All parties to the conflict tried to exploit the Church when it suited them to do so.

The British Army or RUC or NIO became quite upset when criticised by the Church. However, in the case of these agencies, as well as making public criticism of their excesses – for example, use of plastic bullets, use of informers, intimidation and harassment of individuals or families, and, in some cases, summary execution – there was also the possibility of expressing criticism in a more focused and perhaps more cogent manner, privately by letter or face to face with a senior officer. This was often used to back up a public statement. One could write to or phone the local commander of the British Army or Chief Constable of the RUC, but it was difficult or impossible to write or phone the local OC of the Provisional IRA or INLA! Although one could make a fair guess at the name, the address or phone number was not available. Sometimes one could make contact through an intermediary. But criticism of paramilitaries, at that time, was primarily voiced or conveyed through the public media, normally by means of a press release usually issued on a Monday or Thursday night to catch the twice-weekly issues of the local newspaper, the *Derry Journal* on Tuesday or Friday morning. The IRA used the same method in communicating with me.

While some people in the Unionist community believed that I was in daily touch with the IRA, the only official communication I ever knowingly received directly from the Provisional IRA, between late 1974 and the early 1990s, was the summons to the meeting in April 1975. However, this situation had a serious disadvantage in that it gave the impression to the general public that the criticism was biased in one direction. The impression given was that the preponderance of criticism was directed against the Republican Movement.

Comment on evil deeds perpetrated by the various agencies of death and destruction presented many problems for me. The media required and insisted upon instant comment. There was often great difficulty in establishing the precise truth about what happened in any particular incident – rumours abounded – the warring elements constantly wished to create their own particular spin on any action. By the time a statement was researched and prepared, it often was the case that another atrocity had occurred in the meantime, making the prepared statement irrelevant. There was also the problem and worry that one or other agency would exploit the comment on one atrocity as a pseudo-justification for perpetrating another. From time to time such a reaction was alleged – where people said 'if you had not made that statement, this would not have happened'. I found myself trapped, at times, by what was termed as 'the politics of the last atrocity', or even 'the theology of the last atrocity'. This could be summarised as responding to the last terrible thing that had taken place. It was a difficult and heavy responsibility, which generated much anxiety and caused many sleepless nights. I felt strongly that I had a primary responsibility to give moral leadership to people who proclaimed themselves to be members of the Catholic Church, however tenuous those links might be. As a result, the bulk of these comments were directed towards Republican paramilitaries. However, I was also consistently critical of injustice perpetrated on the community by the British Army, the RUC or Loyalist paramilitary groups. It was said to me on a few occasions by one side or the other 'Why should we listen to you when the other side does not listen to you?'

Truth is often a major victim in conflict. For paramilitary groupings and some military groupings, truth is what is expedient at any given point in time. What promotes the cause is true. Anything that would potentially damage the cause is untrue. Everyone was conscious that there was a battle for minds going on. That battle was as important as the armed struggle. Since paramilitary spokespersons were not permitted by law to present their case personally in the media or be interviewed in the media, the press release became very important. As a result, the press statement or release had the potential to be a lethal weapon. It is my personal belief that the law against paramilitary spokesmen appearing in the media gave them a decided advantage in the battle for minds. It was an ill-judged law. As a result, in the immediate aftermath of atrocities, paramilitary spokespersons or their political representatives did not have to explain or be challenged publicly on the terrible actions that they engaged in.

The continuous sequence of horrific events disrupted economic, social and community life. It also disrupted the life of the Church, particularly at a time in the immediate aftermath of the Vatican Council when the Church should have been undergoing extensive renewal. I remember once, while I was a priest in the Bogside, hearing a commentator on an Irish television programme complain that she had walked and made her way to Mass in St Eugene's Cathedral through a riot and that the riot was not even mentioned by the celebrant at Mass. She did not mention that at that time there had been rioting in the streets around the cathedral every single day for eighteen months, apart from Christmas Day. Other subjects had to be preached and taught and reflected upon as well as rioting. Some attempt had to be made to keep the normal life and preaching of the Church going in this abnormal situation and to realise that there was a life outside the conflict but we were never permitted to ignore what was happening on our streets. It dominated all our lives.

I received letters from priests in England and in the South of Ireland critical of what I said from time to time. They had every right to be critical. But it is extraordinarily difficult to preach God's word consistently and objectively in the course of a protracted conflict that is taking place literally outside your door. It is difficult to remain detached, when day by day, neighbours and acquaintances are suffering and the sights and sounds and smells of conflict are all too present. I tried to spell out the broad principles of morality regularly, in homilies, press statements and media interviews. I also endeavoured to confine my comments to events that occurred within the boundaries of the Derry Diocese or impacted on the diocese. This gave rise to many of the critical letters, 'Why did you not comment on such and such? Why did you comment on this and not on that?' It seemed rather pathetic to respond to someone in England or in South of Ireland, 'Well, it did not happen in the Derry diocese'. I acknowledge that I failed dismally at times in this responsibility. I certainly failed to live up to the commitment I made about instant comment in my homily in St Eugene's on the day after my episcopal ordination.*

In the midst of all this mayhem, priests and bishops felt obliged to preach all the other aspects of the Good News of Christ and the

---

* See Chapter One, p. 16.

CHAPTER 10

International Eucharistic Congress – Philadelphia 1976

Early in 1976, I received an unexpected letter from Cardinal John Krol, Archbishop of Philadelphia in the United States. He invited me to attend and preach at the 41st International Eucharistic Congress there during the first week of August 1976. I was honoured by the invitation and excited by it. I had never attended a Eucharistic Congress. In my childhood, I had heard many stories from my parents and older people about the Eucharistic Congress that took place in Dublin in 1932, the year before I was born. The memories of that event were treasured by many in Ireland. Tales abounded about how people travelled there and the experiences that they had. Almost everyone remembered the singing of John McCormack. An International Eucharistic Congress only takes place once every three or four years. 1976 was the Bicentennial Year in the United States and the city of Philadelphia had a special place in those celebrations. 'The Eucharist and the Hungers of the Human Family' was chosen to be the theme of the Congress. There was a great deal of thought and preparation put into the planning of the Congress and the development of the theme. Eight daily themes were agreed upon – the hunger for God; the hunger for bread; the hunger for freedom and justice; the hunger for the spirit; the hunger for truth; the hunger for understanding; the hunger for peace; the hunger for Jesus, the Bread of Life. The Congress was scheduled to begin on Sunday, 1 August 1976.

My anticipation was heightened by the fact that Philadelphia was the city to which thousands of people from the North West had emigrated in the previous 150 years, among them a number of my own relatives and neighbours. I grew up hearing stories about

Philadelphia and the life and opportunities and prosperity and also the hardships that people had experienced there. Although I had previously visited the United States on a few occasions, I had never been to Philadelphia.

Initially, I was invited to preach at one Mass – the Mass for the Irish community on the Saturday morning of the Congress. This was to take place in the open air in the grounds of St Charles Borromeo Seminary in Overbrook, a neighbourhood in the north-west outskirts of the city. I was subsequently invited to speak at an additional ceremony described as a 'Mass for Scouts and other Youth Groups'. This celebration was to take place in the Spectrum Arena – the huge indoor sporting arena in which the fight scenes from the *Rocky* series of films were shot.

I spent a lot of time that summer carefully preparing my talks and left for Philadelphia a few days before the opening of the Congress. I was accommodated in the rectory attached to Our Lady of Mount Carmel church. On the night I arrived I went into the church to say a prayer before going to bed. In the summer evening light, the stained glass windows were illuminated and I was drawn to them. On closer observation, I was fascinated to note that several of the windows were donated by families and individuals with surnames that were very familiar – surnames that had their origin in Donegal and the North West of Ireland. Apparently, around the end of the nineteenth century and the beginning of the twentieth century, this parish had been largely populated by Irish people from my part of Ireland. I felt an immediate and uncanny familiarity with the place. I thought of the hundreds of thousands of people who had sailed out from Derry to the New World – their hopes and fears. I thought of the poverty and suffering and conflict that they had left behind. I thought of the contrast between that teeming area of a great city and the beautiful, quiet but blighted countryside that they had left behind. I thought of the faith that they had brought with them and this place of worship that they had erected in their new home.

Sholto Cooke's fascinating book *The Maiden City and the Western Ocean* about shipping between Derry and North America in the nineteenth century points out that:

More Derry passengers were landed at Philadelphia than at
any other port in the United States, including many hundreds
in the famine years; during the Spring of 1847, Messrs
Cookes alone despatched eight vessels, carrying 1,197 passengers to Philadelphia, and the demand for passages could not
be met.*

The Eucharistic Congress was officially opened by Mass at noon on
Sunday, 1 August in Philadelphia's brownstone Cathedral of Saints
Peter and Paul. It was a spectacular occasion attended by thirty-one
cardinals, one-hundred-and-sixty bishops, the royal family of
Monaco and thousands of clergy and laity. (Princess Grace of
Monaco, the former film actress Grace Kelly, originally came from
Philadelphia.) The leaders of the Episcopal Church, the Lutheran
Church and other Protestant leaders sat in the sanctuary. The music
was magnificent and befitted the occasion. I had never been part of
a religious occasion of this magnitude outside Rome.

Thus began a week to remember. As one of the designated speakers at the Congress, I was treated extremely well. I had a car and
driver at my beck and call and had access to every Congress event
that I cared to attend. I had the opportunity to meet and listen to
people I had only heard of and read about – like Mother Teresa of
Calcutta, who despite her diminutive size, was a powerfully magnetic
figure who spoke with great passion and conviction; she and
Dorothy Day** addressed 10,000 enthralled participants at the
women's conference – an extraordinary occasion. Archbishop Fulton
Sheen was there and gave a stunning lesson in how to preach and
communicate God's word in an effective, witty and attractive
manner. He was a superb and spell-binding communicator and a
great teacher. One of my great heroes, Dom Helder Camara,
Archbishop of Recife in Brazil was there and promised me that he
would come to Derry, a promise he fulfilled the following year when

---

* Sholto Cooke, *The Maiden City and the Western Ocean* (Morris & Co.,
  Dublin [undated]).
** Dorothy Day was a social activist and co-founder of the Catholic Workers
  Movement. She fiercely criticised the Eucharistic Congress organisers for
  scheduling a military Mass on the 31st anniversary of the Hiroshima bomb-
  ing. She was a most charismatic person who died in 1980.

he attended a conference I had helped to organise in our city. Cardinal Suenens of Brussels spoke on the Holy Spirit; he had been one of the great figures of the Second Vatican Council. On the Tuesday night, Cardinal Karol Wojtyla of Cracow celebrated the Mass on the theme of 'The Eucharist and Man's Hunger for Freedom'. I was a concelebrant at the Mass in the packed Veterans Stadium with an attendance of nearly 70,000 people: I had never heard of the Cardinal before. His sermon was the first time that I had heard English spoken in that Polish accent that would become so familiar just a few years later. He spoke of the manner in which the faith had been 'an inspiration and first hope' for the Polish people during their long and many struggles for freedom. He did not lash out at the Communist regime in his country – his criticism was much more subtle and nuanced than that. Speaker after speaker, men and women, made memorable contributions. There were various liturgies and workshops that continued throughout the week.

My own participation was very fulfilling. The Mass in the Spectrum on the Tuesday afternoon was attended by Scouts and young people from all over the United States, about 17,000 of them. They were mainly in their mid-to-late teens. It was a colourful and vibrant occasion generated by the flags and banners, the multiplicity of uniforms and the high school bands. The singing was quite overpowering – rock, country and gospel music were mingled with familiar hymns. I spoke to the young people about the value of scouting and the fact that it does not pamper young people but treats them as adults and asks something of them. I spoke to them about St Patrick, with whom they were all familiar. I then went on to encourage them to be generous in the way they lived their lives. I spoke about the parable of the Good Samaritan:

> I would ask you, as young people today, which world do you choose? Do you want to serve or be served? Are you also going to ignore the Samaritan lying on the roadside? Surely the only way of living life is the Christian way. It gives meaning to life. It gives the person living that life the satisfaction of knowing that he is doing what his Creator meant him to do. It gives one a purpose. Man needs a creed. Man needs some-

thing to follow. The Church offers this to you and to me. Christ offered this to the Church. Each one of you, as young Christians in this world of ours, can make an impact on your own particular world, whether it be in the home, or high school, or college or university campus. Perhaps, it might be in an industrial plant or an office. Each one of you can be another Christ. Because it is not enough that the Good News of the Gospel be announced from pulpits or within liturgical assemblies. God calls man in the world, man in the mammoth industrial plant, man in the university, man in the inner city, man in the suburban area. God speaks to man in scripture, but He must also speak to men through other Christs who proclaim by their lives that God has entered human history, that God can so change a man by His Spirit that he lives in the love of Christ which knows how to serve and work in close union with others for goals which are truly human. We can recall the disappointment of Mahatma Gandhi who grew to love the teaching and person of Christ, but looked in vain for Him in the Christians he met. He is not the only one who has felt the same. There are many today, who sincerely seek a life of communion and service, and search in vain for proofs that action makes this life possible, because many of their fellow workers, their colleagues and friends who are Christians show no apparent concern for bettering this city, this country, this world, which, according to their faith, God loved enough to send His Son. Those with failing faith, or no faith, know that Christ taught His disciples that mutual love and unity were to be the recognisable signs of their belonging to Him, yet they meet too many Christians who cannot get along together or work together, or who live unconcerned in the midst of crying social injustice.*

The young people gave me a very attentive hearing. It was a somewhat daunting task speaking to a congregation of American teenagers in the mid-1970s. In the event, I found those that I met, in many ways, more mature and much more interested in religious issues than

* Derry Diocesan Archive.

similar young people in Ireland. Almost without exception, they expressed an intense pride in their parish and in their Church. Whilst preparing my talks, I had consulted with a large number of people who would have had more familiarity with the Church in the United States than I had. Their advice was most helpful.

My biggest challenge lay ahead, however. The Saturday of the Congress was to be Peoples of the World Day whose theme, 'The Eucharist and the Hunger for Peace', expressed the universality of the Church and the world's desire for harmony. The Catholic population of the United States is drawn from many nationalities and cultures and includes generations of people who had been denied freedom and opportunity in their own countries. Many of them had fled from war and religious persecution. On that sunny Saturday morning of the Conference, Masses were celebrated in various locations around the city to recognise the ethnic and national origins of the Catholic Church in America. There were Masses in Spanish, French, Vietnamese, Chinese, Portuguese and many other languages, a bewildering array of peoples and nationalities – a reflection of the kaleidoscopic nature of Catholic America. The Mass for the Irish attracted more than 40,000 people to the beautiful grounds of St Charles Borromeo Seminary at Overbrook. In addition to the many people of Irish extraction in the Philadelphia area, people travelled from New York and Boston and other parts of the US. Cardinal William Conway of Armagh was the principal celebrant of the Mass. He was joined by two American Cardinals, Cardinal Timothy Manning of Los Angeles and Cardinal Terence Cooke of New York; seven of my colleagues from the Irish Episcopal Conference were joined by more than twenty Irish American bishops and hundreds of priests in the concelebration. In that exalted and overpowering company I was a very nervous homilist.

I was preoccupied by several issues while preparing this homily. During the previous five or six years, many terrible things had happened in Northern Ireland. The country and our people had received a lot of bad publicity worldwide and especially in America. America itself was just recovering from the trauma of defeat in the bloody Vietnam War that had ended just a year earlier. So many young Americans had lost their lives there. I was also conscious of the fact that a large number of Irish Americans had a romantic notion of Ireland and particularly of the conflict in Ireland, notions that were not linked to the harsh reality of the situation that prevailed in 1976. The majority of Irish Americans, at that time, had never been to Ireland, and they were comfortable with the dreams and horrors and romantic notions that their parents and grandparents had conveyed to them of the mother country. Few of the Irish Americans who had visited Ireland had ever been to the North. Despite all that, I perceived the Irish Americans as a potentially powerful influence in our situation. I believed that it was of importance that they should have a clear understanding of the issues and that an erroneous understanding based on British or Irish propaganda should be challenged. I was anxious to set the record straight and within a religious context, as I saw it. I was also anxious to register my appreciation of the immense generosity and assistance of Irish Americans to their home parishes in Ireland, especially during the latter part of the nineteenth century and the earlier decades of the twentieth century. The construction of many churches in our diocese, at that time, would not have been possible without the generous support of parishioners in the United States. I endeavoured to address all these issues in my homily.

After Mass was over, there was a huge picnic in the sunshine on the extensive lawns of the seminary. Signs were erected designating the assembly areas for people from different Irish counties. I met many people with their roots in the Derry diocese and in the North. I also managed to meet people who had their roots in Fermanagh and Donegal. They had settled in Boston or New York or New Jersey or Chicago and had travelled long distances to take part in the celebration. I stayed there until late in the afternoon. We had many interesting conversations. There was a delightful atmosphere of happiness and friendship. Several families told me that Derry was the embarkation port from which their forefathers had sailed to America.

I had the afternoon free on the Thursday of the Congress week. With the help of the local pastor who was my host, Father Tom Wassel, I set out to see if I could find a distant relative – a second cousin on my mother's side who had emigrated from Donegal to

Philadelphia in the late 1920s and had never been back to Ireland since then. She had left Ireland before I was born and had never returned! There had been very limited contact with her and I had only scant information about her. Nobody was sure whether she was alive or dead. Before leaving home, I was given an address where she had lived in the 1940s. The man who gave me this address was unsure whether she was alive or dead. So, with the pastor, on that Thursday afternoon, I went to seek out the listed address. It was in a very old area of the city. To my great joy, she was there! She was in poor health, very weak but alert and able to communicate with me. There was a remarkable similarity in appearance between her and my mother. She told me about her life and all its ups and downs. I told her about life at home and various members of the family. We had an amazing and emotional meeting and spent much of that afternoon together. It was wonderful to meet her and her family. She died a few years later in the late 1970s but members of her family have visited Ireland since our first meeting.

On the Sunday afternoon, the final Mass of the Congress was celebrated in the John F. Kennedy Stadium. President Gerald Ford attended and addressed the congregation. Pope Paul VI, with the aid of a live television link, also addressed the assembly. It was an unforgettable week. It was a great privilege to have an active involvement in the Congress. I returned home with a new spring in my step and a new understanding and appreciation of the gift of the Eucharist. The International Eucharistic Congress in Philadelphia was an inspirational experience.*

During my years as bishop, I made other visits to the United States. Some of these visits were to spend time on holiday with friends and relatives. On some other occasions, I was invited to speak at various gatherings. I also took part in two speaking tours accompanied by Bishop James Mehaffey, the Church of Ireland Bishop of Derry and Raphoe. On one of these visits, in March 1988, we went to Richmond, Virginia, where we spoke at Virginia State University and in several churches of various denominations in the city. We developed a technique where we preached a dialogue sermon

---

* The 50th International Eucharistic Congress will take place in Dublin in 2012.

together. It worked quite well. We never plucked up the courage to attempt to do this in Derry! One cold and sunny morning in Richmond when we had no engagement, we went for a walk and accidentally came upon an old church there, painted all in white – a classic American wooden church. It was quite near where we were staying. It was St John's Episcopal church, the oldest church in Richmond, built in 1741. It was the site of two important conventions in the period leading to the American Revolutionary War, and is most famous as the location where Patrick Henry gave his closing speech at the Second Virginia Convention with the famous quotation 'Give me liberty or give me death'. The church itself was not open that morning, and we wandered into the churchyard and began reading the old headstones. To our amazement, we came across a headstone on which was written 'Here lies John Doherty of Fawn (sic), County of Donegalle (sic), Ireland who died on ...'. I cannot now remember the precise date of his death but it was a date in 1819 and he was aged 21, as far as I remember. Doherty is one of the most frequently found surnames in this part of Ireland. We both wondered how a young man like John Doherty of Fahan, just a short distance from Derry, had reached Richmond in Virginia in 1819. I was not aware that Richmond was a regular destination for Irish immigrants in the early nineteenth century. We thought about John Doherty and his story and we often spoke about this in our subsequent talks in the United States when mentioning the Irish diaspora.

In October 1990, Bishop James and I also engaged in an extensive speaking tour for a week in the Midwest, visiting Milwaukee, Chicago, Davenport, Iowa City, Des Moines, Notre Dame University in South Bend, Indiana, and finishing up with a weekend of talks and sermons in Washington DC. This tour was organised by the US Catholic Bishops Conference and the Presbyterian Church in the US. Such tours were very intensive and involved a lot of travel. But they were full of surprises.

The talks in some situations, particularly in universities, were extremely challenging – there was criticism and questioning, on occasions, from both extreme Republican and Unionist sympathisers. There were organisations like Noraid on the Irish Republican side and Protestants for Truth in Northern Ireland on the Unionist side.

The audiences were always large and incredibly attentive. Many Americans were baffled at how a Catholic and a Protestant bishop from Northern Ireland could be friends and agree to speak together. We discovered that ecumenism in Derry was more developed than it was in some parts of the United States. In Chicago, we had the delightful experience of being assisted and chauffeured by a glamorous young Presbyterian woman who was mother to a little baby, just a few weeks old. She was our PR lady for the visit to the city. She handed one of us the baby to nurse whilst she drove us to our various speaking venues. Our entrance into some of these venues, in full episcopal regalia, carrying an infant in our arms caused considerable interest and some mirth. In Washington DC, we preached in an Episcopal church dedicated to St Columba. As far as I remember, it was in the Georgetown district. It contained a splendid stained glass window depicting the departure of St Columba from Derry to Iona. Among the worshippers in the congregation at that service was Mr James Baker who at that time was the US Secretary of State. There were all kinds of vehicles outside bristling with antennae and secret service men in the church trying to be unobtrusive. (There was some kind of security alert in some part of the world at that time.) A significant feature of that occasion was that it was followed by what was called a preacher's forum – where both of us met the congregation, including Mr Baker, and discussed the sermon! We enjoyed coffee and cookies whilst having an interesting exchange of views.

There were all kinds of surprises on these tours. For my enlightenment, in Milwaukee, I was given a lengthy and animated lecture on Bloody Sunday in Derry by a gentleman with distant Irish ancestry who had never been outside the United States and who admitted subsequently that he had never been outside Wisconsin. He ended his contribution by asking me had I ever heard of Bloody Sunday! I resisted the temptation to respond to him.

One of the most pleasant surprises occurred in a most unlikely place. Bishop James and I were invited to speak in Davenport, a city in Iowa, on the Mississippi, right in the centre of the United States. We gave a press conference at the airport when we arrived and then we spoke at a Rotary Club lunch, went on to St Ambrose University and at night we spoke and took part in an ecumenical service in the

Sacred Heart Catholic Cathedral in Davenport. Just as we were entering the cathedral in procession, I was greeted loudly by a familiar voice speaking in the Derry vernacular! It was Tillie Doherty, a woman from Derry at whose wedding I had officiated in the late 1960s or early 1970s. She was married to a member of the US Navy who was based in Derry at the time. They lived about fifty miles south of Davenport and, to her surprise, she had seen me on the local television news coverage of the airport press conference. I had not met them since their wedding day. She and her husband and children decided there and then to drive to Davenport to meet me and they were at the cathedral for our presentation and we had a wonderful reunion afterwards. Her husband had been posted to Vietnam shortly after they were married. Thankfully, he survived that terrible war.

Visits to the United States were most interesting and challenging. Getting the message across was always difficult in such a huge country with many problems of its own. While there were always a few senior individuals in American public life, political and Church figures, who took a constructive and informed interest in our problems from the beginning, there did not appear to be all that much interest in us at the highest level of American public life until the 1980s, when John Hume gained access into those circles. The British had considerable influence in the State Department and their point of view seemed to be uncritically accepted there.

I was always fascinated by Irish Americans or American Irish, as some of them prefer to describe themselves. A few such people sent me some of the most vitriolic hate mail that I received. Most were the friendliest, kindest and hospitable of people. There were some who studied the Northern problem with great care and diligence. There were others who merely swallowed propaganda. However, most Irish Americans did not care all that much about our issues in the 1960s and early 1970s, except, perhaps, around St Patrick's Day, and many of the few who did had a largely skewed understanding of things. One of the big problems in the early years was that media outlets in the United States were largely dependent on reports from the international news agencies. There were few international news agency bureaux in Ireland. Most of the news from the North was filtered through agencies in London, news that gave a largely British angle on things. A few of the major US newspapers and media outlets sent reporters to Derry and the North from time to time when major events occurred, but the coverage was generally scant, superficial and shallow. Then there were the Irish American publications, some of which did their best to give balanced reporting, but one of which was a somewhat notorious and vicious mouthpiece for Republican propaganda. Someone told me that it was edited by an ex-nun. I certainly was not one of her favourite people! By and large, the Irish American population was poorly informed on Northern issues until after the mid-1980s. Things improved enormously in the late 1980s and 1990s. Most of the major news agencies established bureaux in Dublin or Belfast – and access to the internet and World Wide Web improved understanding vastly. New and better-informed journalists were writing in the Irish American media. Interestingly, most of my hate mail from the US stopped at that time. Gradually, US Government at the highest level, and major and influential figures in the Irish American business community began to take a constructive and vital interest in our problems. Some of these people subsequently played a vitally important role in our peace process.

John Hume must take most of the credit for informing Americans of the truth of the situation here. He travelled to the United States repeatedly, often at his own expense, to seek investment from America and to explain to influential Americans in politics, commercial life and the media the reality of the situation. He ploughed a lonely furrow for many years. Subsequently, the Irish Government, its Department of Foreign Affairs, and Irish Ambassadors in Washington broadened this understanding. Persuaded by John Hume, Senators and Congressmen travelled to the North and gradually came to a better understanding of our situation. As a result, largely thanks to John Hume, the United States had a major influence on the ground-breaking political events in the North in the 1990s.

CHAPTER 11

Ecumenism

On a recent visit to my dentist, I met a delightful young couple from Iran in the waiting room. They are studying here. They had brought their young daughter to receive dental treatment. We began to talk. Early in the conversation, they asked me about the origins and the causes of the conflict between Christians here.

When people think about Northern Ireland, they usually think of a polarised society split along a politico/religious divide. One of the great tragedies of the partition of Ireland was that it divided the island on the basis of a religious head count. Sadly, the political and religious divides are coterminous to a considerable extent. Most of the Catholic community are Nationalist or Republican seeking union with the rest of the island of Ireland and most of the Protestant community are Unionist wishing to maintain the union with Britain. The historic reasons for these sad divisions are well chronicled elsewhere. They are inherited and, in some cases, irrational.

The conflict in Northern Ireland was sometimes described as a religious war. I cannot agree that this was or is an accurate description of our problems. It is often used as journalistic shorthand when writers struggle to portray the situation here. It is a simplistic description. The reality is much more complex than that. There are many dimensions to the problems in our community – social, political, post-colonial, cultural and religious dimensions. For someone who is a member of the Christian clergy, someone who is committed to living and preaching the teaching of Jesus Christ about love and forgiveness, these divisions and tensions present a huge challenge.

Just as there are divisions between the two main communities, there are internal divisions within each of these communities. We live in a much-fractured society. However, interestingly, I believe that it is less fractured now than it was prior to the outbreak of conflict in the late 1960s. This is particularly true of inter-Church relations.

Prior to the pontificate of Pope John XXIII, there was little or no contact between the Churches here. The current situation is quite different. The Ecumenical Council of the Church, the Second Vatican Council, changed a perception of inter-Church relations that had existed since the Council of Trent, held in the middle of the sixteenth century. One of the decrees published by the Second Vatican Council was the Decree on Ecumenism (*Unitatis Redintegratio*). A paragraph in Chapter 2 of this decree has always struck me as being particularly pertinent to our situation here.

> Let all Christ's faithful remember that the more purely they strive to live according to the Gospel, the more they are fostering and even practising Christian unity. For they can achieve depth and ease in strengthening mutual brotherhood to the degree that they enjoy profound communion with the Father, the Word and the Holy Spirit.*

I was fortunate in that I grew up in a situation where some of my childhood friends were members of other Christian Churches. So from the very beginning, friendship with people of other Churches was not a problem. It was natural. When I came to Derry in the early 1960s, I became deeply involved in theatrical production and music. Over a period of eight or nine years, I staged and produced a lot of shows, plays and concerts. People of all denominations came to those performances, including several Protestant clergymen and their families. The Church of Ireland bishop, Bishop Tyndall, and his wife were frequent visitors. We got to know one another extremely well through our common love of music and the theatre. This friendship became surprisingly useful in the early stages of the conflict when the communities in the city were becoming more and more polarised. In an attempt to calm the immediate situation, in April 1969, I accompanied my predecessor, Bishop Farren, and Bishop Tyndall on an afternoon-long visit on foot to both the

---

* Walter M. Abbott SJ, *The Documents of Vatican II* (Geoffrey Chapman, London, 1967), p. 351.

Bogside and the Fountain areas of the city where they met and received a friendly greeting from residents in both communities. From then until now, I have had very good relations with many members of the clergy and laity of the other Christian Churches in Derry. The quality of the relationship stuttered a little in the aftermath of Bloody Sunday, when many Unionists perceived that I allowed myself to be an instrument of Republican propaganda when, in fact, I merely endeavoured to witness to the truth of what happened on that day. However, throughout my period as bishop, and since then as chaplain in the Foyle Hospice, relationships have been very good.

Personal relationships are the basic building blocks of any community. During my years as bishop, I endeavoured to build up personal relationships with the leaders of the other local Churches. By and large, this was successful. The number of changes in leadership personnel that had taken place in that period presented great difficulty. During my term as bishop, there were three Church of Ireland bishops, nineteen moderators of the Derry Presbytery and four Superintendents of the Methodist Church!

Relationships with the Church of Ireland bishops were the easiest to establish. Our situations in our respective Churches were similar. I had a very good relationship with Robin Eames during his five years in Derry (1975–80) before he went on to greater things. I attended his episcopal ordination in Armagh in 1975. As far as I know, it was the first time a Catholic bishop attended the ordination of a bishop of the Church of Ireland. We were both the youngest bishops in Ireland in our respective Churches at that time and we had a lot in common. We worked together on a number of issues. We endeavoured to seek a pastoral solution to the issue of mixed marriages with a degree of success. Robin was very astute politically and he and I held different political views. However, we developed a friendship that lasts until this day. While we never publicly discussed our differences, we agreed to disagree on many political issues. Together we tried to encourage and develop a fellowship among the clergy of the various Churches. We decided to arrange meetings of the clergy in Magee College in the mid-1970s to help improve understanding of the respective positions of the Churches on various issues and to enable clergy to meet socially and to get to know one another. These meetings were very successful. About 90 per cent of the clergy from the various Churches in the city attended these meetings. Most had never met one another previously. We invited speakers and discussed issues on which we were united and faced up to issues that divided us. We read or listened to psalms or passages from the Bible and prayed and reflected on them in moments of silence. We tried to inform one another of the concerns of our respective communities. The most useful product of these meetings was that all the clergy in the city came to meet and get to know one another for the first time.

In the third week of November 1976, there was a spate of sectarian tit-for-tat murders in the city. This shocked and saddened us. It was a new phenomenon that had not been experienced in the city before. Bishop Eames and I decided to call on the clergy of the city to make a protest about this and highlight the threat it posed to our community. On Saturday, 27 November 1976, virtually every single clergyman in Derry City, except the Free Presbyterians, led by the two bishops, walked in silent procession across the city from Altnagelvin Hospital to the City Cemetery. Nothing was said apart from a few prayers. There were no speeches; but the protest attracted considerable interest from the public and the media. It was the first time ever that the clergy of the city had made such a statement, such a witness, albeit without words, together. Few know the precise impact of that witness, but what is certain, is that that particular bout of sectarian bloodletting stopped after that Saturday. Derry diocese, by and large, was relatively free of that dreadful phenomenon compared with some other areas of the North.

Robin was succeeded as Church of Ireland Bishop of Derry and Raphoe by James Mehaffey in 1980. James and I developed a very close friendship and we worked together very closely while we both served as bishops in our respective dioceses. We served together as founder Trustees on the Inner City Trust, which will be dealt with in a later chapter. We were founders of the Waterside Churches Trust, now known as the Churches Trust. From time to time, we issued joint statements in the wake of some atrocities. We spoke on various occasions at different functions in Derry and elsewhere. On the suggestion of the respective cathedral organists, we initiated the annual Two Cathedrals Festival in Derry in the early 1990s – an international music festival centred on Derry's two cathedrals. In the 1980s, we initiated a joint service at Christmas each year, in which a well-attended Christmas Service of Reconciliation was begun in one cathedral and then after a processional walk by the congregation through the city centre, the service was concluded in the other cathedral. This procession annually attracted a protest by Free Presbyterians opposed to ecumenism. They were noisy but harmless. At that time, these bigots tried to disrupt virtually every ecumenical service in the area. Bishop James and I took part jointly in many civic and religious services of an ecumenical nature particularly during the annual Week of Prayer for Christian Unity in January each year. I remember participating in a joint carol service in the Guildhall one Christmas when a car bomb exploded outside without warning, blowing in some of the windows, showering everyone with glass and causing widespread terror among the assembled congregation. A good friend and committed member of the Church of Ireland, the late Flo Lewers, suffered deafness as a result of that bomb. She had been sitting beside me. James and I also dealt with the vexed question of mixed marriages, whereby we agreed on a common policy that we oversaw ourselves, rather than subjecting couples to the various interpretations of the laws by different clergymen. This worked very well.

We went on various trips to the United States. We discovered that in many parts of the US there was not the same friendly cooperation between bishops of various denominations as we had experienced and practised. I consider that we both benefitted from our activity together. I never ever experienced any antipathy from the Catholic community because of this relationship. In fact, I always received encouragement from my community for such activity and witness. I recall that Bishop Mehaffey once experienced heated public criticism from a minority of people in the Protestant community for attending a football match with me on a Sunday afternoon in the mid-1980s. A press photographer pictured the two of us together enjoying a soccer game featuring the local professional team, Derry City. This generated controversy among some people.

I am not quite sure whether the controversy was because of the ecumenical dimension or because it was construed as a breach of the Sabbath or because some wrongly perceived Derry City football club as an expression of Nationalist culture! I have been a life-long supporter of Derry City FC.

I still keep up contact with James and his wife, Thelma. We are both retired from our positions as bishops and meet from time to time. Apart from sharing a similar office, we have also shared and continue to share a deep friendship and mutual respect.

Whilst there were minor protests at ecumenical activity in Derry, I once experienced a more dramatic form of protest about ecumenism. In early 1975, I was invited to Scotland by an organisation called CUE (Christian Understanding Everywhere) to speak at a major Ecumenical Conference that was being planned for the following September in Edinburgh. Subsequently, I received a letter on 16 January 1975 from the Minister of St Giles' Cathedral in Edinburgh, the Reverend Gilleasbuig Macmillan. The Conference was scheduled to take place on Saturday, 6 September 1975 in the cathedral and the Reverend Macmillan invited me to preach at an Evening Service there on the Sunday of that same weekend. I wrote to Cardinal Gordon Gray, Archbishop of Edinburgh and St Andrews, advising him of the invitations and asking him if it was in order for me to accept. He encouraged me to accept and invited me to stay with him at his residence during my stay in Edinburgh. I accepted both invitations.

I arrived in Edinburgh on the Saturday morning and attended the Conference in St Giles' and gave my address, examining Christian alternatives to violence as a means of countering unjust situations and regimes. There was a very large crowd in attendance and the address was well received. There was no controversy whatsoever. After the Conference had ended, I joined the Cardinal for a meal at his home. He then told me that he was a little apprehensive about the service in St Giles' the following day. As far as he understood, I would be the first Catholic to preach in St Giles' Cathedral! I was not aware of this fact. The Cardinal told me that he knew Reverend Macmillan, said that he was new to the position and he was a good man. I decided to go ahead. I had prepared a very simple talk on St Columba for the

Evening Service and planned to reflect on the Christian links between Ireland and Scotland, between Iona and Derry. There was nothing remotely controversial in it, so I was confident that no ecumenical feathers would be ruffled. Evening Service in St Giles' is quite a significant event. There was a very large congregation and the music and singing were magnificent. I robed in choral dress, with my purple cassock, white surplice and purple zucchetto (skull cap). The service proceeded as normal with a selection of Bible readings and hymns. Then the verger came to me and escorted me up the steps to the pulpit in St Giles' – I remember him clicking the lock or bolt in the door behind me – it was quite a loud click – I put down my script, took a deep breath and said 'My dear brothers and sisters' and all hell broke loose! People began shouting and chairs started to fly through the air. I was left in no doubt that I was the target of the protest. I tried to begin my talk a couple of times but it was obvious that any effort to speak was pointless. Those protesting only appeared to be a small minority of the congregation, but they created widespread fear and panic among other members present. Everyone was on their feet – I waited for what seemed like an age for the verger to return and unlock the door so that I could retreat from the pulpit. When I got to the bottom of the pulpit steps, several police officers were waiting for me; they rushed me to the vestry and escorted me out of the building with a coat over my head. I felt like one of the Great Train Robbers, a criminal! I was taken in a police car to a college where the Reverend Macmillan and others joined me and we had dinner. They apologised profusely. The protest was organised by a group that styled itself as the Protestant Action Society and they chanted such pleasantries as 'Burn him at the stake' and 'No Popery'. They had objected to me, a Roman Catholic, preaching in St Giles' Cathedral. The Reverend Macmillan and I issued a joint statement later that evening about the events in the cathedral. The little reflection on St Columba was not heard but seen! *The Scotsman* newspaper published it the next day in full in the context of a report on the events of the previous night.

In the last number of years since I retired, ministering in the Hospice, there have been further opportunities to engage in happy and positive relationships with the other Christian Churches. There

CHAPTER 12

The Birmingham Six – Justice Denied

The Birmingham bombing shocked and angered me. When it occurred on 21 November 1974, I was filled with a mixture of sorrow for the victims and their relatives and families and anger at those who had perpetrated such an atrocity. Twenty-one people were killed and 182 injured by bombs that were detonated without warning in crowded pubs in Birmingham city centre. I had had first-hand experience of such evil deeds here in Derry, but never anything with loss of life to this extent. I noted the arrests and was pleased. Initially, reading the news reports, I was convinced of the guilt of those arrested and then, with the passage of time, I began to hear stories that cast doubt on that belief.

On 29 May 1975, during the 1975 ceasefire, I received a letter from Kenneth Curtis & Co., a firm of solicitors in Birmingham representing Richard McIlkenny, John Walker and Gerard Hunter, telling me that the men had

> maintained their innocence of these charges or of any other involvement with the explosions that occurred then or at any other time.*

The letter went to say that 'Unfortunately, however, some of the six men arrested, including two of our clients, signed written statements admitting their involvement in these offences.' The letter continued,

> We understand that you have in the past been able to assist in arranging contacts between the representatives of the British

---

* Derry Diocesan Archive.

Government and the IRA and took a major part in bringing about the present ceasefire. Our clients have suggested to us that we should write to you to see whether through your offices the IRA Command in Dublin could be persuaded to make some definitive statement concerning the explosions on 21st November. Our clients believe that those men responsible for those explosions are at present in Éire. If such a statement were made in which the IRA Command made it clear that the men charged were not responsible, then it could well be that this would be published by the British Press. Such a statement at this time would be of considerable importance.

I gave the letter some thought and then made contact as requested, through an intermediary. There was a complete denial of any IRA involvement in the bombing. I conveyed this information to the solicitors. Then, with their permission, I approached a senior civil servant in the Northern Ireland Office whom I knew. I apprised him of the case and the claims of innocence. I had heard from another source that there were doubts about the men and their alleged involvement. I expressed my personal concern. He passed my letter to someone in a more senior position. However, the trial was fast approaching and nobody wanted to get involved. The Birmingham Six were not the flavour of the month. A shaky IRA truce was in place and local events rather than events in England got priority of the attention of most people here. I have to confess that, like many others in the North, I became distracted by other matters nearer home.

The six men were convicted of the murders in August 1975. They were John Walker, Paddy Hill, Hugh Callaghan, Gerry Hunter, Billy Power and Richard McIlkenny. John Walker was a native of Derry City and I knew some members of his family. The six men were given multiple life sentences.

Some considerable time elapsed before I gave serious thought to the case again, but it was always at the back of my mind. Among my diocesan duties were prison visits and work on behalf of people who had been arrested. Apart from Theresa Walker's visits to me from time to time, I cannot recall one instance during that period when the Birmingham case or the conviction of the six men was mentioned in my presence. (Theresa Walker was John Walker's wife. She and her children had to leave her home in Birmingham because of intimidation. She came to live in Derry shortly after the bombing and is still here. I offered her some assistance from time to time.) I read the late Father Denis Faul and Father Raymond Murray publication, *The Birmingham Framework*, published in 1976, and the case came back to my attention. The carefully and accurately researched work by Fathers Faul and Murray renewed my concern and stirred up my interest once more. There were so many local cases of injustice competing for attention, cases of local young people whom I knew and whose families I knew. And whilst, after reading Father Faul's book, the Birmingham case renewed my interest, I never seemed to get time to pay proper attention to it at that period in the mid-1970s. However, Father Faul and Father Raymond Murray ensured that the case of these men was not forgotten.

It was a young Derry man in an English prison who brought the Birmingham case to the forefront of my attention in the late 1970s. Since 1975, I had been writing to the already mentioned Shane Paul O'Doherty and visiting him in Wormwood Scrubs and in various English high security prisons – Long Lartin, Wakefield and Gartree. In his letters and during visits, he began to mention the case of the Birmingham men. I was campaigning to get Shane brought back to a prison here in Ireland. Finally, during a visit to Shane in an English prison, he told me quite unequivocally that these six men were completely innocent of the Birmingham bombing and something ought to be done about it. At that time, I was in fairly regular contact with some other people in English prisons. They corroborated what Shane had said. Few people outside were interested in the Birmingham men and there was little or no publicity about their case. The hunger strikes in the North were dominating the news at that time. As a result, I began a correspondence with Paddy Hill in 1982. In a letter dated 25 February 1983, Paddy informed me that he and some of his colleagues had decided to go on hunger strike on 1 June to draw some attention to their plight. Shane asked me to plead with him not to go on hunger strike, and to persuade him that nothing could be achieved by such action. I decided, on Shane's insistence, to visit Paddy Hill, although he had no connection with the Derry diocese. Paddy was originally from Belfast. He was in Gartree Prison, near Market Harborough in Leicestershire, a difficult place to access.

After a visit to some of the high security prisons in England, you begin to realise the awful hardship that such visits placed on the parents, wives and families of those imprisoned there, especially if they had to travel from Ireland. Some of these prisons, such as Long Lartin and Gartree, are out in the countryside. It is not easy to gain access to them by public transport. Getting there involved long journeys on ferries, trains and coaches. Travelling from Derry to Long Lartin or Gartree leaves one quite exhausted. Over the years, in making visits to English prisons, I experimented with all the various travel permutations and combinations and I finally decided that the best and most efficient way was to bring over my own car and drive to each of the various prisons on my itinerary. A routine trip involved more than 1,000 miles of motoring. Another major difficulty in visiting Category A (high security) prisoners in English prisons was that such prisoners could be moved without any notice to a prison in another part of the country. A wife might arrive at Wakefield Prison in Yorkshire accompanied by children and learn on arrival that her husband had been moved hundreds of miles to a prison on the Isle of Wight on the previous day!

I visited Paddy Hill in Gartree. Paddy was a very interesting individual. Extremely open and honest, a gregarious type of character, he was pale, strong and tough. He talked with enormous urgency and energy and feeling about his plight. Like many long-term prisoners, he could roll incredibly thin cigarettes at high speed without even looking at his fingers or hands. He then lit the cigarette with a rather ingenious flint device the mechanics or physics of which I never was quite able to fathom! I will always remember my first meeting with him. I came to like Paddy very quickly. After that first meeting, I was deeply disturbed. I promised him that I would try to heighten interest in the case outside. I pleaded with him not to embark upon a hunger strike. He promised me that he would consider my appeal. Whether because of my appeal or not, he did not go on hunger strike.

I first visited a parishioner in prison in 1960. Up until 1968/9, there were few other occasions to visit people in prison. However, from 1969 until I retired, I visited prisons and prisoners regularly in the North, in the Republic and in England. I did not confine such visits exclusively to those convicted of political offences. When time permitted, I visited any prisoner from my diocese who wished to see me. There were some who clearly expressed in no uncertain terms that they did not wish to see me because of my stated views on violence or paramilitary activities. I corresponded regularly with people in various prisons on either side of the Irish Sea. I considered this to be part of my ministry as bishop. After some years of regular visits to prisoners and correspondence with them, an insight is acquired into those with whom you are in contact and a relationship is built up with them. I feel that, after a time, you can make a fairly accurate distinction between those who are telling the truth and those who are not. It has been my experience that, in most cases, prisoners are truthful. The actions for which they have been convicted are public knowledge. Their story has been dragged through the courts and reported in the media. They have little reason to be untruthful about what it is alleged they have done. Within the prison community, it is rather pointless for long-term prisoners to plead innocence when, in fact, they are guilty. Such pleas cut little ice with fellow prisoners unless they are well based in fact. I began to form my opinions on the innocence of the Birmingham Six on the basis on my long personal contact with people in prison and on what I was hearing from other people within the English prison system. I must stress that not all of those in the latter category were prisoners. Service as a priest and bishop in one of the most troubled areas of the North and contact with people who had perpetrated or were victims of some dreadful atrocities, I think, equips one with a fairly keen insight in such situations.

After my initial visit to Paddy Hill, I sought permission to visit Derry man, John Walker, in Long Lartin Prison. My visit with John Walker further convinced me that a most dreadful injustice had been inflicted on these men. John was wiry and thin, a much quieter and less loquacious individual than Paddy Hill. He was keen on sports and kept himself fit in prison. Although he spent most of his life in England, he had a Derry accent that was well preserved. There was very little acrimony expressed against those who had deprived him of fourteen years of his life and liberty. He was always anxious to know all the news from Derry.

In the period after those visits, I took every possible opportunity to speak to as many people as were prepared to listen to the plight of these men. In Derry, a large number of print and broadcast journalists called at Bishop's House on a fairly regular basis. Scarcely a week went by without contact with some journalist from Ireland or abroad. During that period in the early 1980s, I mentioned the Birmingham case to almost every journalist who called with me. I spoke about their case to politicians and other churchmen, to everyone who was prepared to listen. I kept in contact with Paddy Hill and John Walker as often as I could and I had the *Derry Journal* posted to John twice a week to keep him in touch with things at home in Derry.

In the following years, I endeavoured to visit John and Paddy at least once a year. I wrote to them from time to time. On the suggestion of a senior prison officer, I also came to meet Hugh Callaghan in the course of my visits to Paddy and John. The officer told me that Hugh was 'going through a bad patch' and thought that it would give him some encouragement if I were to ask to see him. I considered this to be significant. Hugh had a different personality than the other two. He looked delicate and unwell and very nervous and fragile at times. The years in prison had exacted a very heavy toll on Hugh's health. Life in a top security prison for a Category A prisoner is not easy, particularly for someone in middle age – and for someone who knows that he is completely innocent, it must have imposed an almost unbearable strain.

Some of the men were at last beginning to get some effective legal advice. Ms Gareth Peirce had arrived on the scene. Gareth is a most remarkable woman of enormous skill, compassion, courage, integrity and considerable humility. She has done an incalculable amount of work for Irish prisoners in English courts and prisons and in various aspects of human rights. She is a brilliant lawyer. We all have reason to be grateful to her. I have great admiration and respect for her.

In a moment of inspiration, Paddy Hill decided to contact the MP for the constituency in which he 'resided' and the unlikely figure of Sir John Farr, the local MP and a prominent Conservative, came to visit his 'constituent' in Gartree. Paddy's own patent honesty and his passionate explanation of the background to his conviction obviously raised questions in Sir John's mind, too, because he soon became a very effective and influential advocate on behalf of the six men. Coming from the right wing of the Tory Party, his interest in the case had a considerable impact. Then came the television programmes, which were quite powerful. Chris Mullin, later to be an MP, was the key researcher for the most important television programme on the case in late 1985. He did a remarkable job of work. Chris also wrote a splendid book on the case entitled *Error of Judgement*.* The demand for a review of the case was increasing in volume and intensity. More and more people were becoming concerned and interested. Even more significant than the numbers of people who were expressing concern was the fact that those expressing concern were from various British political parties and included prominent establishment figures. I wrote to many people whom I thought could help, including the Archbishop of Canterbury, Robert Runcie. I had known Robert previously when we had served for several years on CRAC† when he was Bishop of St Albans.

He replied to me on 25 March 1986:

> As regards the Birmingham Six, I did, in fact, take up their case with the Home Office in August of last year. I did not get an encouraging reply then, and, nor I understand, did Cardinal Hume when he wrote to Douglas Hurd on this matter only last month. In the circumstances, I feel the best we can do is to await the outcome of the Home Office Review.**

I was one of many correspondents to the Home Secretary about this matter. The Home Secretary repeatedly stated that he was reviewing the case, but he did not offer much hope.

---

* Chris Mullin, *Error of Judgement* (Chatto & Windus, London, 1986).
† CRAC – acronym for Central Religious Advisory Committee on Broadcasting – a committee that advised the BBC and IBA on religious broadcasting matters.
** Derry Diocesan Archive.

The first great breakthrough eventually came in early 1987. I received a letter from Douglas Hurd, the Home Secretary, dated 20 January 1987. It was headed '*Birmingham Pub Bombings, Guildford and Woolwich Pub Bombings, The Maguires*' and it said

> You have written to me previously expressing concern about the safety of the convictions in these cases. I have, as you know, been carrying out reviews in all three cases.
>
> I am now writing to enclose a copy of a statement that I am making this afternoon in which I am announcing the conclusions which I have reached.
>
> You will see that I have decided to refer the Birmingham case to the Court of Appeal, but that I do not think there are any grounds which could justify this course in the other two cases. My reasons are set out in greater detail in the statement and, in particular, in the two enclosed memoranda. The brief point is that there is, in my view, no new evidence or consideration in substance which would provide a proper basis for a reference to the Court of Appeal.*

He asked the Court of Criminal Appeal to examine it. It was the first great breakthrough in many years. It raised hopes, albeit cautious hopes, in the hearts of the men and in their families and in those who had been associated with them. I came to like and respect Douglas Hurd. It took considerable political courage to make such decisions. Doing what he did involved considerable political risk, particularly for a Tory.

I visited John, Paddy and Hugh in July 1987. We had lengthy discussions about the pending appeal hearing, which seemed ages away in November. They were exceedingly calm and very sensible about the hearing. They all looked quite well. Even Hugh looked much better, I thought. They had significant confidence in the legal team that was being assembled to present their case. During that visit, I also happened to meet Gareth Peirce. She was seeing a client in Long Lartin Prison. We had a long conversation and she brought me up to date on the preparation for the appeal. She was utterly

---

* Derry Diocesan Archive.

convinced of the innocence of the men but not very optimistic about the outcome of the appeal hearing. She asked me if I would be willing to prepare an affidavit and to give evidence at the hearing if called upon to do so. I assured her that I would be very happy to assist the men's case in any way possible. She wished me to explain to the judges that, in Northern Ireland society, more people than IRA supporters attend the funerals of IRA members and to elaborate on the whole custom and tradition of funeral and wake attendance in the North. (Five of the men were arrested at Heysham, as they were about to board a ferry, on their way to an IRA funeral in Belfast a few hours after the bombing.) Paddy Hill was in sparkling form during that visit in July 1987. He had reams of printed material about the case. He was busy preparing and contacting various prominent people. I could not help contrasting his morale on this occasion with his morale on the first occasion I met him, when he was contemplating going on hunger strike.

I prepared the affidavit for Gareth on the funerals and attendance at funerals. Little did I know at that time, that this particular piece of evidence was going to have an added personal significance for me when I was eventually called to give evidence some months later. During September/October, I was in fairly regular contact with Theresa Walker and with Gareth. There were a lot of journalists enquiring about the case. There was a tremendous amount of interest building up both here in Ireland and in Britain, and also beyond these islands. I found this to be most encouraging.

The appeal hearing was set to begin in the Old Bailey in London on Monday, 2 November 1987, at 10 a.m. I made arrangements to stay in Archbishop's House, Westminster and made travel bookings about a week beforehand. I was asked by the Irish Episcopal Conference to represent the Irish Catholic Bishops at the hearing.

On the Wednesday before the appeal hearing was due to begin, just after lunch time, I received a phone call from a priest in Creggan in Derry to tell me that he had just administered the Last Rites to two men who had been killed by a bomb that they appeared to have been carrying. Within a few hours, the IRA in Derry claimed that these two men were their members. Several months earlier, after guns were discharged at an IRA funeral in the grounds of a Derry

City church, I had ruled that such funerals would not be permitted to enter church grounds in Derry City until further notice. As this was the first funeral since the ruling was made, I felt bound to stand by the ruling, despite the considerable natural sympathy I felt for the families of the two dead men. In view of the fact that I was likely to be asked to give evidence on such funerals in the Old Bailey a few days later, I anticipated a few very difficult days ahead. My worst fears were realised. I was subjected to very powerful pressures over those days. The media kept pressing me for statements and interviews. There was a torchlight procession to my house appealing to me to abandon the ruling on the funerals. There were non-stop calls on the telephone, day and night. Some of the calls were supportive, but most of them were extremely abusive and intimidating. They were very difficult and distressing days.

Our Diocesan Youth Congress took place in Strabane that weekend, 30 October–1 November 1987. It was attended by 400–500 young people from all over the diocese. The Youth Congress took place every two years; months of planning went into its preparation. As was my custom at previous Youth Congresses, I attended the opening ceremony on the Friday night. I attended for some time on the Saturday and spent most of Sunday with the young people in Strabane. I was also keeping in constant touch with developments in Derry. After celebrating and preaching at the concluding Mass of the Congress on the Sunday afternoon, I drove from Strabane directly to Aldergrove Airport to catch a flight to London. I arrived at Cardinal Hume's house at 11 p.m. Cardinal Hume was in Rome attending a Synod of Bishops. The IRA members' funerals in Derry still had not taken place. I spent a long time in the chapel in Archbishop's House in London that night. I prayed that the six men would get a fair hearing and that the truth would emerge and that the problem of the Derry funerals would be resolved in a peaceful and dignified manner as soon as possible. It was the eve of All Souls Day. I did not sleep for a single moment that night. I thought a lot during that night about the six men who had been brought to Wormwood Scrubs for the appeal hearing. I am sure that they were not sleeping that night either. They must have been so tense and anxious. I thought also of the two families in Derry who were concerned about the burial of their loved ones. And I thought of the Derry priests in St Eugene's Cathedral who had the difficult and complex task of handling this very delicate and sensitive problem. I felt very guilty about being away from Derry on such a night, but I felt that, as I had worked for so long on the case, I had to be present when the Birmingham Six were brought into the Appeal Court in the Old Bailey. In my mind, I went over all the different possible eventualities and this went on the whole night through. I heard Big Ben chiming out every single hour as I lay on that bed.

On the Monday morning, I celebrated Mass at 6.30 with the Sisters who were members of the staff in Archbishop's House. After phoning Derry to find out the latest situation, I left for the Old Bailey shortly after 8 a.m. I had never been at the Old Bailey before. When I got there, there were already a few television camera crews around the entrance. I met an Ursuline nun from Sligo whom I knew. She worked in the pastoral care of Irish immigrants in London. We could not gain access at the main entrance, so we queued for the public gallery. Quite large numbers of people arrived to join the queue during the following hour. About 9 a.m., one of Gareth Peirce's staff called me from the queue and asked me to come to the main entrance of the court, the familiar entrance that one often sees on television. There was very heavy security there. Once I got upstairs, after a lengthy task in satisfying the security people at the entrance that the Clerk of the Court had authorised me to be there, I met many of the journalists who were covering the case. There were members of some of the families of the six appellants, politicians, a young man from Amnesty International, the Irish Ambassador to London, Father Bobby Gilmore of the Irish Chaplaincy Service in London, individuals representing the Irish Justice and Peace Commission and many others. The three judges had to decide whether or not to permit me to sit in the body of the court in view of the fact that I might be called upon to give evidence later. They decided, to my relief, that I could attend. I was permitted to enter the court shortly after the hearing had begun. With other observers, I was placed in the jury box. I first looked to see the appellants, all six of them together. I had thought so much about these men for so long. I knew three of them. I had never met the other three. It was a most dramatic moment to see them all there sitting together. Paddy Hill and the others nodded and smiled. They all looked smart sitting in the dock in their civilian clothes. They looked pale and tense but composed. They looked so different from those six awful police photographs with which everyone was so familiar. I found myself sitting beside a middle-aged man with spectacles. In the course of the morning he told me that he was Michael O'Riordan, General Secretary of the Irish Communist Party, and during breaks in the court procedure, we quietly chatted amicably. He was a most interesting man. I am afraid it was the only manifestation of *glasnost* or *perestroika* that I experienced in the Old Bailey during that week.

The first day's hearing was largely taken up with the various leading counsel for the appellants and the Crown making their opening submissions. At the lunch break, I tried to get to a public phone to find out what was happening in Derry. (There were no mobile phones at that time.) It was very difficult to find a public phone in the building that was not already being used. Eventually, I found a phone in the basement and got through to one of the priests in the cathedral in Derry. The two funerals had presented themselves for the regular 10 a.m. morning Mass and, after an objection had been registered, they had been permitted to enter the cathedral for Mass. By a happy coincidence, it was All Souls Day, 2 November, and all Masses were Requiem Masses. The Mass had proceeded without incident. However, there was a confrontation with the RUC when the cortege sought to leave the cathedral grounds and the two coffins and hundreds of mourners were still in the cathedral grounds. There was stalemate. That was the situation reported to me when I phoned on that Monday at lunchtime. A lot of journalists outside the Old Bailey sought comments from me on the funeral situation. I told them that I was unwilling to comment until things became clearer. It was the first time in my fourteen years as bishop that I was away from Derry for a critical situation of this nature. During the lunch adjournment, a group of London people who were working on behalf of the Six, asked me to attend a press briefing with a few of the other observers and members of the families. I went and spoke at the briefing. It was a low key and very constructive affair. That afternoon when the hearing was adjourned for the

1 Ordination as bishop by Cardinal William Conway, 31 March 1974.
Also in picture: Archbishop Alibrandi, Papal Nuncio.
2 Ordination as bishop, 31 March 1974.

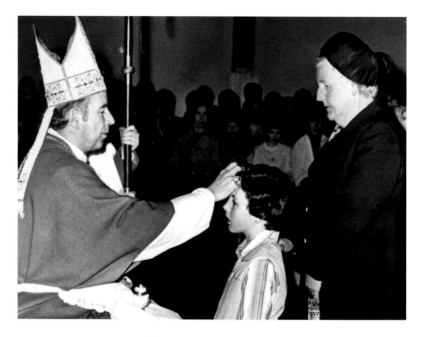

3 Confirmation of niece, Trudi Daly;
Bishop Daly's mother is sponsor, 1975.
4 With Archbishop Helder Camara, at a
conference in Derry, April 1977.

5 Marriage of Dana (Rosemary Brown), St Eugene's Cathedral, Derry,
5 October 1978 (*l to r*): Damien Scallon, Fr Kevin Scallon,
Bishop Neil Farren.
6 Archbishop Tomás Ó Fiaich visits after cancer surgery
in Altnagelvin Hospital, November 1977.

7 Papal Visit, Dublin Airport, 29 September 1979.

8 Papal Visit, audience for media, Cabra, Dublin,
29 September 1979.

9 H-Blocks, Long Kesh (photograph courtesy of the *Derry Journal*).
10 IRA funeral, Long Tower church grounds, Derry, March 1987
(photograph courtesy of the *Derry Journal*).

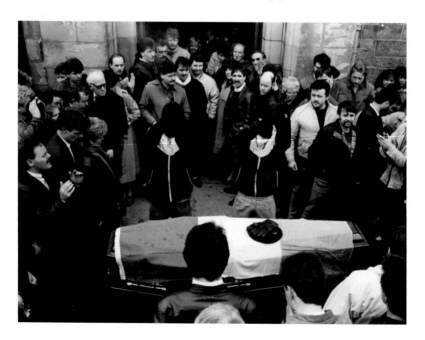

11 Cardinal Basil Hume and Father Tom Kelly at the ordination of
Father Kelly, Sunday, 26 April 1981, St Mary's church, Creggan, Derry.
12 New Ireland Forum in Dublin Castle, 9 February 1984. *L-R*:
Archbishop Joseph Cassidy, Dick Spring, Charles Haughey, Bishop Cahal
Daly, Bishop Edward Daly and Garret FitzGerald. Cahal Daly was
Bishop of Down and Connor at that time, and was not yet a Cardinal.

13 With Bishop James Mehaffey.

14 Signatures of the Birmingham Six, March 1991.

15 Paddy 'Bogside' Doherty (photograph courtesy of the *Derry Journal*).
16 With sisters, Anne (*left*) and Marion (*right*), receiving Honorary
Doctorate from the University of Ulster, 8 June 1994.

17 Celebrating Mass with Pope John Paul II in his private chapel.
18 Golden Jubilee Mass at St Eugene's Cathedral, March 2007
(photograph courtesy of the *Derry Journal*).

19 Golden Jubilee Mass, St Eugene's Cathedral, March 2007.
L-R: Hugh McMonagle, Charles Glenn (who assisted Bishop Daly on
Bloody Sunday) and Jackie Duddy's sisters, Kay and Bernie.
20 With John and Pat Hume at the Golden Jubilee Concert,
St Columb's Hall, Derry, March 2007
(photograph courtesy of the *Derry Journal*).

21 Golden Jubilee, March 2007. *L-R:* sister Dympna, brother Tom, Edward Daly and sisters Anne and Marion.
22 Group function held in the Foyle Hospice to celebrate Golden Jubilee: *from left*, seated, Rosemary Peoples and Dr Tom McGinley (founder of the Hospice), standing, Hannah Healey, Marie Dunlop, Father Eamon Graham, Helen Foley and Julia McIvor.

23 On the steps of the Derry Guildhall after the publication of the Saville Report, 15 June 2010 (photograph courtesy of the *Derry Journal*).
24 Thousands of people gathered in Guidhall Square for the publication of the Saville Report (photograph courtesy of the *Derry Journal*).

25 Relatives of the Bloody Sunday victims on the steps of the Guildhall, as they acknowledge the cheers from the gathered crowd, after the publication of the Saville Report (photograph courtesy of the *Derry Journal*).

26 At the Bloody Sunday Monument, Bogside, Derry, with leaders of other Christian Churches the day after the publication of the Saville Report, 16 June 2010 (photograph courtesy of the *Derry Journal*).

day, I could not get through to Derry on the telephone. I did not know what was happening at home. I was besieged by journalists at the door of the Old Bailey and eventually was rescued by Seamus Mallon MP, who got a taxi and took me with him to the House of Commons. From there, I managed to contact home and learned that the funerals were over at last and the burials had taken place despite further ugly confrontations on the way to the cemetery. I watched the reportage on the funerals and the Old Bailey appeal on the early evening television news in a bar in the House of Commons. I was relieved to know that the Derry funerals were over at last. I left for Archbishop's House shortly afterwards. I spent a lot of time in prayer that night. I kept thinking of the six men who were in Wormwood Scrubs. I was very tired and went to bed about 9.30. It was the first night for some time that I got a good, sound, uninterrupted sleep.

On Tuesday and the other days during the week, I came to the Old Bailey rested and able to give full attention to the business in hand. The witnesses began to appear. Their counsel took them through their evidence. They were cross-examined by the opposing counsel. The court took on an atmosphere akin to theatre. Michael Mansfield was most accomplished and flamboyant. His grasp of complex technical detail and feats of memory were exceptional. Richard Ferguson made a big impression on me. The various witnesses made varying impacts. I thought that the leading counsel for the Crown was very bright. I was alarmed and very disturbed, however, at the attitude of the judges and the nature and tone of their interventions on occasions. To my mind, they revealed a considerable degree of bias against the appellants. They also displayed an inability to grasp the difficulties and behaviour of poor people who are unemployed. There was an apparent unbridgeable culture gap between the judges and the appellants, between upper-class English and working-class Irish. At the back of the court, sitting along the wall directly opposite the judge's bench sat the six appellants through all those days. They did not say anything publicly. None of them gave evidence. They always looked interested, at times they smiled, but the tension in their faces was obvious. Their dignity was most edifying. During that week, too, I met some members of the six families. They, too, were very dignified and impressive. The suffering of the years was patently obvious in the faces of some of the women. At the end of the first week, I must confess that the attitude of the three judges caused me considerable anxiety and worry. I was satisfied in my own mind that some of the evidence in the court had raised the most serious questions about the quality of the admission statements that the appellants had made and the manner and circumstances in which these statements were taken. Much of the evidence given raised questions in my mind about the safety of the men's conviction. I attended the entire hearings for the first week. I had to return then to attend to duties at home in Derry. Dr Pat Hannon, Professor of Moral Theology in St Patrick's College, Maynooth, a barrister as well as a theologian, was present for almost the entire appeal hearing representing the Justice and Peace Commission of the Irish Episcopal Conference. Cardinal Ó Fiaich and a number of other Irish bishops attended on various occasions during the remaining weeks of the appeal hearing.

I was called to give evidence on the Thursday of the first week and briefly taken through the cultural and social dimension of attendance at funerals in Ireland and the fact that people other than IRA supporters attend IRA funerals. I pointed out that neighbours, relatives, work colleagues, friends of the family etc. would also be present at such funerals and that relatives and friends from England and abroad regularly travelled to attend funerals in Ireland. It was my second time to appear as a witness before a British Lord Chief Justice. The last time was at the Widgery Tribunal in Coleraine in 1972.

During the remainder of the hearing, at home in Derry, I carefully read the newspaper reports of the appeal hearing. I thought that the quality of writing and coverage by Nuala O'Faolain in the *Irish Times* and Kevin Dawson in the *Sunday Tribune* was quite outstanding. As the hearing went on, I spoke with various people who attended the hearings on different days. They all considered that the appellants' lawyers were making an excellent case. They were profoundly unimpressed by forensics expert Dr Skuse and felt that the forensic evidence at the original trial had been brought very much into question, if not completely discredited. They were convinced that the original conviction was unsafe. They were equally convinced, from observing the attitude of the judges, that these three 'learned and wise' men would throw out the appeal.

After the appeal hearing ended, there was a general sense and atmosphere of pessimism among almost all of those associated with the appellants. Despite the strength of the case of the appellants, it was felt that the three judges would not order a retrial or find that the convictions were unsafe. At Christmas time, I exchanged letters with John Walker and Paddy Hill. They were back in Long Lartin and Gartree. I was also in touch with Theresa Walker. I got the impression that they were hoping for the best and preparing for the worst.

Gareth Peirce contacted me in late January to tell me when the Appeal Judges were to give their judgment in the Old Bailey. I immediately made arrangements to travel over. Once again, I stayed in Archbishop's House. I made the early morning journey by Tube to the Old Bailey. The security at the court was tighter than ever. Everyone was checked with great care, even though most of the people concerned had already attended all or part of the earlier hearing and most of those involved in the security seemed to have been involved in that hearing also. Just in front of me entering the court, former Irish Foreign Minister, Mr Peter Barry, was thoroughly searched. I could not imagine a former British Foreign Secretary being subjected to this treatment if he were attending a court in Dublin. If it did happen, I could imagine the outcry that would ensue. There were members of the families of the appellants there. There was a big attendance of media people. Nobody was very hopeful of a positive outcome. The judgment was to be given in Court Number 2, a different courtroom than that in which the hearing had taken place. The entrance hall on this floor of the Old Bailey is quite magnificent. It is much more like a basilica than a court of law. The reason I had time to notice this was that we had such a long wait in a queue before getting our security clearance.

The judgment took several hours to read. Each of the three judges read parts of it. Within the first few minutes, it was obvious that they were going to throw out the appeal. As time went on, I felt more and more angry and dismayed, not just with the decision, but with the whole tone and manner of the judgment. Every aspect of the case made by the appellants was rejected in almost every detail. When the last few sentences of the judgment were read, and the full harsh verdict was given, I felt quite distraught. I was heartbroken for the men and for their families. I was deeply moved by the dignity with which the six appellants reacted to the judgment. Even at the conclusion of this travesty of justice, there were no hysterics, no demonstrations, no futile gestures from the six victims. In my opinion, the six men in the dock had demonstrated considerably more dignity in that courtroom than the three men on the bench. I spoke to Gareth Peirce and some of the legal team. I answered questions and gave interviews to some journalists. I looked around for some of the relatives outside the court to sympathise with them, but I could not find any of them. Like me, they all seemed to wish to get away quickly. In the gloom and darkness of the late afternoon, I headed straight for the nearest Tube station, travelled out to Heathrow and caught the first flight to Belfast. On the way home from Aldergrove Airport to Derry on the motorway, I noticed the great blue motorway sign for Coleraine picked out in the car headlights. And I thought of Lord Widgery and his hearing in the County Hall, Coleraine, many years before in 1972 and I thought of Lord Lane and his hearing in the Old Bailey in London in 1988. And I thought of so many people in graves in Derry and Birmingham and six men in prison in England. I thought of all the obscene futile violence and all the injustice in our society and all the innocent victims of these two evils. And I wept.

I was determined that these six men and their dreadful plight must not be forgotten. I was more convinced than ever of their innocence. They and their families were the victims of a horrendous injustice. I looked forward to visiting them again sometime in the next few weeks. I was more determined than ever that the case must be kept alive.

At the end of the first week of the appeal hearing, I stayed on in London to attend the annual function of the Derry Association in London on the Saturday night. On the Sunday morning, 8 November, I caught a mid-morning shuttle flight from Heathrow to Aldergrove Airport in Belfast. As I set out for Derry, I switched on the car radio to hear the news. 'Reports are coming in of an explosion at a Remembrance Day service at Enniskillen. It is feared that there are casualties'. Gradually, on that journey home from Aldergrove, the shocking immensity and obscenity of the horror of Enniskillen began to emerge in subsequent news flashes and reports.

I was filled with a fierce anger and sadness. I could only imagine how the men in a London prison would feel when they heard that news; they were in the midst of an appeal for which they had worked so long and hard. They hoped for justice. I could only imagine how the people of my own county town, Enniskillen, would feel.

It was the second time that a Provisional IRA atrocity had intervened directly in something that I had worked for and planned. The first time was in 1979 when the Mountbatten murder wrecked the plans to bring the Pope to Armagh, and now this latest atrocity had the potential to generate so much bad will in England at a time when the six innocent Birmingham men needed all the good will possible from that quarter to have their innocence recognised.

Over the next few weeks, while the Birmingham case was still being heard in London, I visited several of the Enniskillen victims on numerous occasions in Altnagelvin Hospital in Derry where they were being treated for their terrible injuries. They impressed me and moved me deeply with their dignity and with their Christian forgiveness. Out of the darkness of those days, Gordon Wilson emerged. His daughter, Marie, was killed in the Remembrance Day bombing. In a television interview with the BBC in the aftermath of the atrocity, Gordon Wilson, a Methodist, described with anguish his last conversation with his daughter as they both lay trapped in the debris:

> She held my hand tightly, and gripped me as hard as she could. She said, 'Daddy, I love you very much.' Those were her exact words to me, and those were the last words I ever heard her say.

He added,

> But I bear no ill will. I bear no grudge. Dirty sort of talk is not going to bring her back to life. She was a great wee lassie. She loved her profession. She was a pet. She's dead. She's in heaven and we shall meet again. I will pray for these men tonight and every night.

Gordon Wilson's Christianity and forgiveness were brilliant and noble beacons of light and hope at a time of great darkness.

There are many types of victims and many forms of violence and injustice in our sad society. Those weeks in late 1987 and early 1988 highlighted for me once again the wickedness and immorality of violence and the cruelty of injustice and the sheer futility of attempting to achieve political objectives in this country through the use of violence.

What price justice for the innocents
Locked up in prison cells
What price respect and peace of mind
For those who know and will not tell
What price the horror of the beatings
The torture and the cries
Of honest men who in terror signed
Perverted statements filled with lies
What price hunger and deprivation
Threats with guns and growling dogs
Of minds now blank and wandering
As if lost within a fog
What price the cries of wives and children
Of families torn apart
Whose moans and wails of anguish
Come from deeply wounded hearts
What price the long lost years filled
With loneliness and pain
And the longing to be held
In loving arms again
What price the lost love and joy of children
All now fully grown, left without a father
Now with children of their own
What price, what price!!
What price for honesty and truthfulness
For dignity and pride restored
For the innocents to be set free
Exonerated and recompensed
To rejoin society once more*

Richard McIlkenny

---

* Richard McIlkenny, one of the Birmingham Six, gave me this poem and a collection of other poems in his own handwriting when I visited him in Gartree Prison in July 1990.

CHAPTER 13

The Birmingham Six – Free at Last

After the appeal judgment, I received a torrent of letters reacting to the judgment and comments I had made on television outside the Old Bailey. I had said among other things, 'I lost my faith in British justice many years ago. I had hoped this might repair it. I feel very sad and distressed for the men and their families. I am satisfied of their innocence in my own mind'.* Most of the letters were supportive but some of them were critical – a few letters from English people were virulent and expressed deep hatred for the men and a scarcely concealed hatred for me. One correspondent who described himself as 'a Catholic and regular church attender', expressed the view 'You, sir, are not a man of God, but tantamount to a murderer yourself and should rot in hell with these men'.† This 'courageous' correspondent gave a name and address but when I responded, the letter was returned; a postal official had written on the envelope, 'not known at this address'.

But there were other English people who were very courageous and showed great moral and physical integrity and stood up to be counted; at this stage a forensic scientist, a few newspaper and television journalists and some politicians put their heads above the parapet. Others chose to stay silent. RTÉ was particularly shameful in its silence. Many people including the legal teams, with more determination than ever, worked quietly to right this wrong.

In the six or eight months after the appeal judgment, there did not seem to be much activity on the surface but a lot was going on. I visited Paddy, John and Hugh in Gartree and Long Lartin in the summer of 1988. I was permitted to go on to the prison wings and, on a corridor, I met and had a conversation with Gerry Conlon, one

* *Irish News*, 29 January 1988.
† Derry Diocesan Archive.

of those wrongly convicted of the Guilford bombing. I thought that whilst they were in outwardly good spirits, they did not appear to be in good health. Paddy Hill appeared to have lost a lot of weight. Gartree was a dreadful place. The men in Long Lartin appeared to have had comparatively better treatment. I wrote again to Douglas Hurd, the Home Secretary, expressing my concern for them. I asked him to exercise the Royal Prerogative.

In the meantime in Derry the Provisional IRA continued its atrocities. On 31 August 1988, two good and caring Creggan people went to investigate the disappearance of a young neighbour in their parish. They were concerned for his welfare. He had not been seen for several days. An IRA booby trap bomb, intended for security forces, exploded and killed them both. The IRA subsequently issued a pathetic apology. I spoke at the Requiem Mass for the victims, Sean Dalton and Sheila Lewis, on 3 September in St Mary's church, Creggan. I addressed the issue of the murders and the apology:

> We mourn the tragic death of two people who were outstanding in their goodness. Sean Dalton was mourning the death of his wife. He was a good husband and a good father. Sheila Lewis had attended daily Mass both here and in St Eugene's Cathedral for years. They were both here at daily Mass on Wednesday morning. Unlike many of us, they did not confine their faith to the church building. They brought the Gospel outside and lived it in the community in their care and Christian concern for their neighbour. With Gerry Curran, who thankfully survived, they went to check out the welfare of a neighbour who lived alone and who had not been seen for some days. And it was in following the Gospel of love for neighbour that Sean Dalton and Sheila Lewis died. The parable of the Good Samaritan was rewritten in Kildrum Gardens last Wednesday.
>
> Every community needs people like Sheila Lewis and Sean Dalton. Let it be said that there are many such people here in Creggan, people who care for their community, people who care for their neighbour, people who put love of God and neighbour before any flawed and distorted ideology. Such people of genuine charity and concern present the true pic-

ture of Creggan. The events of last Wednesday highlighted the stark contrast between those who serve and build community and those who intimidate and destroy it.

It has to be said clearly that the explosion last Wednesday did not go tragically wrong. It did exactly what it was designed to do. It killed the people who came to that flat out of concern for the missing occupant. For many years, every social and caring organisation in this city has encouraged people to care for their neighbour, especially those living alone. That concern and work must continue even after the events of last Wednesday.

It must also be said that we do not want to hear any more apologies from the IRA or anyone else. We seek an end to all of this death and destruction that is destroying our people and destroying our city. It must be patently clear after all the death and suffering and misery and destruction in this city over the last 20 years that our political problems must be solved by dialogue and reconciliation rather than by war and conflict. Surely the events at Kildrum Gardens last Wednesday give everyone food for thought.

Listen again to Christ's teaching. A man once asked Jesus 'Who is my neighbour?' And Jesus told the story about the man on the road from Jerusalem to Jericho being attacked and beaten and left lying on the roadside. And He spoke of how people passed, ignoring the victim, and then the Samaritan, someone whom the Jews despised, came along and he took the man, bound up his wounds and cared for him. And Jesus said to the listeners, 'Go you and do likewise'. Jesus repeats those words to all of us this morning. He addresses them to me and to you. I hope that all of us, including those who engage in violence and those who support them will listen to those words and respond to them. The events of last Wednesday are a powerful parable contrasting good and evil. We all must clearly decide which side we are on.*

It was discouraging and disheartening that the very organisation that detonated that explosion in Birmingham all those years

---

*   Derry Diocesan Archive.

ago,* bringing so much misery and suffering to so many, were still intent on carrying on their murderous campaign.

I had a letter from Douglas Hurd, dated 13 September 1988, in which he wrote

> I know that you remain concerned about the safety of the con-victions of the 'Birmingham Six', but I am afraid that there is no further action which I can properly consider taking in respect of them or the life sentences which the men are serving. The deci-sions of courts are free from interference by the Government and its Ministers. The Court of Appeal reviewed the case fully and found no grounds for quashing the convictions. I must accept that view, and I cannot think it right in the absence of any indication from the Court of Appeal or of any further significant evidence to bring about the release of any of the six men by rec-ommending the exercise of the Royal Prerogative of Mercy.†

He added in his own handwriting

> I try to follow all your efforts for understanding and against violence.

Rightly or wrongly, I gathered from this letter that Mr Hurd was more concerned about the case than he cared to admit. I had known him reasonably well when he was Secretary of State for Northern Ireland and I had come to respect him as a caring person.

Paddy Hill was busier than ever writing to people in Ireland, England, Europe and America – politicians, church people (includ-ing twenty-nine cardinals), campaign groups of every kind. He understandably expressed concern about the cost of postage and I helped with his expenses.

I visited the men again on 24/25 July 1989. They were brighter and more hopeful. I remembered Denis Faul's quip many years earlier about 'digging a tunnel'. I got the sense that 'a tunnel was being dug', albeit metaphorically. There were developments and they were sig-nificant developments. On 20 August, Chris Mullin MP, in a detailed

---

*   Although the Provisional IRA denied the Birmingham bombing, I always believed that they were responsible for it.
†   Derry Diocesan Archive.

submission to Douglas Hurd, drew the Home Secretary's attention to recent events in the Serious Crimes Squad in the West Midlands. This squad had been disbanded by their Chief Constable and fifty-three officers connected to that squad were transferred to non-operational duties. This was the very squad that investigated the Birmingham Six case and had elicited 'confessions' from four of them. He argued that 'the recent developments in the West Midlands police force have a direct bearing on the pub bombing convictions'. He went on to state: 'If the jury at the pub bombings trial had known what we know today, there is at least a reasonable chance that they would have rejected the police evidence'. He respectfully requested the Home Secretary 'to refer this case back to the Court of Criminal Appeal'. Chris Mullin's role in this case can never be underestimated.

In late 1989 and early 1990, the atmosphere began to change. The Guildford Four had their convictions quashed and were released in October 1989. The interest in the Birmingham men increased. The focus of attention was now on them. The public outcry internationally could no longer be ignored.

I visited the men again on 23/24 July 1990 – Paddy Hill and Richard McIlkenny in Gartree and John Walker and Hugh Callaghan in Long Lartin. Richard McIlkenny gave me a collection of his poems in his own handwriting. They are deeply moving and full of insights and Christian meaning. Richard was such a good and impressive person. (One of these poems is printed in full at the end of the last chapter.) On that visit, I also met Gareth Peirce at Gartree and we had lunch together in a pub in Market Harborough. She brought me up to date with new and significant developments in the case. She was cautiously hopeful. I also was beginning to grow hopeful.

On 30 November 1990, the Director of Public Prosecutions declared that it was his intention 'to invite the Court of Appeal to review all the evidence and to decide afresh whether the convictions are safe and satisfactory'. There were to be no shortcuts. In the early months of 1991, there was huge international media interest in the case. I did dozens of media interviews, among them one for the American CBS programme *60 Minutes*. The story was now being carried by media all around the world.

After several preliminary hearings, the Appeal Court was set to begin in the Old Bailey on 4 March 1991. I was allocated a seat in the well of the courtroom for the hearing. There was a palpable atmosphere of excitement as the case began. The men looked relaxed; but they were also anxious to walk out of the court totally vindicated. The hearing lasted for ten days. I could only attend for the first three days. Again, Michael Mansfield was magnificent. I was overawed by his mastery of such a complex and technical brief. He exposed what he described as 'a web of deceit' and effectively dismantled the forensic evidence piece by piece. The case made was unassailable. The convictions were clearly unsafe and unsound. The men were innocent. The tone of the hearing was markedly different from that of 1987. The judges were courteous and fair in their dealings with all parties.

I returned for the final days of the hearing. It concluded on 14 March and Lord Justice Lloyd announced that the Court upheld the men's appeal and that it would give reasons for this decision at a later date. He told the six men that their appeal had been granted and that they were free to go. There were scenes of unbounded happiness and tears of joy in the court and subsequently in the street outside. It was an occasion that will live in my mind forever. It was like winning the World Cup and the All Ireland final on the same day. I summed it up by saying 'It is a day of sheer unadulterated joy and relief that ultimately the truth has emerged and the innocence of these men has been proclaimed for the world to see'.

It was a long, difficult struggle. It was particularly difficult for the men and their families who suffered cruelly and terribly for more than sixteen years. The journey from London back to Derry was so different on this occasion. Even in the departure lounge in Heathrow, people whom I did not know came over to me and told me how happy and pleased they were with the decision of the court. I shared their pleasure. I was particularly moved that quintessentially English people like Gareth Peirce and Chris Mullin were the people who eventually and successfully brought these injustices to light. The brilliance of Michael Mansfield was particularly memorable. I did not know then that I would have further reason to admire Michael's wonderful skills ten or fifteen years later in the Saville Inquiry.

The families of those who lost their lives and those who were injured in the Birmingham bombings should never be forgotten. People recall the Birmingham Six but forget the twenty-one people who were murdered in that obscene act of savagery. They and their families were the primary victims of that atrocity. The six men who were wrongly convicted and their families were also victims of that atrocity. The 'brave' people who placed a bomb in a crowded pub, the murderers, are utterly beneath contempt. They were the agents of unspeakable suffering to a huge number of people and they seem to have escaped justice on this earth.

The visits to English prisons continued. There was one female life sentence prisoner whom I regularly visited in Durham Prison – a dreadful place. I visited her for many years, because she had few other visitors. She was originally from Derry and I had known her since the time I served as curate in St Eugene's Cathedral. She was not involved in paramilitary activity. She had been convicted of murder; alcoholism sadly was at the root of her problems. As she approached the end of her sentence, she was moved to a lower security prison in a charming little village called Askham Grange in Yorkshire. On one occasion when I visited her in this prison, the Prison Governor permitted me to take her out for a few hours. Another priest from Derry, Father Aidan Mullan, accompanied me and the three of us drove to Scarborough for the day. It was only when we were having lunch in Scarborough that I realised that if the lady decided to make a dash for freedom, there was little I could do to stop her. I suddenly had terrifying visions of the tabloid headlines that could ensue – the circumstances would provide a tabloid sub-editor's dream. However, she behaved impeccably and we reported back at the agreed time and we had a delightful and enjoyable day. She was finally released from prison shortly afterwards.

When speaking of Irish prisoners in English prisons, I really have to give special mention to one individual – a diminutive Irish nun – Sister Sarah Clarke. Sarah was indefatigable and immensely courageous. At the time when she began visiting Irish prisoners in English prisons, it was not the most popular thing to do. However, she brushed aside all kinds of criticism and intimidation. She was tough as nails. She was afraid of nobody. She took on Special Branch officers, bishops, prison governors, politicians and government ministers. She accommodated members of prisoners' families in her convent when they were over in England on visits to family members or attending court hearings in the London area. I can still see her, in my mind's eye, with her shopping bag, peering at me through her glasses, asking awkward questions and demanding clear answers. She died in 2002. Her work should not be forgotten.

Whilst visiting prisoners from my own diocese in English prisons, I could not but notice the number of Irish people who were held there. The vast majority of these were serving sentences for ordinary crimes as opposed to politically related crimes. It was notable that while those imprisoned for paramilitary activity received many visits, letters and social support, other Irish prisoners were not so well catered for – they were sometimes abandoned and disowned by their families and communities. In this regard, a development worthy of mention is the ICPO (Irish Commission for Prisoners Overseas). This was an agency established in 1985 by the Irish Episcopal Conference in response to serious concerns regarding the number of Irish men and women in UK prisons. It was established largely as a result of the concerns of Bishop Eamon Casey and some other bishops who were experienced in visiting Irish prisoners in England. It was founded primarily on the basis of Christ's teaching about how peoples' lives will be judged or evaluated, 'I was in prison and you visited me' (Matt 25:35). Whilst initially established to work for prisoners in England, the Commission developed into caring for all Irish prisoners abroad wherever they are: it makes no distinction in terms of religious faith, the nature of the prison conviction, or of a prisoner's status. During the last twenty-five years the ICPO has worked for Irish people in prisons all over the world. President Mary McAleese and other prominent legal figures have been deeply involved in its work from the beginning. Nuala Kelly served for many years as Director, and she offered fine leadership and did great work.

Visiting those in prison is one of the most challenging and thankless corporal works of mercy. The ICPO has been responsible for good Christian service to those less fortunate over the last twenty-five years and deserves great credit.

CHAPTER 14

Two Men of Derry

John Hume and Martin McGuinness were the two most prominent figures in the political life of Derry during my years as bishop. They grew up a short distance from one another. Yet they were completely different from one another. They shared similar political objectives but radically differed on the means to achieve those objectives. Both were quintessential Derry men. Both were major figures locally and internationally and each represented a facet of the Nationalist people of Derry.

For most of the last four decades, John Hume was the major political figure within the Derry diocese and one of the major political figures within the island of Ireland. He established a huge international profile and was, and still is, universally respected. He was involved in the establishment of the Credit Union in Derry and Derry Housing Association with Father Tony Mulvey and Paddy Doherty in the 1960s. He represented the area in Stormont, Westminster and Strasbourg. He did pioneering work in attracting US and international investment to the North West. He succeeded in internationalising our political problems. He was associated with virtually every positive and constructive political, economic and social initiative in Derry during the last forty years. He is widely accepted as the primary architect of the peace process that led to the establishment of the current devolved administration in Stormont. He worked and travelled tirelessly throughout his political life, at considerable cost to his health.

John first came to public prominence whilst he was a young teacher in St Columb's College. He wrote a brilliant thesis for his MA under the direction of Professor Tomás Ó Fiaich in Maynooth, later to be Cardinal Archbishop of Armagh. The subject of the thesis was the social history of Derry – a seminal document that is an indispensable source for anyone studying the social or political history of the city. He led the campaign to protest against the decision to locate the second university for Northern Ireland in Coleraine. The first time I heard him speak publicly was at a protest meeting in the Guildhall in the mid-1960s. As a result of that meeting, there was a motorcade of cars from Derry to Stormont to protest the decision not to locate the university in Derry. Stormont, of course, went ahead regardless and built the university in Coleraine.

John became an articulate leader of the Civil Rights Movement here in the 1960s, drawing inspiration from the US Civil Rights Movement and the Reverend Martin Luther King Jr, one of his heroes. He was one of the few public figures in the Nationalist community who foresaw the potential danger of the Bloody Sunday march in Derry. He had very good political judgment and a keen sense of what was possible and what was not. He won every election in which he stood, whether it was for Stormont, Westminster or Europe. He was a passionate advocate of non-violent methods of solving our conflict and the suffering and grief of the people here weighed heavily on him. He articulated these methods clearly, repeatedly and courageously.

I was always fascinated by the contacts John established in Europe and the United States. He had to start this from scratch. Gradually over the years, largely on his own and at his own expense, he established a powerful network of friends in political and commercial life. He travelled frequently to the United States and educated major Irish American political figures in the reality of our problems and issues and relieved them of the simplistic romantic and unreal notions that many of them had in relation to Ireland – ideas that I repeatedly encountered on visits to the United States in the early 1970s. He invited and encouraged many of these people to come to the North and experience the situation for themselves at first hand. I had the pleasure of meeting many of these people during their visits to Derry. There were intense discussions with many of these individuals who were anxious to grapple with and understand our situation and willing to do what they could to assist us. I particularly remember the visit of the late 'Tip' O'Neill,

Speaker of the House of Representatives. The Speaker's forebears came from Buncrana, near Derry. This legendary Boston politician was particularly interested in our problems and was a fascinating individual. At the instigation of John Hume, O'Neill collaborated with fellow Irish American politicians, Senator Edward Kennedy, Governor Hugh Carey of New York and Senator Patrick Moynihan. They became known as the 'Four Horsemen'. They made a declaration on St Patrick's Day 1977 denouncing violence in Northern Ireland and suggesting a political way forward. This culminated in the establishment of the hugely important International Fund for Ireland after the signing of the Anglo-Irish Agreement in 1985. The 'Four Horsemen', counselled by John Hume, persuaded both the President Carter and the President Reagan administrations to pressure the British Government on Northern Ireland issues. Out of the Four Horsemen arose Friends of Ireland, a very influential body of Senators and Congressmen who put our case before the highest levels in US political and commercial circles. There were Senators, Congressmen and women, journalists, commentators, industrialists, business executives and bankers from the US – there were MPs from Westminster and TDs from Dublin, and Eurocrats from Brussels and Strasbourg – a myriad of powerful and influential people visiting Derry at that time. It is to John's great credit that many of these people came to the city during the height of the conflict, at a time when people from much nearer would not dream of coming here. Almost on his own, John urged influential people in Europe and America to take a constructive interest in us and to make political and economic investment here. This happened despite all kinds of obstacles – such as devastating explosions or murders occurring during the visits of people that were being encouraged to set up business or industries here. The Provisional IRA, apparently as a matter of policy, carried out bombing and other atrocities when such people came to visit. It was part of their so-called 'economic war'. They even murdered the managing director of DuPont's operation here, Jeffrey Agate, in February 1977. DuPont, an American industrial giant, was Derry's most important industry and a huge local employer at that time. Apart from the horrible crime of murder of an innocent man, one can only imagine the impact of this murder on

isolated. (I knew Mary since she arrived in Derry as a young journalist in the late 1960s.) I had decided before Mary called with me, that, in the course of my talk at the funeral, I should express public support for John and his initiative. John was present at the funeral Mass. The community was like a tinderbox – there was the potential for a bloodbath such as we had not seen before. It was a time to appeal for calm and reason. Among my remarks at the funerals were the following:

> And how should we respond as a Christian community? In the first place, we must remain calm and eschew any ideas of engaging in violence, verbal violence or physical violence. We should do everything we can to promote harmony in our communities, to reach out to others, and this applies especially to Church leaders. We have had too many bloody days and nights, too many funerals. People are bleeding and heartbroken and we must listen to their cry. We must appeal to Governments and those charged with political responsibility to treat this intolerable situation with the urgency and priority it deserves, not just in the immediate aftermath of atrocities but until the political problem is finally resolved and conflict is ended. We must assist the police in their investigations into this crime and other similar crimes. Finally, we must appeal and appeal repeatedly in every way we can to those faceless heartless murderers of all organisations who operate behind balaclavas and to all those who identify with them to stop their diabolical activities. Unless such murderers repent, they will face a terrible judgment.
>
> Above all, people who have the courage to engage in dialogue with these people in good faith should not be rejected by anyone but should have the support of everyone.*

I further developed the last paragraph and made it more explicit during the delivery of my remarks at the end of the Requiem Mass.

In the adjoining cemetery in Faughanvale after the burials, John was embraced tearfully by the relatives of one of the Greysteel vic-

---

* Derry Diocesan Archive.

tims who pleaded with him to continue the talks. It was a very important moment for John at a time when he needed such affirmation.

A few hours later, at the funeral of another of the Greysteel victims, John Alexander Burns, in a nearby Presbyterian church on Killylane Road, I met Alan McBride, a young man whose wife, Sharon, and his father-in-law had been murdered in the Shankill bombings. His forgiveness and Christian attitude moved me deeply. Once again, it was my experience that those who had suffered most were among the most forgiving.

On Wednesday, 31 August 1994, John spent much of the late afternoon in my home. We both sat together tensely waiting for news of the announcement of the Provisional IRA ceasefire. It was an afternoon of great tension and anxiety. John felt that everything was in place and he nervously awaited telephone communication to confirm that the decision had been finalised. In the late afternoon, the good news came – 'the complete cessation of military operations' was to be announced within a few hours. John was hugely relieved. He was one of the primary influences in this decision and had endured so much personal suffering in bringing it to reality.

John had been enormously inspired and influenced by his European experience. He often spoke about the European Union being a powerful example of conflict resolution and respect for diversity and about how the establishment of institutions that would accept and respect diversity was an essential constituent in the quest for peace here. He was hugely impressed by the manner in which France and Germany had effected reconciliation in the wake of the Second World War.

He was centrally involved in the talks that ultimately resulted in the signing of the Good Friday Agreement on 10 April 1998. Historians will analyse that agreement, but whatever their evaluations of it, they will have to conclude that it could not have taken place without the efforts and political wisdom and nous of John Hume. I believe that much of John's political success came out of the lived experience of his Derry background, from his understanding of community, of what a community needs, a profound Christian understanding of how a community should address its problems and differences added to the influence of Catholic social teaching. He has always had a strong sense of neighbourliness and a sense of duty and service towards his fellow citizens, a powerful Christian social conscience. He displayed this understanding consistently through his involvement with the Credit Union, the Derry Housing Association, the Civil Rights Movement and ultimately in political leadership and peacemaking. This profound sense of duty and self-lessness has taken a considerable toll on John's health.

John was a most worthy winner of the Nobel Peace Prize in 1998. He honoured me with an invitation to be a personal guest in Oslo City Hall at the presentation on Thursday, 10 December 1998. It was an amazing event that I greatly enjoyed. The prize-giving ceremony was dignified and carried out with great style and taste.

Deaglán de Bréadún of the *Irish Times* described the scene memorably and accurately:

> Great hatred, little room. Much sadness, sparse joy. Many days of misery and tears, very few grand occasions. That's been the history of the Northern Ireland Troubles for the last 30 years.
>
> But yesterday, at last, it was time for a celebration. There were fanfares by cockaded soldiers in fairytale uniforms who blew silver trumpets. There was a king and a queen and they looked the part, too. There was snow on the streets with Christmas just around the corner and children in bright clothes cheering as they sang about peace and lit eternal flames.*

It was like a fairytale, quite magical in those Scandinavian surroundings. One thought of some of the esteemed previous recipients – it was a seal of recognition and appreciation by the international community for John's efforts against all the odds. John made a superb speech at the ceremony. Among other things, he said,

> Throughout my years in political life, I have seen extraordinary courage and fortitude by individual men and women, innocent victims of violence. Amid shattered lives, a quiet heroism has borne silent rebuke to the evil that violence rep-

* *Irish Times*, 11 December 1998.

resents, to the carnage and waste of violence, to its ultimate futility. I have seen a determination for peace become a shared bond that has brought together people of all political persuasions in Northern Ireland and throughout the island of Ireland. I have seen the friendship of Irish and British people transcend, even in times of misunderstanding and tensions, all narrower political differences. We are two neighbouring islands whose destiny is to live in friendship and amity with each other. We are friends and the achievement of peace will further strengthen that friendship and, together, allow us to build on the countless ties that unite us in so many ways.

There was a particularly exclusive banquet to honour the prizewinners, the Nobel Peace Prize Banquet on the day of the prize-giving. The table setting is used just once each year for the Nobel Banquet – the only occasion when I had the experience of using golden cutlery! It was exquisite. It was rumoured that the guests had to pass through metal detectors on the way out! I sat at a table with James Galway and other notables and the conversation was sparkling. John greatly enjoyed the occasion. He was happy and relaxed and seemed less preoccupied than he often seemed to be with the various burdens he had to carry. Typically, when he returned home, he donated the substantial cash award he received from the Nobel Committee to the Salvation Army and the Saint Vincent de Paul Society. Even in his moment of greatest triumph, he was conscious of those less fortunate than himself, just as he had been when he was involved in the foundation of the Credit Union in Derry all those years ago.

The Oslo newspapers on the following day featured John's elderly aunt, Bella Kerrigan, a delightful lady who almost stole the show.

On the following night there was the Nobel Peace Prize Concert featuring an eclectic and glittering cast of artists ranging from The Cranberries, Shania Twain, Alanis Morissette, Phil Collins and Enrique Iglesias to James Galway, Phil Coulter and the superb bass singer, Willard White.

David Trimble, leader of the Ulster Unionist Party, was a joint recipient of the prize. Unlike John, he appeared to be somewhat uncomfortable and ill at ease for much of the time spent in Oslo and some of the sentiments expressed in his speech at the prize-giving, I thought, were rather gauche and out of harmony with the spirit of the occasion.

John Hume's wife, Pat, and his family have been a wonderful support to John. Pat Hume is a remarkable human being. Ever patient, ever serene, ever wise, she combined and coped with her multitude of responsibilities as a mother of a large family, a full-time teacher, a wife and a political manager without fuss. All of this was carried out at a time of political turmoil. During all those years, John's home in West End Park was a frequently frantic place – constantly populated by journalists, political activists from various parties and places, and local constituents who required John's advice or assistance. Nothing was a problem for Pat. She made a major contribution to John's success.

A little story will serve to underline her calming influence. I remember one evening in John's home in West End Park. John and Pat invited me to dinner when their main guest was Sean Donlon, who had just been appointed as Irish Ambassador to Washington. I had come to know Sean over the years when he visited Derry as a listening ear on behalf of the Department of Foreign Affairs in Dublin. The other dinner guests that night were Michael O'Kennedy, the then Irish Minister for Foreign Affairs and Brian Friel, the playwright. It was a time of great unrest. Early on during the dinner we realised that I was the only male present who was not an ex alumnus of the Irish national seminary at Maynooth! All the others – Sean, John, Michael and Brian had spent some time studying there. As the main course was being served, there were noises and shouts from outside the house and then stones began hammering on the windows and doors. After some degree of alarm among her guests, Pat assured us that the windows and doors were bulletproof and continued serving the dinner as if it had been a mild hail shower outside! It was just one of many nights when John's house was under attack by so-called patriots. He and Pat live in the same house on the edge of the Bogside to this day.

Ever since the Sunningdale Agreement in December 1973, John has worked for a stable political future for Northern Ireland. He has striven for political dialogue rather than armed struggle, for dignified harmony rather than sectarian bigotry. When one studies any of the major political developments in the last forty years in Northern Ireland, John's huge influence can be seen. His fingerprints are obvious on almost all the major documents. The great tragedy is that many of his political colleagues did not show the same political astuteness or moderation until more than 3,000 people had lost their lives.

I considered myself blessed to have had such a charismatic and inspiring political figure in Derry during my entire episcopate. During my years as bishop, John was a good friend and valued confidante. John was always his own man. We disagreed on a few issues and we agreed to disagree on others. Whilst we always gave one another space and respect, John had a considerable influence on my political thinking.

In more recent years, John Hume has suffered indifferent health. He has retired from active involvement in the political scene. He just seems to have burnt himself out over almost four decades of nonstop activity and international travel and unceasing pressure. We still keep closely in touch, almost on a weekly basis. He is a regular caller to my home. I always keep encouraging him to write his memoirs. He has such a wonderful story to tell. I hope that his story will be told, because it needs to be put on record. Like many in this community, I feel deeply indebted to him.

John Hume is one of my great heroes.

During the years of conflict in Derry, one of the most significant figures was Martin McGuinness. I first noticed Martin in the late 1960s. He did not reside in my pastoral area. I did not really know him. I met his late mother, Peggy, from time to time, and greatly respected her.

I often observed Martin taking a prominent part in the early riots and protests in Rossville Street and William Street. He was one of several individuals who were particularly noticeable. Even at a very youthful age, he seemed to be respected by his peers. He was a focus of attention. Other young people and rioters on the street seemed to turn to him for guidance and leadership.

I remember that he was on the platform at a press conference at which Dáithí Ó Conaill presided in the Gasyard sometime around

1970. He and a young Dublin woman, Maria Maguire, were very effectively presented as the new face of Irish republicanism, youthful, attractive, urban and trendy. More and more, it became obvious to any observer that Martin was increasing in stature as a leader on the streets in those earlier years. However, I cannot remember ever having a conversation with him at that time.

At the time of my ordination as bishop, I think that Martin was in prison in the Republic.

Over my years as bishop, Martin and I directed many verbal assaults at one another from afar, usually through the columns of the *Derry Journal*. I had met Martin on a few very brief occasions during the 1970s and 1980s when I was officiating at the Confirmation of some of his children. But prior to the early 1990s, amazingly, I cannot recall ever meeting with or speaking to Martin, in any substantial way, even on the telephone. Senior British Army officers, NIO types and journalists who came to see me from time to time were convinced that I was in regular contact with Martin and were amazed and somewhat sceptical when I told them that I had no contact with him. I had my contacts within the IRA, usually indirect contacts during all of those years, but Martin was not one of them. Senior British Army officers seemed to be fascinated by Martin.

The first substantial meeting that I ever had with Martin was at the beginning of the 1990s. As far as I remember he was accompanied by Mitchel McLaughlin. The Hume/Adams talks were in progress and I met Mitchel and Martin in my office at the cathedral. I had known Mitchel, his parents and his family very well for many years. That first meeting with Martin was memorable. We had an intense and lengthy discussion about the morality of the armed struggle. I believed that the armed struggle conducted by the IRA was morally wrong and unjustifiable. That is still my belief. Martin believed passionately that the armed struggle was morally justified. He argued his point cogently and forcefully. We had a very protracted discussion. It was very reasoned and temperate. At the end, we had to agree to disagree.

From our conversation, I was convinced that Martin had no problems in conscience about the armed struggle. He had, at some stage, obviously given considerable thought to the issue and he was convinced that he was engaged in something justified, necessary and moral. In every other aspect of his life, as far as I ever knew, Martin was and is an upright man. He was devoted to his wife, Bernie, and his family. He always had and still has a very modest lifestyle. He was a regular churchgoer. He is temperate and I have never known him to use foul language. He is very articulate and highly intelligent. My only problem with Martin was his attitude to and involvement in armed struggle. We fundamentally differed on that issue.

In those years since the 1990s, I have frequently met Martin. Our relationship is now very friendly. I respect him and I think that he respects me. I have been hugely impressed by his political achievements and his ability to argue his case politically. I have also been impressed by his courage and particularly by the manner in which he forged a relationship with Ian Paisley. He has adapted to his position as Deputy First Minister in a most impressive manner. He has been successful far beyond expectation.

I remember one of the more humble British Army brigadiers in Derry remarking to me in the 1980s 'McGuinness should never be underestimated'. It was a very perceptive comment.

It is about twenty years since we had our lengthy discussion on the morality of the armed struggle. We have never discussed it since then. I doubt if our positions on this issue have changed. In many ways, Martin McGuinness has come nearer to John Hume in recent years in the manner in which he has now embraced political dialogue.

Martin is a most interesting and fascinating individual. I hope that someday he also takes time to write his memoirs. Like John, he also has a most absorbing story to tell.

CHAPTER 15

The Inner City Trust

1979 was a very difficult year in Derry. There were bombs and shooting virtually every day. Sometime during that year, I was approached by a remarkable local man known by the sobriquet Paddy 'Bogside' Doherty. He had been involved with John Hume and Father Tony Mulvey in the founding of the Credit Union in Derry and establishing the Derry Housing Association. He had been a major player in the aftermath of the RUC confrontations with the Civil Rights Movement marchers in the late 1960s and the subsequent riots and battles that took place in the area. Paddy had previously worked very successfully as a site foreman in the construction industry and took part in the building of Altnagelvin Hospital among other major projects. After his involvement in the earlier unrest, he had difficulty in finding employment and went abroad to the West Indies in search of work. He arrived back in Derry in the late 1970s. He was a dynamic figure imbued with a great love for his native town and full of ideas about how to bring life back to an embattled and slowly dying city.

The city was on its knees economically. The centre of Derry had been devastated by multiple IRA bombs over the previous ten years. Ferryquay Street, one of the city's most attractive shopping streets and on which there had been some wonderful old shops with magnificent antique shopfronts, had been destroyed by several huge car bombs on one terrible day. Many buildings lay in ruins, others had fallen into neglect. Few shoppers came to the city from outside. Business people were demoralised and discouraged. There was no building and no investment in the city centre, especially inside the walled city. Derry's inner city was, to all intents and purposes, dead as an economic entity.

Paddy came to me and to others with the idea of setting up a charitable Trust with the objective of trying to inject commercial and social life into the almost-defunct inner city. He proposed bringing Church leaders and people with various kinds of expertise from across the community together as members of this Trust. He had researched sources of possible funds in Europe and the United States. He also had researched various schemes for job creation in Northern Ireland. With his background and expertise in the construction industry, he suggested that the new Trust might be able somehow to acquire some city-centre properties and reconstruct and redevelop those properties. He further suggested that the Trust should set up a scheme for unemployed young people from the most deprived areas of the city in this project to participate in this reconstruction. They would work under guidance from skilled instructors and tradesmen. He had the conviction that young people who would be involved in construction would not subsequently allow themselves to be involved in destruction; he believed that involvement in such a project would give young people a sense of ownership of their own city centre and ultimately a sense of self-esteem and pride in their community.

Although I had some reservations, I was enthralled by the idea. I felt that it was a constructive and imaginative attempt to address, albeit in a small way, both the economic problems of the city and the disaffected young people who were easily recruited into negative and nihilistic activities. At the very least, it was a daring initiative to do something positive at a time when we were surrounded by negativity.

The charitable Trust was formed on 17 July 1980. We called it the Inner City Trust and subsequently established it legally as a charity. The Board of the Inner City Trust consisted of Bishop James Mehaffey and me, the two bishops of the city, Revd James Young, a Presbyterian clergyman, Michael McCafferty, an architect, John McDaid, a chartered accountant and Joe Fagan, the Mayor of Derry at that time. Paddy Doherty was Chief Executive. We began with the purchase of two small derelict houses in the inner city and they were renovated and rebuilt by young people under guidance. Then we set our eyes on bigger properties that lay vacant or derelict. Paddy tirelessly raised funds from various charities around Europe and the

United States. We also raised loans from various banks – Paddy regarded the two bishops as ideal collateral! I was rather unnerved when I found myself acting as guarantor for large loans from various banks. Paddy used us two bishops shamelessly to prise funds from all kinds of unlikely sources. I found myself signing documents under-writing seven-figure sums. If truth be told, my only asset was my car and a few hundred pounds in savings. I was not sure where I stood either in canon law or civil law; in fact I suspected that I was on the wrong side of both legal systems! But the banks did not seem to be unduly worried and the projects went successfully ahead. The Trust ultimately met its entire loan and grant commitments to banks and other agencies. As time went on, we became more enterprising and managed to purchase some large and significant sites in the city centre and put together packages of property and ground in order to develop these sites. The restorations were of a high quality and several fine and significant new buildings were constructed in the inner city during the 1980s. Over the years, we gave good employment, under various schemes, to more than 700 young people. A large body of young people came to realise that construction was a much better idea and activity than destruction. It is interesting to note that none of our buildings was ever attacked or bombed.

Largely as a result of our initiatives, the inner city of Derry began to become alive again. Gradually, when they witnessed our success in the early and mid-1980s, commercial investors began to get interested in the city centre once again and started to invest and build. Late in 1984, the Richmond Centre was opened and, in subsequent years, more and more business and office spaces were constructed.

The Inner City Trust continued its work utilising the sites that had been acquired. Among other developments, we built the Craft Village, the Calgach Centre, the Tower Hotel, the Nerve Centre and the Tower Museum, all significant features of modern Derry. We provided accommodation and opportunities for people coming out of prison to pick up the pieces and endeavour to re-integrate into society and work. We provided office space for various community and voluntary groups at reasonable rentals. We provided the Nerve Centre to facilitate and encourage and provide a Centre of Excellence for local young artists in film and music and the creative arts. It is a centre for popular music, film, video, animation and interactive multimedia together under one roof and promotes creative collaboration and fusion between artists. It has provided a cultural outlet and venue for many young people who feel excluded from what is traditionally regarded as the 'arts sector'. The Nerve Centre has been hugely successful. One of the short films emanating from there, *Dance Lexie Dance*, was nominated for an Oscar for best short film in 1998.

When I retired from the board of the Inner City Trust in 2005, the Trust owned well in excess of STG£20 million worth of property and had cleared all its debts and commitments to the banks. The derelict buildings and sites that we purchased at knock-down prices and reconstructed or redeveloped were then extremely valuable. The portfolio of property was earning a substantial income from rentals and the Trust was able to provide grants to assist young people from deprived backgrounds with their education.

I always believed that the Inner City Trust was a very imaginative kind of Christianity and a very constructive kind of ecumenism. It offered support and help for neighbours; it offered opportunities for employment and useful work experience for young people who otherwise would not have had that experience; it involved three of the major Churches in the community and it served to bring what was an essentially dead community back to life. It offered hope in the midst of darkness. After the success of the popular uprising in Egypt earlier this year,* President Barack Obama said that 'We need not be defined by our differences, we can be defined by the common humanity that we share'. I believe that the Inner City Trust embodied that ideal.

The Inner City Trust, since its inception, has attracted a lot of interest from across the world. It has inspired others to initiate similar projects in other places. It is a good example of something useful and constructive to do when one is engulfed in conflict. I believe it helped people to see beyond conflict. It is much better to do something constructive in such circumstances than to wring one's hands and lament. The Inner City Trust is, I believe, a very fine example of generating hope and light in a situation of civil and economic darkness.

* 11 February 2011.

In September 1992, the Trust and agencies of the Trust were heavily involved in convening a Conference in the Guildhall in Derry with the theme 'Beyond Hate: Living with our Deepest Differences'. The Conference was endeavouring to look beyond the years of conflict and examine how human beings could live with their deepest differences. It was an enlightening Conference bringing together all kinds of disparate people – Spaniards and Basque separatists, Israelis and Palestinians, South Africans of different political and racial hues, different elements from Yugoslavia, Professor Kadar Asmal of the ANC, and William Flynn, Chief Executive of Mutual America, who subsequently became centrally involved in the NI peace process. Four men who had been hostages in Beirut, Terry Waite, Father Lawrence Jenco, Brian Keenan and Terry Anderson, gave an unforgettable presentation at one of the sessions. Martin McGuinness and John Hume took an active part. President Mary Robinson gave the keynote address on the opening night of the Conference. Regrettably, relatively few representatives from the Loyalist/Unionist community participated. Despite this, it was an incredible gathering of interesting people and much useful networking went on. I believe it served to give a nudge of encouragement to the peace process here. Eighty-eight delegates from twenty-two countries took part. The key organiser was a remarkable American religious sister, Carol Rittner.

Paddy Doherty is an amazing man – a powerful public speaker – and an indomitable salesman. I was often present as he sold the idea of the Inner City Trust to various people whom he persuaded to visit Derry. He is a superb communicator and his multimedia pitch for the Inner City Trust in such situations was a classic of its kind. Hardheaded business executives and trustees of large charitable foundations and various government agencies were encouraged and successfully persuaded to invest substantially in the Inner City Trust. Paddy was particularly successful in attracting funds from the United States and ultimately from an initially sceptical and cautious group of local civil servants and Direct Rule ministers here at home. There is a wonderful story about a Jewish diamond merchant in Hatton Garden in London who found himself seated beside Paddy on the short flight from Amsterdam to Heathrow. After being relentlessly subjected to Paddy's charm offensive for less than an hour, he visited Derry and became a significant backer of the Trust and funded one of our projects. Prior to that fateful flight, he had never heard of Derry and had never been to Ireland. Paddy had the wonderful philosophy that it is much better to ask forgiveness than to ask permission – an ethical principle that could and did cause planners and some of his board members a few sleepless nights.

In recent years, Paddy has turned his attention to another project. For years, he has had the idea of constructing a monument to St Columba, the founder and patron saint of Derry, in the middle of the river Foyle near the city centre. This would be a mammoth project and would provide a significant feature and landmark for the city. He is suggesting a statue of large dimension. This idea has had a mixed reception locally. However, from my personal experience of working with Paddy and my knowledge of his ability to raise finance, to dream dreams and get things done, I would not be surprised if the river Foyle had an unexpected visitor within the next ten or fifteen years! As I am now a pensioner and a retired bishop, I consider myself both canonically and financially ineligible to act as guarantor for any multi-million bank loans in association with the Columba Project – but I wish it well.

Paddy taught me many things. Above all, he exemplified for me the triumph of hope over despair. A man of great vision, he taught me to dream. When things were at their very worst in Derry, he persuaded me to take part in a project that seemed impossible and almost ridiculous at the time. It was a stunning success far beyond our wildest dreams in the dark days of 1979. I was greatly honoured and privileged to be associated with it.

CHAPTER 16

Paramilitary Funerals

One of the issues that caused me great anguish during my years as bishop was the management of paramilitary funerals in churches and church grounds. I spent many sleepless nights over this issue. These occurred very frequently – they occurred in rural parishes and in urban parishes. Some priests were subjected to enormous pressure and were extremely nervous about them. I tried to help them as best I could but I had to admit that I found these funerals particularly difficult. The circumstances in which the person died varied. The attitude of the deceased family varied – sometimes there were different feelings within a family about whether the funeral should have paramilitary trappings or not.

I have mentioned this issue in an earlier chapter, but I would like to address a particular sequence of events in 1987 that caused me and others great heartbreak. I think that it is important now, more than twenty years later, to put this issue in context.

On the evening of Monday, 23 March 1987, three people were murdered in Derry by the Provisional IRA. About 9 p.m. on that dreadful Monday evening, Leslie Jarvis was shot dead as he sat in his car outside Magee College, where he was attending night classes. He was a mature student engaged in further studies after he had been made redundant. He was a part-time instructor in leatherwork in Magilligan Prison. He was an innocent man, an active member of the Church of Ireland. To add to this obscenity, after murdering him, the Provisional IRA booby trapped Mr Jarvis's car, so that anyone coming to his assistance would be killed or seriously injured. Two RUC officers, Austin Wilson and John Dennison, were killed by this booby trap bomb when they came to investigate the shooting. I was outraged by these murders and appalled by the fact that the body of a murdered man was used deliberately as bait to murder others. Firemen, clergy and ambulance personnel, people living nearby and passersby regularly came to the aid of people who were shot or attacked in their cars and tried to assist them. I had done that myself.* The booby trap illustrated just how depraved the killers were. Good people concerned for the welfare of another human being were being targeted, not for the first time and, unfortunately, not for the last.

On Tuesday, 24 March, the very next morning, in a hugely tense situation because of the triple murder the previous evening, there was an IRA paramilitary funeral in the Long Tower church in Derry. It was the funeral of Gerard Logue, an IRA member who had been killed accidentally a few days earlier by his own weapon. After that funeral, in the church grounds, in the presence of a large crowd and in full view of television cameras, shots were fired by two masked men over the coffin. Shamefully, many of the crowd applauded these shots. Handguns were used; it was believed that these weapons had been concealed in one of the confession boxes in the church prior to the funeral. There was a large number of RUC and British Army troops in the near vicinity and, as the shooting incident took place in a very confined area, a massacre could easily have followed. There was uproar about the incident. It was repeatedly shown on television news bulletins. I considered the action as a sacrilegious abuse of church grounds. A line had been crossed. I decided that, in view of the sequence of events, strong action was needed.

I met with priests in the city the day after these events. Unfortunately, I did not keep a record of that meeting. In January 2010, whilst preparing this book, I was told that one of the priests who attended that meeting advised me against taking any action and that the other priests attending the meeting agreed with him but did not voice their views. That is not my recollection of the meeting but I accept that it may well have been the case. My recollection of that meeting in 1987 is that various views were strongly expressed and voiced for and against action – opinion was divided. No clear view emerged. After considering the matter for forty-eight hours, I still believed that strong action had to be taken. I subsequently issued a statement on the afternoon of Thursday, 26 March, as follows:

* See Chapter 9.

Whilst I fundamentally disagree with the intimidating and heavy-handed security presence of the RUC at Tuesday's funeral, I was disgusted that St Columba's church, Long Tower and its sacred and historic grounds were desecrated by the carefully planned discharge of firearms by the Provisional IRA. Rather than being the occasion of a religious ceremony which was intended to invoke God's comfort for the bereaved and to implore mercy for the soul of the deceased, this was cynically exploited as the occasion for a cheap paramilitary propaganda stunt for the benefit of the media. Not even the Long Tower church or its grounds, the very centre and fount of the Christian faith in Derry, are sacred any more for these people. Up until now, agreements to respect churches and church grounds during such funerals have been honoured in Derry City. Now that this trust has been broken, I would be failing in my duty as Bishop and Parish Priest of Templemore, if I did not take the most serious view of this situation. And when several hundred people who, by some stretch of their own imagination, profess themselves to be Christian, applaud and cheer an act of desecration of this nature, it gives us all even more cause for concern. For these reasons, I wish to state, with great regret, that, in future, <u>with regard to funerals of this nature in Derry City</u>, whatever assurances may be given by the bereaved family to the priests in the parish or to me, Requiem Mass may not be celebrated in any city church with the remains of the deceased present. We cannot permit our church grounds to become battle grounds for anyone. We do not want armed men of any kind in our church grounds on the occasion of funerals. As happens on many occasions in this city in the ordinary course of events, the Requiem Mass may be celebrated, if the family so wishes, at a different time and independent of the burial ceremony.

As I have said on several previous occasions, those who engage in immoral campaigns of murder, intimidation, cruelty and deception will eventually have to answer for these terrible deeds, either in this life or in the next. Constant involvement in such evil activities clouds judgment and blinds conscience.

Here in Ireland and elsewhere, such movements have a history of ultimately tearing themselves apart after a protracted period of activity. Involvement in activities of this nature eventually corrupts those involved, however noble their original intention may have been. In such organisations, today's comrade is potentially tomorrow's supergrass or the person who will be hunting you down to kill you or kneecap you in a year or two. However frustrated or angry young people may be as a result of unemployment or being harassed by police or Army, they should not be tempted to associate themselves with such organisations or become involved with them and they should become fully aware of the immense evil that is inherent in them. These organisations offer the young person a road to nowhere apart from an early grave or years in a prison cell.*

It should be remembered that it was the practice in Derry City at that time for some funerals to take place without the remains being brought to the church. The Requiem Mass was celebrated at a different time and even on a different day than the burial of the deceased. Funeral Masses, for example, at that time, did not take place on a Sunday in any church in Derry City. The burial took place on a Sunday afternoon and the Requiem Mass was celebrated on Monday. So this ruling was not as draconian as it might have appeared to some. I received a huge reaction to this ruling. There were many letters in support and almost as many letters opposing the ruling. Some diocesan priests in the city supported it but others were very unhappy about it and made their unhappiness known to me. Many considered it as an over-reaction. But I believed that the incident itself, allied to the triple murder on the previous evening, was so serious that it merited an equally serious response. The statement drew a furious reaction from Sinn Féin and the Provisional IRA and their supporters – it also drew a predictable reaction from the Unionist community.

It was not the first time that paramilitary organisations had abused the Long Tower church; on at least two previous occasions,

---

* Derry Diocesan Archive.

people were held hostage there after their vehicle had been hijacked and made to sit in the church for several hours accompanied by armed men. Whilst the vehicle was being used in the pursuit of some paramilitary action, the unfortunate owner was held at gunpoint inside the church. The holy ground that is the Long Tower church and its environs were repeatedly treated with utter disrespect.

Two months after the Magee College murders, on 23 May, Dermot Hackett from Castlederg was murdered by Loyalist paramilitaries outside Drumquin, as he was going about his work delivering bread. Whilst Dermot was completely innocent, he had been subjected to constant harassment by the RUC in the months before his murder. I preached at his funeral in Castlederg on Monday, 25 May and, with some justification, alleged that undue and unwarranted attention by the RUC had contributed to his murder:

> Dermot Hackett was cruelly murdered as he went about his daily work. And there is no greater crime than murder. And there is no sin more grave than the murder of the innocent. Let me state quite clearly that Dermot Hackett was a completely innocent man and not merely that, but an outstandingly good man, a Christian man, a Catholic man who cared about the needy in his parish through his deeply committed work in the St Vincent de Paul Society.

I then quoted St Paul's Epistle to the Romans (14:7) and said:

> I hope that his life will have influence on others.
>
> I hope that his death, too, and the terrible circumstances of his death will have an influence on others. I hope that it will point out the callous evil and cruel deed which murder always is – an action which is completely contrary to every Christian teaching, whoever the victim might be, whoever the perpetrator might be. I hope that it will point out to the RUC the blatant injustice and inherent danger of picking out patently innocent people for their special attention and thus leaving them vulnerable to attack by some of the psychopaths who abound in our society. Such arrests and harassment of

completely innocent people have been occurring all too frequently in this area of West Tyrone in the past year.*

These comments drew a furious reaction from the RUC and people
in the Unionist community. I felt it necessary to issue another statement standing over my comments on the following day, 26 May.

In October 1987, I was asked to submit a sworn affidavit for the
appeal hearing against the conviction of the Birmingham Six.†
Ironically, the main thrust of this affidavit was to explain the
Catholic tradition and culture of attendance at funerals in Ireland. I
was summoned to appear as a witness at the Old Bailey in London
to give evidence on Monday, 2 November 1987.

On Wednesday, 28 October 1987, two IRA volunteers, Paddy
Deery and Eddie McSheffrey, were killed in Derry in a premature
bomb explosion. The funerals were to be the first paramilitary
funerals to take place in Derry since the ruling delivered on 26
March, seven months earlier. Both men were married with children.
The families requested that both funerals take place with Mass in St
Eugene's Cathedral on Monday, 2 November, All Souls Day. The
period between the deaths and the funerals was filled with frantic
activity. There were numerous protests and torchlight processions
outside Bishop's House and endless telephone calls demanding that
the ruling be withdrawn.

At 10.30 p.m. on Thursday, 29 October, I received a typed statement. This same statement was issued to the media a few hours earlier in the late afternoon of that same day. The names of the wives of
both men were typed at the bottom of the statement. It read as follows:

> The wives and families of Edward McSheffrey and Patrick
> Deery have issued a joint appeal to Bishop Edward Daly
> asking that he change his ruling on the funeral of IRA Vols.
> Following the funeral of Gerard Logue the IRA issued a
> statement saying that they had decided that there would not
> be any more instances of volleys of shots being fired in

---

* Derry Diocesan Archive.
† Derry Diocesan Archive.

churchyards or their precincts. We ourselves have approached the IRA and they have told us that this remains their policy.

Given that guarantee we would hope that Bishop Daly would allow us to bury our loved ones in peace with dignity. This is our deepest wish and we hope sincerely that Bishop Daly, as a caring and humane man, will recognise how important it is to us at this most tragic time.

We also hope that the RUC and the British Army would respect our grieving families and leave us at peace.*

The grief of the families, both of whom were known to me, made the greatest impact. Nana McGilloway, the mother-in-law of Eddie McSheffrey, had been a very close friend of mine for many years. She was someone whom I greatly admired and respected. I had known her when I was a curate and had kept up contact with her over the years. She was a regular church attender in the cathedral and a very good woman. I also had known the mother of Paddy Deery. Peggy Deery was one of those shot on Bloody Sunday. There was considerable pressure orchestrated and exercised by Sinn Féin. I was keenly aware that this was perceived by them as a major propaganda exercise. The Army and the RUC were also very active. The media kept calling – the telephones and doorbell rang almost non-stop for forty-eight hours. Several priests called asking me to change the ruling. It was a most difficult and excruciating time, possibly among the most painful days of my time as bishop. My heart tended in one direction, my head in another. After the most careful consideration and much prayer and reflection, I insisted that the ruling had to be upheld.

On the morning of Friday, 30 October, I wrote to each of the two widows and had the letter delivered by hand:

I acknowledge receipt of your appeal last night. I only received your letter at 10.30 p.m.. The media had copies of it four or five hours earlier. I would like to reply to you personally before speaking to anyone else.

First I wish to offer you and your family my sympathy on the death of your husband. I also wish to point out that your

* Derry Diocesan Archive.

husband is not being denied Christian burial. He can be buried with peace and dignity.

The situation is that, as a result of unseemly events in the grounds of the Long Tower church after a similar funeral last March, I decided that, in future, whatever assurances were given, Requiem Mass, in the presence of the remains, would not be celebrated in any city church at funerals of this nature. That decision, I regret to say, still stands. Those events in the Long Tower church constituted a complete breach of a trust which had been honoured for many years. I cannot accept the guarantee given in your appeal.

I know that the priests in the parish have been in regular contact with you since your husband's death and are ministering to you. If you wish, you may have a Requiem Mass celebrated in a church for the happy repose of your husband's soul at a different time and independent of the burial ceremony. This is quite regular practice in Derry City.

However, I genuinely regret that I cannot permit Requiem Mass in a church with the remains present. I would ask you to understand the circumstances. I may issue a public statement on the matter later today. I am sending this letter to you first of all, so that you will hear the decision first from me rather than from anyone else.

I am keeping you in my prayers. I pray that the Lord will comfort you and your family in your sorrow.*

At 2.30 that afternoon, I issued a statement to the media reiterating what I had written in the two letters and adding:

I do not wish any of our churches or church grounds to become once again the setting for gunfire, battles or political exercises by anyone. A Christian funeral is intended to be a dignified peaceful religious ceremony, not a carefully orchestrated propaganda exercise.

I appeal for calm over the next few days. I appeal to those who will be attending the funerals and I appeal to the Police

---

* Derry Diocesan Archive.

and the Army. The Police and Army have been insensitive in the extreme during a number of these funerals in the last year both here and elsewhere.

The Catholic Church policy on these funerals in Derry City will be kept under review.*

Later that evening, I received a second appeal from the two widows – this time the appeal was signed by both in their own handwriting.

All of this was taking place during days when I had a number of out-of-town diocesan engagements. There were four diocesan clergy conferences in Derry, Strabane, Carndonagh and Maghera on the Wednesday and Thursday of that week. There were other commitments and appointments to fulfil. I discussed the issue with senior clergy in the diocese. They had mixed views on the matter. Meanwhile, there were demonstrations outside the house and the phone kept ringing.

I had to attend and address a Diocesan Youth Congress in Strabane on the Friday evening, Saturday and Sunday. More than 500 young people had gathered for this Congress that had been planned for months.

On the Sunday night, I had to leave for London to give my evidence at the Birmingham Six appeal at the Old Bailey, as described earlier. I felt guilty about leaving Derry at such a time and leaving the cathedral priests with such a daunting problem on their hands. However, in hindsight, I think that it was just as well that I was in London on that All Souls Day. Father Neil McGoldrick, the cathedral administrator, and his colleagues responded to the challenge in a sensible and realistic pastoral manner.

On the Monday morning, All Souls Day, both coffins were carried to the cathedral accompanied by thousands of mourners and a huge media presence. The coffins were laid at the main cathedral doors. It was made clear to the clergy that the coffins would remain there until they were admitted to the cathedral. There were hundreds of heavily armed police and soldiers in the surrounding streets. Father McGoldrick, after a delay, wisely and prudently, after registering a protest, permitted the funerals to proceed in the cathedral

* Derry Diocesan Archive.

in the best interests of maintaining peace in the cathedral environs on All Souls Day. The man on the ground had to make a decision and he made the correct decision in the circumstances. I was indebted to him.

It was one of the most difficult, angry, direct and public confrontations between the Church authorities in Derry and the Provisional IRA during the years of conflict. None of us came out of the situation untarnished. We were all losers. Hopefully, all concerned learned from it. From that day forward, to the best of my knowledge, guns were never fired in church grounds at a Provisional IRA paramilitary funeral anywhere in the North and the heated confrontations, which were a feature of the past at such funerals, became less and less frequent. So perhaps both sides learned from that chastening experience. I would like to think so. Church funerals, whoever the deceased may be, should be pastoral not political events.

There is an interesting corollary to the All Souls Day funeral. After the cortege left the cathedral grounds en route to the cemetery, a volley of shots was fired over the coffins. Police later recovered spent shells at the scene. Ballistic tests showed that the same weapon had been used in the shooting of Leslie Jarvis in the Magee College grounds.* His callous murder set in train this painful sequence of events.

A few days after those two funerals, on Sunday, 8 November 1987, the Enniskillen Remembrance Day bombing took place, murdering eleven people and causing serious injury to many others. The Provisional IRA, once again, was believed to be responsible for that dreadful atrocity.

---

* David McKittrick, Seamus Kelters, Brian Feeney, and Chris Thornton, *Lost Lives: The Stories of the Men, Women and Children Who Died as a Result of the Northern Ireland Troubles* (Mainstream Publishing, London, 1999).

CHAPTER 17

Coshquin – The Stolen Years

In the early hours of the morning of 24 October 1990, I was awakened by a huge explosion. It rocked my house and the echoing reverberations rumbled on for some time. Within a few minutes the haunting wails of the sirens of ambulances, fire engines, police and army vehicles filled the air. Shortly afterwards, the sound of helicopters was heard. It was obvious that a very serious incident had taken place.

As the facts emerged later in the morning and throughout the next day, it became clear that the Provisional IRA had perpetrated the most obscene, cynical and callous of murders. An innocent person had been used as an instrument of multiple deaths. Patsy Gillespie, a married man of 42 and a civilian worker at an Army base, was taken from his home and compelled to drive a van loaded with explosives to the Army checkpoint at Coshquin on the outskirts of Derry on the main road to Buncrana. He was fastened to the van's steering column and told that he was being followed by the IRA who would detonate the bomb if he did not carry out their orders. When he reached the checkpoint the bomb was detonated by remote control. Patsy and five soldiers were killed in the explosion. One can only imagine the anguish and terror that Patsy Gillespie experienced on that last journey. One can only despise the organisation and individuals who could plan and execute such an odious plot. Every murder is obscene, but this murder had a further dimension of obscenity.

I visited Patsy's wife, Kathleen, and her three children several times over the next few days. Kathleen and her daughter, Jennifer, had been present when Patsy was taken from his home. Kathleen was a wonderfully courageous woman. She still is. She is someone for whom I have huge respect. Like many of those who suffered greatly, her dignity far outshines that of those who engaged or supported such vile and heinous actions. People like Kathleen are the real heroes of our thirty years of useless and pointless conflict. There is something worrying and discomfiting about a society that celebrates the murderers who detonated that van bomb and air brushes Kathleen out of history.

I officiated at Patsy Gillespie's funeral on Saturday, 27 October, in St Brigid's church, Carnhill. I came home from visiting Kathleen and her family on the night before the funeral and began writing a homily when I was full of rage and tears. Earlier in the day, some anonymous 'hero' rang me to argue that the murder of Patsy Gillespie was justified and to be careful with my words. I am not sure whether he was referring to comments made in media interviews since the murder or to the funeral homily.

This is the full text of my homily that Saturday morning:

> A sermon at a funeral in our Catholic tradition should be a reflection on death and an application of Christian teaching to the occasion, an application of Christ's teaching to everyone involved. It tests the preacher to the full to apply Christian teaching to a death which was as cruel as that of Patsy Gillespie, a dreadful murder carried out by people from his own town, by people who would dare to call themselves Christian. Over the past few days, and during the preparation of this sermon, I am ashamed to admit that I found myself almost overcome with anger and distress on several occasions. I ask God's forgiveness for that.
>
> I am angry and distressed because I believe that a new threshold of evil was crossed by the Provisional IRA in the early hours of last Wednesday morning. Patsy Gillespie was taken from his home and from his wife and children and deliberately sent to his death and used as the instrument of five other murders. Over the years, the Provisional IRA has used people's homes to launch their vile attacks. They have used people's cars to launch their vile attacks. They have now descended a step lower to use people's lives to launch their vile

attacks. It is a cynical and outrageous abuse of human life. We weep for the Gillespie family this morning. We weep for the families of the soldiers who died. And we weep for Derry this morning. We weep for our own city, a city we all love deeply. And we weep because we have among our citizens men who are capable of planning and carrying out and even attempting to justify such evil. There has been a cloud over our city these past few days. The ordinary decent people of Derry are out-raged and dismayed by the events of this week.

It is an occasion to recall the passage in St Matthew's Gospel about the manner in which God will judge us – our judgment will be based on the way we see God in others – 'in so far as you did it to one of these the least of my brethren, you did it to me'. Could I bring that scriptural reference a little more into focus and say that we have in our midst a group of people very similar to the Good Friday rabble out-side Pilate's palace, the rabble described in the Gospel reading at this Mass, and they still cry 'Crucify him', 'Crucify him'. Because all those who engage in and all those who support or condone atrocities against their fellow human beings are cru-cifying Christ, they are crucifying the least of his brethren. When you kill those whom Christ calls brothers or sisters, you kill Christ. All kinds of lame and spurious excuses may be used about 'the British presence', about 'regrets that anyone should die', about 'collaboration or working for the security forces', about 'legitimate targets', about 'the right to self-determination' – they are like the excuses of the Good Friday rabble when they shouted 'we have no king but Caesar' – but they simply all amount to one cry and that cry is 'crucify him … away with him' … because these excuses are merely futile and hypocritical attempts to justify the unjustifiable.

St Paul wrote in Chapter 6 of his Epistle to the Ephesians, 'Put God's armour on so as to be able to resist the devil's tac-tics. For it is not against human enemies that we have to struggle, but against the Sovereignties and the Powers who originate the darkness in this world, the spiritual army of evil in the heavens'. There is and there has always been much evil in the world and it is a powerful force. It should never be under-estimated. I believe that the work of the IRA is the work of the devil. I say that very deliberately. And I say it as a Catholic bishop charged with preaching the Gospel and charged with the pastoral care of the people of this diocese. Jesus Christ said 'by their fruits, you shall know them' – and the fruits of the IRA are strewn all over Europe from a murdered infant in West Germany, to murdered Australian tourists in Holland, to murdered pensioners in Enniskillen to murdered Good Samaritans in Creggan in our own city. And on last Wednesday morning, they attempted to do to two other men in Newry and Gortin, what they did to Patsy Gillespie – an act of unspeakable cruelty. These are the fruits of the Provisional IRA – by their fruits you shall know them.

Everyone is now at risk from these evil people with their foul and obscene actions. They corrupt every thing and every person they touch. As well as causing serious physical damage, they have caused very serious moral damage in this community over the years. It is dreadful and quite shocking to think that we have now reached the stage where some people would even attempt to justify something as crass and as cruel and as inhuman as what happened in Coshquin on Wednesday morning. These people and their supporters are the complete contradiction of Christianity. They may say that they are followers of Christ, some of them may even still engage in the hypocrisy of coming to church, but their lives and their works proclaim clearly that they follow Satan. I appeal to these people to repent, to change their ways, to realise that Christ speaks a Gospel of love and tolerance. Until they do repent, until they come round to living that Gospel of Christ, they certainly should not engage in the pretext of following a God whom they mock in everything they do and say.

So we must put on God's armour, as St Paul teaches us – by endeavouring to live Christ's teaching more fully, by rejecting everything that is evil including the use of violence and by doing so unequivocally – by absolutely rejecting violence and rejecting and marginalising those who engage in it. People have to make a choice. Remember this – and I quote Bishop Cahal Daly – 'this struggle against violence and for peace in our country is a struggle for the survival of values which are not only inseparable from Christian faith and basic Christian morality but are also the condition for all civilised living'.

Patsy Gillespie was not the only murder victim on Wednesday. Five British soldiers were murdered at Coshquin and one in Newry. A taxi driver in Dungannon was the victim of a sectarian murder on that same terrible Wednesday. We think this morning of all those victims. We think of all the families left behind to mourn both here and in England, families devastated by sorrow. They all have our deep and heart-felt sympathy and prayerful support.

At least the families of all these victims can hold their heads high. They can look back in pride. You have borne your grief and heartbreak with great courage, Kathleen. You have the sympathy and support and understanding of countless people here in Derry and elsewhere. Be assured of that. We are with you in our thoughts, in our prayers and in our presence here today. Patsy was a good husband, a good father. You and Patrick and Kieran and Jennifer and all his relatives and friends can be proud of him, very proud of him. You have many happy memories. We pray that God may comfort you all and give you courage and strength.

In our Church we pray that God may grant rest and peace to those who have died in His grace. We do that today. Patsy Gillespie led a good life. He was a good and decent man. He never sought to hurt anyone. He simply wished to be a good husband and father and to continue in his lawful work to provide for his wife and for his family. And he did that and he did it well. We pray that God may grant rest to Patsy Gillespie.

May he rest in peace.*

There was an interesting reaction to my words. I was encouraged by the widespread support I received, but I was even more comforted by the relatively small number of objectors. Compared with num-

---

*   Derry Diocesan Archive.

bers in the past, there were very few who telephoned or wrote to complain. I think a corner was turned, particularly in Derry. Patsy Gillespie's murder was a murder too far. Most people in Derry, including committed Provo supporters, were appalled at the callousness of this crime. It was almost the last major Provo action of the Northern conflict in Derry City and its immediate environs.

At the time of the Coshquin murders, the Northern Catholic Bishops were engaged in talks on the way forward in Northern Ireland, critically examining our own roles in the years gone by and looking at what we should be doing in the future. We had a full day meeting on 23 November 1990 in Monaghan and further full day meetings in January and February 1991 in Armagh. We were addressed by various speakers, lay and clerical, male and female. These speakers were drawn from various walks of life, and from North and South. They were engaging and constructive meetings. I prepared a paper in early December 1990 and submitted it to the discussions. It is a summary of my feelings and views, in the immediate aftermath of the Coshquin murders and at a time, I believed, when there was an opportunity for radical change in the North and a possibility of bringing an end to the conflict.

For that reason I include the full text of my written submission. It encapsulated my views at that moment in 1990, after more than twenty years of continuous conflict:

> Our conflict has now gone on for twenty years. There is great weariness and hopelessness among our people. Almost 3,000 people have died. The conflict has inflicted suffering on many people and families. It has corrupted others. It is now a cancer, which threatens the moral well being of our entire society. As the spiritual leaders of the single largest religious grouping in the North, we should be prepared to make some significant and determined effort to break the current deadlock even if it involves taking some risks.
>
> I would submit that we should not commit ourselves to a document. Rather we should commit ourselves to a process, which, in itself, could be an instrument of reconciliation. A document may well emerge at the end of the process.

However, I would suggest that the process itself is at least as important as any document that may or may not result.

I would also suggest that it should be clearly seen that it is the Bishops of the Armagh Province who are engaged in this process, rather than the Bishops of the Irish Episcopal Conference as a whole. As well as being less unwieldy, I believe that such an arrangement would offer us greater freedom and have much more impact. It would give our efforts a sharper focus. Other members of the Irish Episcopal Conference should, of course, be kept fully informed of developments.

THE PROCESS

1. A NEW WORD

Someone used this expression at our last meeting. We need a new word, a new approach, and a new way of presenting Christ's teaching in the North and about the North.

Whilst most members of the Church have paid attention to and agreed with what we have said and taught over the years, a significant number of people who claim to be members of our Church have not been persuaded by what we have been saying or doing over the past twenty years and have acted accordingly. I refer especially to the members and supporters of Provisional Sinn Féin and the Provisional IRA as well as to an increasing number of other people on the opposite political pole of the Catholic community who feel that we have not been sufficiently robust in meeting the threat of the IRA. This must be a cause of major concern.

It is not so much that the IRA and Sinn Féin are defying our teaching authority as bishops. They would suggest that we do not have such authority or that we do not know what we are talking about. They quote and refer to liberation theology. They quote and refer to some 'maverick' clergy. There are mixed signals going out from the teaching Church. Catholic Bishops are dismissed as people who 'always side with the establishment, with the status quo. They always did the same in Ireland'. They also allege that we do not answer questions or challenges, which they repeatedly put to us, especially the question on 'the morality of the British presence'. They say that, in any case, the Church (Bishops) will always side with the winners at the end of the struggle. And they propagate these ideas very effectively through their education officers, some of whom teach or have taught in our schools and they also do it through publications like *An Phoblacht*. These arguments have quite a powerful and persuasive influence on some young people, even among some young people who would not engage in or support the acts of violence perpetrated by such organisations. For example, a priest from Nicaragua recently spoke to a large audience of young people in Derry under the auspices of Sinn Féin and praised the ideal of armed struggle as a most Christian and noble activity. These developments cannot be ignored.

We have to challenge those views and attitudes and meet them and respond to them in a convincing manner. And we must do it in the proper context and circumstances. It is not enough to channel the main input of our popular teaching and theology of violence and justice issues through our reaction to particular atrocities in statements or funeral homilies. Whilst that may be considered as an unfair observation, it is the perception of many people.

Sadly, we must admit that we, the Catholic Bishops of the North, have not, over the last seventeen years, jointly discussed or considered, in any comprehensive or profound manner, a response to the conflict in our midst. (I mention seventeen years because I have been a member of the Episcopal Conference for that period.) We have prepared documents and statements from time to time, mostly in reaction to specific events or atrocities. There have been some excellent statements and papers from individual bishops and from the Episcopal Conference. The issue of violence was addressed in some pastoral letters from the IEC. However, we have not come together to discuss, over an adequate period of time, a detailed and comprehensive and coordinated pastoral and teaching response to the conflict in our community.

There has not been evidence of a local Magisterium (if that is not a contradiction!). And this, I believe, is a major spiritual and pastoral challenge facing our Church.

I believe that we must formulate and communicate a theology of struggle against oppression, a theology of non-violent struggle, a theology of justice, a theology of tolerance and accommodation of different ideals and ideas specifically addressed to our situation. We should teach and exemplify that dialogue is preferable to and more effective than confrontation and we should develop and promote a European model rather than a South American or Latin American model. A European theology of liberation should now be emerging out of the experience of the past forty years. That theology has not yet been articulated. The reconciliation of France and Germany in the 1950s, the removal of the Iron Curtain in the late 1980s, all achieved without violence, should be the basis of such a model. Perhaps we could invite some of the leading European theologians from France and Germany and Eastern Europe to join some of our own leading theologians and historians to take part in a major and prestigious international theological conference or dialogue on these issues as part of our process. Such a conference could take place at a venue in the North. The main papers could be published subsequently. Perhaps from such a dialogue or conference or colloquium, a new word might emerge.

2. DIALOGUE/CONSULTATION

If we wish to teach the importance or value of dialogue, perhaps we might begin by exemplifying such activity ourselves.

Over the years, as a group of Bishops, we have never formally spoken to any of the various political groupings or parties in the North. We did attend the New Ireland Forum. As far as I know, the other main Churches have had meetings with the Official Unionists and SDLP on several occasions over the years.

I believe that we should now consider such meetings as part of our process. We should seek to talk to all the main political groupings, Unionist, DUP, SDLP, Alliance and Sinn Féin, as well as to the NIO and the Dublin Government. Some may decline our invitation. So be it. We will seek to talk to the others. We can both speak to them and listen to them.

The agenda for such discussions would be carefully determined beforehand. I would see the primary purposes of these discussions as an effort to remove misunderstanding and to improve understanding, an opportunity for each party to listen to the other, to seek ways of effecting reconciliation and moving out of the current hopeless impasse.

Whilst all these discussions would be important, I would consider the meeting with Sinn Féin to be possibly the most important of these meetings. We have much to discuss with that particular group.

A parallel dialogue could take place simultaneously with the three Protestant Churches if only to inform them of what is going on. Unlike the political groupings, there has been considerable dialogue with the other Churches in the past.

3. JUSTICE ISSUES

We are perceived in the Catholic community as people who are opposed to the violence of the IRA but somewhat less vocal and less opposed to the violence of the RUC, UDR, British Army etc. This is not true, but it is the perception that is widely held in our own community.

Perhaps we might consider setting up an office here in the North to deal with all issues of violence and injustice – something similar to the work that has been magnificently carried out by Father Denis Faul.

I would like to see a person appointed or office established to whom or to which such cases could be referred, so that there could be detailed and accurate documentation and recording of cases as well as the presentation of such cases to the authorities concerned and, if and where considered necessary, to the media.

I believe that we have fallen down on this matter. It is left to individuals or to organisations that are sympathetic to paramilitary groups. It is often very difficult to discover exactly what happened in any given instance.

I would not see this as a full-blooded sub-office of the Justice and Peace Commission – rather as a central clearing house for such matters. Many of us are approached about such cases. Investigating them can take up an inordinate amount of time and can be most frustrating.

The establishment of such an office would certainly put our genuine concern much more clearly on public record and offer a useful service to many of us and to our priests.

4. ATTITUDES TO THE POLICE

We are perceived in the Protestant community as people who are somewhat equivocal in our opposition to the deeds of the IRA and suspect in our attitude to the RUC, UDR, British Army. Our position on paramilitary funerals and on the excommunication of IRA members continues to upset even some moderate Protestants. (The Lefebvre comparison is brought up again and again.) There is a wide gap of misunderstanding allied to distrust. I also suspect that there is a certain degree of guilt and insecurity among some members of the Protestant community because of the manner in which they mistreated the Catholic people in the past.

The position of Royal Ulster Constabulary is one of the most difficult and delicate of the issues here in the North.

There is vagueness, possibly deliberate, about our position on the police – about the advisability of Catholics joining the RUC – even about the morality of membership of the RUC.

Quite a number of young Catholics, interested in policing as a career, have joined the Garda Siochana or various constabularies in Britain.

There is a feeling of resentment among some Catholics in the RUC because of their perception of our attitude to them. Many of these are good men who do very good and even heroic work for our community.

This matter needs to be addressed. It should be part of the

process. Those police officers and their families are also part of our Church.

5. EDUCATION

We need to ask ourselves some searching questions about our schools. Whilst much superb work is done in our schools, the question has to be asked 'how can our schools produce so many people capable of the most heinous deeds and many others who have a considerable degree of sympathy with those who engage in such unspeakable activities?'

We exhaust a great deal of energy worrying about the 'threat' of integrated schools. I would suggest that we should worry more about our own schools. If our schools are excellent in the manner in which they prepare young people for life in the moral sense and in the quality of education offered, there is nothing to worry about from the threat of integrated education. More and more, parents will choose schools on the quality of the education offered. Catholic parents will send their child to a Catholic school that offers a first class education. Much more frequently than in the past, they will not send their child to a Catholic school that offers a poor standard of education if there is a good Protestant or controlled school near at hand. In many cases, I feel that we have been much more concerned about the Catholicism of the school rather than the quality of education offered. That is not going to be enough in the future.

I question our current attitude to integrated schools. For example, I do not believe that we should separate Catholic children who attend integrated schools from those who attend Catholic schools on parish occasions such as First Communion and Confirmation. I believe that this policy is mistaken and runs counter to our teaching about the idea of parish as a family or community and the importance of unity in the local Church. Whether we like it or not, over the next twenty years, I am convinced that 10% to 15% and possibly more of our children will be attending integrated or non-Catholic schools throughout the North. With respect, I would suggest that we might be better engaged in examining the most effective means of ensuring and securing the sound Catholic religious education of these children instead of putting up temporary obstacles, rather like Canute. We would be irresponsible to ignore this phenomenon or hope that it will go away. It is here to stay and we need to make provision for the religious education of these children.

I wonder if we are getting from our own Catholic schools value in proportion to the resources we pour into them, especially second level schools. Many priests are very weary of all the endless hours of work and effort involved in school management and the abuse they have to suffer from unions, parents etc. Many of today's younger priests do not wish to have any involvement in the management of schools. In the very near future, we may experience considerable difficulty in finding priests willing to take on this particular chore.

We need to take a long hard look at the members of our Church involved in schools, pupils, parents, governors, teachers, priests and a rapidly decreasing number of religious and devise pastoral policies accordingly. It is chastening to consider that, at any time, up to 40% of our entire people are directly or indirectly involved in education.

Education is going to be one of our most important issues in the next twenty years. It has suddenly become the biggest issue on the Westminster political agenda. The promotion of integrated education is now a plank of Government policy. We will lose out unless we can clearly and convincingly show that our Catholic schools are instruments of reconciliation rather than instruments of division. We must do much more than merely express or indicate opposition to integrated education. That type of attitude or policy will simply not be acceptable to many of our own Catholic people for much longer. At the same time, an ever-decreasing number of religious will be involved in our schools and fewer priests will wish to be involved in management.

I would, therefore, suggest that the consideration of education must also be an important element of any process on the role of the Catholic Church in Northern Ireland in the next twenty years.

CONCLUSIONS

This document is partly an examination of conscience, partly an effort to identify some of the main issues as well as an effort to chart a possible way ahead.

I believe that we simply cannot drift along as we have been doing for the last twenty years without any definite policy or direction apart from a vigorous opposition to the use of violence and hoping that we will wake up one morning and everything will be fine.

We have gone along, too, on the cosy assumption that 99% of our Catholic people in the North are Nationalist and aspire to the eventual unity of Ireland. I wonder if this is still the case. I detect substantial disquiet and even dismay among many of our Catholic people with the situation in the Republic of Ireland. Others fundamentally disagree with some of the manifestations of 'Irishness' that they witness and suffer from in the North. They do not wish to identify with this. Others are disturbed by the manner in which Catholicism is seen as the acid test of Irishness and vice versa. We cannot go along with that cosy 99% assumption much longer. I believe that as well as forty shades of green, there are a few shades of blue in the Northern Catholic community and it is our responsibility to minister to all of those people of whatever shade.

We face a major challenge. We must consider and examine new ways of meeting this challenge. With God's help and the guidance of the Holy Spirit, we will meet it with confidence and eventual success.*

I have quite deliberately included the full text of that lengthy submission and the full text of my homily at Patsy Gillespie's funeral in this book so as to offer a snapshot of how I felt at that particular

* Derry Diocesan Archive.

point in time in late 1990. I was frustrated and on the verge of disillusionment. I articulated many views in that document that had been on my mind for a very long time. It was a good experience to put them down on paper and have them discussed. It was the best meeting of bishops that I had attended since the very first meeting in Mulrany sixteen years earlier. Sadly, like the Mulrany meeting, the wonderful high ideals of the 1990/1 meetings were never fully realised by the Church leadership.

As a result, rather than wait any longer, I went ahead and met Martin McGuinness and Mitchel McLaughlin on my own. This meeting is described in an earlier chapter.

I felt and still feel that the Church must formulate and communicate a theology of struggle against oppression, a theology of justice. It should examine various techniques of non-violent struggle for justice. We have teachings on nuclear war and global war, but very little has been authoritatively published on the type of conflict that has been all too common over the world in the last fifty years, in Europe, Africa and Latin America – small-scale internecine conflicts, struggles against injustice, or sectarian conflict. This is something I raised with the Holy See on more than one occasion, but there was little or no response. The lessons of the experience of the last forty years in the North should be learned. It is perplexing to me that so many gentle docile law-abiding people can be so quickly transformed in a relatively short period of time into an angry, vengeful people – and then be transformed back again to a peaceful community. Sadly, one gets the impression that atrocities like that at Coshquin eventually bring success in the terms of those engaged in the struggle. It is, to my mind, too high a price to pay.

In the course of my life and work, I meet many people who talk to me about their experiences of the Troubles. Some would be sympathetic to the Church's position during the Troubles. Others would be very critical of it. I meet some people who were active Republican paramilitaries. Some of them are very disillusioned that they wasted some of the best years of their life in prison to 'smash Stormont' and to 'drive out the Brits' and now they see their erstwhile colleagues and some of their former leaders administering Stormont and, as they say, 'the Brits are still here and Stormont is unsmashed'. There are people whose family members died and they ask, with some justification, 'What did they die for?' Some of these are people whose family members were active members of paramilitary groups and more often the families of victims of those self-same paramilitary groups. I have this conversation in taxis, in homes, in hospitals, in the course of my work in the Hospice. It is a frequent experience.

There is a generation growing up here for whom the Troubles are irrelevant and already ancient history. It is good that such terrible years can be left behind. But surely more can be learned from those years. However, those years of conflict still cast a dark shadow over many members of our society. For nearly everyone living here at that time, they were the stolen years.

There has been a great deal of discussion about the legacy of the Troubles. Much has been written about it. The Report of the Consultative Group on the Past chaired by Robin Eames and Denis Bradley endeavoured to address this difficult and sensitive subject. I have known Robin Eames and Denis Bradley for more than thirty years and I hold both of them in high esteem. I wished to offer them my support as well as my personal views and, therefore, in July 2007, made the following submission to them and their group:

> I have read about your Commission in the media. I wish you well in your challenging responsibility. I believe that these issues need to be addressed in an imaginative and original manner.
>
> I have served as a Catholic priest for just over fifty years. I have served in various capacities here in Derry City for over forty-five years. I witnessed many dreadful events during the years of conflict. I can clearly recall three events during these years when I was among the first on the scene when there were fatalities. There were many other occasions when I ministered to those who were seriously injured. I ministered to many families who suffered in the conflict and officiated at countless funerals of victims. I continue this ministry to such families. I was traumatised by the accumulation of these events and experiences over many years. I found considerable comfort in my faith and prayer. I also found great comfort in

writing about some of these experiences in a book, something that was most therapeutic.

It has been my experience that most people wish to have the opportunity to articulate their experiences or frustrations and put them in the public domain, so that other people may know them also. They want their suffering to be acknowledged and recognised by others. The inability or lack of opportunity to do this is the cause of much frustration.

During the last fourteen years, I have served as chaplain in the Foyle Hospice ministering to the terminally ill and their families. In the course of that ministry, I have come to appreciate the therapeutic dimension of patients and families talking about and writing down their experiences.

In seeking a solution to our problems, I do not think that the South African model would work here. I have personal experience of tribunals – they are unwieldy and slow and very expensive. I believe that we should opt for something original, practical and finite, addressing our own particular situation and needs.

As a result of what I have experienced and learned during these years, I wish to make the following submission to your Commission.

- A special Council or Commission or Agency should be established to deal with these issues.
- All people who continue to experience anguish or heartbreak or anger as a result of our conflict should be invited to record their feelings and memories in detail and in writing and entrust them to this new Agency. Where necessary, such people could be assisted in this by someone who could record their statement and put it in writing for them. The written statement could then be carefully read by the person and signed, witnessed and formalised. The statement would also be digitally recorded.
- These statements would take some time to complete. The statements of the people should not be challenged or edited but recorded in precisely the way that they are communicated. However, taking cognisance of other peoples'

rights and legal issues there would have to be some guidelines concerning the use of names of people etc. The involvement of lawyers should, however, be kept to a minimum. There should be some kind of privilege, like parliamentary or court privilege, attached to the statements and those making them.

- These statements would then be preserved for posterity in a central Repository or Archive. This Archive would contain a collection all the written statements which could be viewed on site and be accessible online on the Internet so that people anywhere in the world could see and read these statements. If people wished their statement or their names to be confidential, then there could be password provision to take care of that.

- The Repository, ideally funded by one of the major international Trusts, should be housed in a signature landmark building in some central neutral location, standing on its own – easily accessible by public transport – somewhere like Glenshane Pass – and be a place where people could come for quiet reflection – a kind of inter-denominational place of retreat for future generations. It would stand as a monument or memorial to everyone who had experienced suffering during our years of conflict and be a lasting symbol and an acknowledgment of their own pain and the memory of their loved ones.

I make this submission for your consideration.*

The Eames/Bradley Report, published in January 2009, was a thoughtful and considered document. It did not receive the attention or the serious consideration that it deserved, largely because of a suggestion that a financial grant be made to all victims. As so often happens, the media and others focused on this one suggestion to the virtual exclusion of the many good things and constructive proposals in the Report. It skewed attention away from the Report's many other interesting recommendations. The Report made more than thirty recommendations, and it deserved a better response.

---

* Derry Diocesan Archive.

Someone, somewhere in the future, will have to address this issue. It is a vitally important issue. There are still so many people and families here who are feeling deep hurt. There is a danger that these hurts will be transmitted down through generations if they are not dealt with in an effective and meaningful manner. It is a difficult issue.

I do believe that a Repository of some kind should be considered. Although I am not sure of this, I think that something of this nature was used in Spain as an instrument of reconciliation after the Spanish Civil War. Others have suggested the method of reconciliation used in South Africa. The dialogue and debate on this matter must continue and reach a widely acceptable resolution sooner rather than later.

Whatever is put in place, I hope that armed conflict will never again occur in any part of the island of Ireland. It is cruel and disgusting and a pointless waste of precious human life and valuable resources. I consider that it blighted my life and the lives of many of my contemporaries. It would be comforting to think that no future generation of Irish people, North or South, would ever again have to experience armed violence in their streets or communities. It generates nothing but misery and tears. Whatever the historians make of it, I can say, as a witness to almost thirty years of conflict, that there is nothing glorious or noble about such armed struggle.

CHAPTER 18

Injustice Worldwide

I was involved in various international conferences and visits abroad during my years as bishop. A few of these were particularly significant. Each of them gave me new insight into the problems confronting the Church in Derry.

I had a letter from Monsignor Bruce Kent in late August 1976 advising me that Pax Christi International wished to organise an International Consultation on Non Violent Alternatives somewhere in Northern Ireland in 1977. This would be a continuation of a similar conference in Driebergen in Holland and would be convened by Archbishop Helder Camara. I had met Helder Camara at the Eucharistic Congress in Philadelphia in 1976 and greatly admired him. I immediately suggested Derry as the venue. After an exchange of correspondence with Bruce, an officer of Pax Christi in Britain and the international executive of Pax Christi International in the Netherlands, my suggestion was accepted.

The conflict had been going on here in the North for eight or nine years at that time. With many others I felt that there must be better ways to seek justice than inflicting violence on other people. I considered that it would be interesting and useful to examine alternatives to violence or armed conflict in pursuit of justice and to hear the views of people from other nations around the world on this subject. After many meetings, Magee College in Derry was agreed upon as the venue and would also provide accommodation for delegates. The International Fellowship of Reconciliation, a Christian body, and Pax Christi offered to be joint organisers and primary funders for the event. The Consultation was scheduled for 24–28 April 1977.

Speakers were invited from all over the world to come and address the Conference, people who had had long experience of coping with injustice in their own countries. As well as Dom Helder Camara, Archbishop of Recife in Brazil, Bishop Donal Lamont from the country that was then known as Rhodesia (now Zimbabwe) was invited. Donal had just been imprisoned and subsequently expelled from Rhodesia for his public stand against white rule there. He was a Carmelite and a native of Ballycastle, County Antrim. Helder Camara was famous for his quotation 'When I give food to the poor, they call me a saint. When I ask why the poor have no food, they call me a Communist'.

There were forty-five delegates altogether – they came from all over Western Europe, Asia, South Africa and the US – many faiths were represented including Buddhists and Sikhs. Despite all the dreadful things that were going on in Derry at that time and reported around the world, nobody declined the invitation to attend the Consultation.

There were many excellent papers and powerful speeches that highlighted the injustices that were prevalent in many parts of the world and the sufferings that were inflicted on innocent people and how this could be confronted and addressed. There was much discussion about the manner in which the Third World had been, and was still being, exploited by other countries, particularly European countries. A particularly memorable speech on this subject was delivered by Father Tissa Balasuriya, a Jesuit priest from Sri Lanka. (He was subsequently excommunicated by the Church in 1997. The excommunication was rescinded in 1998.) Eileen Egan, one of the founders of the Catholic Worker Movement with Dorothy Day in New York, also made a very thought-provoking contribution. Many alternative strategies were discussed – too detailed to catalogue here. It was a remarkable multi-faith, truly international event and served to open the Derry community to the world at a time of isolation. It also made us aware of so many other communities around the world who were having similar problems to ourselves.

One of the most memorable events associated with the Consultation took place in the Long Tower church in Derry. There was a Mass attended by many of the delegates at the Conference and a huge capacity congregation of local people. There were choirs, musicians and even a brass band in the congregation. Helder

Camara held the congregation spellbound with a sermon in a mixture of Portuguese and broken English that everyone remarkably understood. He was addressing people who understood injustice and they identified with what he was saying. The synergy was quite amazing. Donal Lamont had been prominent in the media in the previous weeks because of his expulsion from Rhodesia. He also spoke very powerfully about institutional injustice and racial bigotry.

In October 1977, I visited Nigeria. It was my first visit to Africa. I travelled there from Rome after completing an Ad Limina Visit there. This visit was in fulfilment of a promise I made to missionaries from the Derry diocese who were working there, a promise made shortly after I became bishop. It was my first experience of a missionary country and it was an unforgettable experience. Visiting Nigeria illustrated powerfully for me the universality of the Church. The words of the Book of Wisdom are very much brought home to a person in those surroundings: 'In your sight, Lord, the whole world is like a grain of dust that tips the scales, like a drop of morning dew falling on the ground' (Wis 11:22). When I read those words, they remind me of arriving early one morning at a little church in a clearing near Abakaliki and suddenly there were smiling people everywhere. In Nigeria, I thought, the words of scripture came to life in a remarkable manner. The scenes in some of the rural areas there at that time could be taken straight from the Gospels.

I travelled all over that vast country by car. I particularly remember visiting south-east Nigeria. This had been the location of the Biafra War only a few years earlier; the detritus of war was to be seen here and there; the roads were in a complete mess, travelling was difficult. The war came about when that area of Nigeria attempted to secede from the rest of the country in 1966. Nigeria only became an independent nation in 1960. The attempt to secede failed. The war was widely covered by the media in Ireland, largely because of the presence of a large number of Irish missionaries, mainly Holy Ghost Fathers, in that area of Nigeria. The Irish people were particularly generous in their support of famine victims in Biafra.

As in every conflict, civilians were the primary victims. The Biafra War caused considerable bloodshed and generated a very serious famine in the area. There were many tens of thousands of victims. When I visited, I found the people to be delightful and friendly and most welcoming. I came away full of admiration for the work of the priests and sisters and lay people who served as missionaries there. The vitality and vibrant nature of the liturgical celebrations will live long in my memory. I was deeply impressed at the manner in which the people had put the conflict behind them and were getting on with their lives in so short a time. However, there are two particular memories of that visit that stand out in my mind. One was a visit to a huge leper colony that shocked me to the core. The second was an interview with a Nigerian journalist about the conflict in Northern Ireland where he virtually did all the speaking comparing the Biafra War with our conflict and comparing tribal and racial conflict in Africa with sectarian conflict here. He spoke with great passion for over an hour. I only had to listen!

In May 1979, at the request of the Irish Episcopal Conference and Trócaire I travelled with the late Bishop Michael Murphy of Cork to represent them at the BISA* V Conference in Asia. It was a Conference on Human Development. The Conference was originally scheduled to take place in Bangalore in India but was subsequently transferred at the last minute to Baguio City in the Philippines – reportedly because of reservations among local Church authorities about the theology and social views of some of the scheduled speakers!

The attendance was made up of Asian bishops, bishops from Oceania, the US and Europe. It was decided that before the Conference, all the delegates from developed countries should spend at least four days living in a Third World community with local families, so that they could have some personal experience of such life before their discussions. This was called an exposure programme.

With a Japanese bishop, Bishop Nobuo Soma of Nagoya, Bishop Patalesio Finau of Tonga and an Australian priest, Father Damien Heath, I spent four days in a tiny village on the island of Eastern Samar in the Philippines. It was an area where martial law was in force. To get there, we travelled miles up a river by motor boat and the final stage of the journey was in a small and rather fragile canoe

---

* BISA is an acronym for Bishops' Institute for Social Action, an agency of the Federation of Asian Bishops' Conferences.

– an experience in itself. The people lived beside the river in huts built on stilts in the middle of a clearing in a rainforest. Their diet was largely made up of fruits from the surrounding forest, rice and fish from the river. It was certainly a humbling and challenging experience. With the help of an interpreter, we listened to people, observed them in their daily lives and ate with them – we saw with our own eyes how people lived in the situation and what factors impeded their human development. They were beautiful people, unspoiled by the world, who lived primitive, simple, very basic lives. In many ways, they had more to teach us than we had to teach them. It was an unforgettable experience.

After the exposure programme we attended the Conference in a college in Baguio City, about a four-hour journey from Manila. Marcos was still in power and his shadow hung over the Conference. The themes of the encyclical letters *Evangelii Nuntiandi*, *Populorum Progressio* and *Redemptor Hominis* were frequently referred to. Also discussed were issues of social justice, the ever-widening gap between rich and poor, the great distance in some countries between people and government, the impact of non-democratic government and martial laws, the plight of refugees, the lack of consensus in the Church as to decisions for action, the explosive situation of a youthful population becoming aware of a most uncertain future. The aftermath of war in South East Asia and concern about the power of China were also addressed in the week-long Conference. It was most interesting.

I returned from the Philippines more aware of the fact that the problems of injustice and discrimination are essentially the same worldwide. I also came away with huge admiration for Trócaire and its work – something of which the Irish people and the Irish Catholic bishops can be very proud.

CHAPTER 19

'Fishers of Men'

On my early visits to Maynooth as bishop, I was regularly button-holed by a retired elderly member of the academic staff who still resided in the college. He reminded me that he was present at the Second Vatican Council and urged me to promote the orthodox teaching of the Church. He implied that some of my colleagues were not as committed to that teaching as they ought to be and was highly critical of one person in particular. He always spoke of himself in the first person plural and was unable to hide his disappointment that he had not been appointed as bishop at some time or another. He certainly considered himself to be much more eligible for such an appointment than some incumbents. I rather liked the man but he became somewhat tiresome after repeated encounters. He lived in a narrow little world that was frozen in time.

I have often thought about this, especially during the years since I retired. Bishops who served in the dioceses of Ireland for the last one hundred years have been largely drawn from a small elite group within the priesthood. I was the first Bishop of Derry appointed in the twentieth century who had not been a President of St Columb's College in Derry. My three predecessors, Charles McHugh, Bernard O'Kane and Neil Farren had all served as President of the diocesan college. Two of their fellow presidents, Eugene O'Doherty and Anthony McFeely, had also been appointed as bishops in other dioceses – Dromore and Raphoe respectively. When I joined the Episcopal Conference, almost all the bishops in Ireland had previously served for many years in full-time teaching posts, either in diocesan colleges or major seminaries such as Maynooth. There were a small number of us who had served exclusively in parish ministry, but we were a tiny minority. In the Irish Church, in the twentieth century, I am sure that more than 75 per cent of diocesan priests served exclusively in parish ministry – yet very few of them were appointed to serve as bishops. More than 75 per cent of the bishops were appointed from less than 20 per cent of the priests, priests who were engaged or who have spent most of their priestly lives engaged in full-time teaching.

This lack of parish pastoral experience was evidenced quite often in the discussions and debates in the Episcopal Conference. There were some bishops who were wonderful theologians and wonderful human beings but who showed little understanding of the problems that many people and priests encountered in living their daily lives in parishes. It was my impression that the powers that be in Rome had always considered, like the retired Maynooth professor, that teaching and orthodoxy in teaching were primary and that parish pastoral experience was secondary. Intellectually gifted men were, in the main, chosen for appointment as bishops in preference to those with practical parish experience. Orthodoxy and intellectual ability are, of course, vitally important in any Episcopal Conference but the pastoral needs of people and a first-hand experience of those needs are also important. In parish ministry, the priest is directly exposed to the rawness and frailties of human life and how difficult it can be – called out at all hours of the day and night to all kinds of dreadful situations. The priest in the parish regularly witnesses human life at its rawest and also at its best. I believe that repeated exposure to such situations is a type of education that cannot be replicated in an academic environment. It serves to makes one more tolerant and generates a tendency to be more understanding and flexible when considering human frailty. I would venture to suggest that the academic common room or dining room is, in most cases, at least one step removed from such mundane experiences.

I do not wish to appear anti-intellectual. Professors and competent theologians and teachers are certainly a necessary element in any Episcopal Conference. There has to be a core of such competent and knowledgeable people in authority in a teaching Church but, in my view, an increased presence of 'fishermen' is required. I am not sure of the situation in other countries. I believe that the virtual absence of pastorally experienced clergy in positions of authority in the Irish Church has been a factor inhibiting the Church in the accomplishment of that renewal promised by the Second Vatican Council.

Things are changing. The shortage of vocations to the priesthood means that fewer and fewer priests are teaching in second-level schools in Ireland. Maynooth is the only major seminary left on the island. So, by force of circumstances, the majority of priests being appointed as bishops in the years to come will possibly be drawn from the parish clergy. That, to my mind, will be a positive development.

I hope that the teaching priests in the episcopate are not now replaced by others from non-parish backgrounds – people who have no experience of being called to a sick person or road traffic accident or the aftermath of a suicide in the middle of the night, the challenges of parish fund-raising, having frequent exposure to the despair and anger that cause human suffering from unemployment, poverty, abuse of alcohol or drugs or broken relationships; people who have no experience of listening again and again to the anguish of women who are struggling with the Church's teaching on birth control and other issues, the challenges of living in housing developments that are laid waste by drug abuse, the devastation of domestic violence. It is enlightening when you are regularly confronted by those who have lost their faith or those who are struggling with Church teaching, those who have been abused and are struggling to live, instructive when confronted face to face by those who are angry with the Church. Only when you have fed the hungry and thirsty, clothed the naked and visited the prisoner, and smelt the smell of poverty and met the unbeliever can you speak and teach Christ's teaching with true understanding and sensitivity, and Christ's words and teaching are so relevant in many of these situations. Whilst there is much that can be learned from a background of teaching or academic studies or senior positions in the Holy See or as major superiors in religious congregations, it is my view that, where priests or bishops are concerned, there is also a great deal to be learned in the university of the parish, particularly the more challenging of parishes. I therefore believe that there should be a preponderance of priests from a parish pastoral background in the ranks of bishops.

When considering 'fishers of men' for appointment as bishop, I also believe that more attention could be given to the younger age groups, rather than those in their more senior years. 'Bishoping' is an immensely complex and challenging leadership position. It makes huge demands, physical and intellectual, on the individual. In society today, be it in business, politics, education or commercial life, younger people are in more and more positions of leadership and major responsibility than in years gone by. The Church could take careful note of this. There are so many things that older clergy can do and do extremely well in the service of the Church, but, in my view, more priests in the 35–50 age range should be invited to serve in leadership positions and particularly as bishops. I also believe that the mandatory retirement age for bishops, now 75, should be decreased.

For the first few years of my priesthood, I celebrated Mass in mostly unheard Latin words with my back to the congregation. Those present were really more spectators rather than participants. I can scarcely remember that experience now. However, I believe that the new Vatican II rite of celebrating Mass in the vernacular is a much more prayerful, fulfilling and inclusive form of celebration. I love Latin as a language and many of my academic theological lectures, textbooks, studies and examinations for six years in Rome were through the medium of Latin. As a result, I was reasonably fluent in Latin. I still enjoy reading it. It is a wonderful and rich language and I have a great affection for it. I have a particular appreciation of Gregorian Chant and especially the singing of various parts of the Mass in that setting when there are singers and opportunities to do this. Gregorian Chant is beautiful and prayerful, one of the great treasures of the Church. However, I have been disappointed and somewhat bemused by the recent efforts to promote the celebration of the Mass in Latin once again. I believe that this attachment to the use of Latin in the Mass is based more on sentimentalism rather than reality. I believe that it is divisive in the Church. Many of those who promote the return to the Latin Mass here in Ireland have very little knowledge and understanding of Latin and most of them have a much wider agenda than merely liturgy. Some years ago, with excited anticipation, I celebrated Mass in Latin under the Indult* for

---

*   '*Quattuor abhinc annos*' issued by Sacred Congregation of Divine Worship, 3 October 1984.

a small group in Derry. I was deeply disappointed with the experience. It was a lifeless and somewhat meaningless celebration. The nostalgic memory and anticipation were much richer than the actual experience.

I am very happy with the liturgy and language of the Mass as we now have it. When it is well celebrated, it is beautiful and prayerful. I write as someone who regularly celebrates daily morning Mass with a congregation in a parish church.

There were liturgical reforms brought about by Vatican II that greatly enriched the pastoral life of the Church. The reform that brought about a new understanding of the Sacrament of the Sick was particularly notable. I have personal experience of the wonder of this sacrament both as a minister and as a recipient. This sacrament in its current form can bring great comfort to the very people to whom Jesus Christ directed much of his ministry all through the Gospels. In the early years of my ministry, this sacrament was reserved exclusively for those who were on the point of death and, on most occasions, the recipient was unaware that a sacrament was being administered. Now it is not so circumscribed.

I also believe that a greater understanding of the Sacrament of Baptism came after the Second Vatican Council. In my early years of priesthood, baptism took place within hours of birth, the parents of the child were seldom present and it usually took place in some secluded corner of the church. Now it is a public ceremony, the parents are usually both present and take an active part in the liturgy and it is preceded by a course of instruction on the meaning of baptism and the responsibilities incumbent on parents who bring their child to be baptised.

I served as a priest for almost a decade before the main Vatican II reforms. I believe that Vatican II brought about a whole new understanding of Church in the modern world and that it was a wonderful blessing for the Church.

Whilst the Church is always renewing itself and is in constant need of renewal, we must be wary of a widespread rowing back on the teaching of the Second Vatican Council – something that seems to be in vogue and gaining in popularity in recent years.

CHAPTER 20

Illness and Resignation

As the years passed, I became convinced that it would be in the best interests of the Church and the diocese that I should retire as Bishop of Derry after serving for twenty years in that capacity. My enthusiasm for episcopal ministry was waning and I was very tired and burnt out. I became more and more frustrated with the multiplicity of meetings and the endless travel. Administrative duties became more burdensome. I also convinced myself that twenty years was a long enough term for a bishop to serve and possibly long enough for the diocese. Being a bishop in a conflict situation is difficult. It makes considerable demands. Besides, in situations of conflict very hard things have to be said and done by anyone preaching God's word and some good people are alienated and hurt as a result. There needs to be healing, new faces and new ideas. I thought that a change would be beneficial for the people and clergy of the diocese, as well as for me. Once every five years, each Catholic diocesan bishop makes a report to the Holy Father and the Congregations in Rome. It is called a Quinquennial Report. In a letter accompanying my Ad Limina Quinquennial Report to Rome in early 1992, I wrote to Pope John Paul II:

> Although I am very tired, I enjoy good health, thank God. However, it is my view that it might be better for this diocese to have someone else serve as Ordinary. Perhaps Your Holiness might consider this matter during the coming Quinquennium. My own preferred wish would be to return to ministry in a parish as a curate. Perhaps, initially, I would serve in a parish elsewhere for a few years and then return to serve in this diocese. I love my priesthood and I love minis-

tering as a priest. I served very happily as a curate for seven-teen years after ordination to the priesthood and before my appointment as bishop.*

Neither the Holy Father nor other authorities in Rome responded to that suggestion, although they did respond to other matters raised in the Quinquennial Report.

In the mid-1980s I had asked the Holy See to appoint an Auxiliary Bishop to assist me in my ministry. Subsequently, Pope John Paul II appointed Father Francis Lagan as my Auxiliary Bishop. He was ordained as bishop in St Eugene's Cathedral on 20 March 1988. Francis was of wonderful assistance and support to me in subsequent years. He shared many of the pastoral and other responsibilities, particularly with regard to Confirmation and parish visitation. He was also a wise and valued counsellor, confidante and a good friend and colleague.

Throughout the years I served as bishop, I desperately missed the ordinary parish pastoral ministry of the priest and the close daily interaction with people in a parish or community. I longed for a return to that kind of life and ministry in some shape or form. I discussed this with a number of episcopal friends, priest friends and lay friends. Some dismissed the idea. Some were sympathetic and supportive, but most of the bishops and priests with whom I discussed the matter thought that I would not be permitted to retire as bishop in my early sixties.

Then, unexpectedly, one Monday morning in February 1993, nature took a hand. I woke up with the radio alarm as usual and listened to the BBC Radio Ulster news headlines at 6.30. After listening to the headlines, I tried to get out of bed but was perplexed when I was unable to do so. My right arm and my right leg did not work; there was no power in them; they did not respond; it was as if they were not there. It was a bizarre experience. I initially thought that the limbs were 'asleep', or that I had slept on that side. I clearly remember experiencing a few moments of complete relaxation, floating on air. There was no pain. Then I gradually realised that something more serious had happened. I then thought – stroke??!! So to further

* Derry Diocesan Archive.

confirm my fears, still lying helpless on the bed, I tried to speak out loudly and I was unable to speak normally – while I could make noises and utter some basic words, my tongue would not move freely and permit me to articulate words properly. That confirmed my fears. I had movement and normal power in my left arm and leg, but the right side was inhibited. I knew that I had suffered a stroke.

I waited for a little while until I heard my housekeeper, Betty, moving around and I called her from my bedside telephone. She called my doctor, Peter Fallon, who came to the house and immediately summoned an ambulance and I was taken to Altnagelvin Hospital, just a few miles away. It is a remarkable experience to be a patient in a speeding ambulance in the early morning with the siren blaring overhead! It certainly concentrates the mind. I subsequently underwent various tests and scans. These confirmed that I had had a stroke. Initially, I was shocked and bemused and frightened. I was worried that I would spend the remainder of my life in a wheelchair, particularly when I suffered a similar experience in hospital that afternoon. There followed a few very difficult and anxious weeks and months. However, with the assistance and encouragement of doctors and nurses and friends, I gradually began to look more positively at things. The people in Altnagelvin were kind, reassuring and professional. After being discharged from hospital in due course, I embarked on long months of rehabilitation with intense physiotherapy and speech therapy, doing endless exercises with my leg and arm and tongue. The physiotherapists and speech therapist were wonderful, skilful and very encouraging. In addition to the other problems, I had great problems with swallowing. Ever so gradually, over the months, power began to come back to my arm and leg – and after hours doing all kinds of tongue exercises whilst sitting before a mirror, my speech began to return. I managed to articulate words again. Slowly my self-confidence began to come back. Profound fatigue in the evenings was, and continues to be, a challenging problem. However, I began to look forward to the future again.

A stroke is a sinister experience. It is like sitting in a car with the engine running, but none of the controls are working. There is little warning. My lifestyle had been somewhat chaotic – early mornings, late nights, irregular meal times and little exercise – hours spent driving a car. I did not have the regular health checks that I ought to have had. I had been reasonably healthy – apart from having a malignant tumour on my kidney in 1977 and subsequently a nephrectomy to remove my infected left kidney. I had been a cigarette smoker for more than thirty years. I gave up smoking in 1983. There was a lot of pressure and worry over the years. As I became older, I found the cruelty and destruction and the murders more and more difficult to cope with. The murder of Patsy Gillespie and the circumstances of that murder had a particularly devastating impact on me. At times, I was consumed with sadness and frustration. I had officiated at the funerals of two murder victims, Michael Ferguson and Martin McNamee, in the weeks immediately before I got the stroke. The Northern conflict persisted throughout my twenty years as bishop, although its intensity had eased somewhat in Derry after Patsy Gillespie's murder. To lose power in a hand and arm, to be unable to swallow or to speak properly is very frightening and devastating to one's self-confidence.

A few months after the stroke I celebrated Mass in public again for the first time. It was a nerve-racking experience. I owe a great deal of debt to the doctors and nurses, physiotherapists and speech therapist, June McCarter. They demonstrated boundless patience. They gave me back my life and, gradually, my self-confidence began to return. After hours and hours of physiotherapy and speech therapy, mostly alone, following exercises advised by the physiotherapists, slowly but surely I recovered almost full power in my right arm and hand and fingers; apart from difficulty on steps and stairs, I was able to walk without assistance; my speech, though initially very slurred, showed definite signs of improvement. My swallowing also improved, but, even, today, all these years later, I have to be very careful when eating. Unless I am very attentive, I am inclined to choke on my food. Fatigue, in the later part of the day, still persists to this day. I was a touch typist – I have been unable to do that ever since the stroke – I am back to using a couple of fingers.

My prayer life was considerably enriched in the wake of the stroke. During the months of recovery from a serious illness, there is much time when you are totally alone with God – much time to think and reflect and time to read. You gain a new awareness of your own mortality, a new sense of the slender fragile hold that one has on life. New dimensions of prayer come into play – meditating at length about various events in Christ's life, various things that Jesus said and taught, rediscovering the wealth of teaching in old prayers that one recited from childhood. Even familiar things take on a new meaning and significance. I particularly discovered the richness of the Psalms. At a time like that, you can receive great comfort, strength and hope from prayer and you can learn a great deal about yourself.

Sometime after I began partial resumption of episcopal duties in the early summer of 1993, my doctor, the late Peter Fallon, asked me about my plans for the future. He said that it would not be advisable to resume my full duties as bishop. He recommended that I should submit my resignation as bishop and seek a less strenuous life. I then told him that I was considering this before I had become ill. He urged me to step down and to do so sooner rather than later.

Eventually, I got back to the office and began to be confronted by all the usual responsibilities. Invitations flowed in for public engagements. People and clergy wished to consult me about all kinds of problems. There were letters and media enquiries. Difficult decisions had to be made on various issues. I knew that I was out of my depth. I could no longer cope and I quickly realised that the doctor's advice was correct. There was no half way. Being a bishop could not be a part-time occupation.

In due course I went to see Cardinal Cahal Daly in Armagh, my Metropolitan Archbishop, and the Papal Nuncio, Archbishop Emmanuel Gerada, in Dublin, and discussed my possible retirement with them. They were very gracious, understanding and sympathetic. They both assured me that they would offer their support for my application to retire on health grounds. The Nuncio suggested how I should construct my retirement letter to the Holy Father, detailing my medical condition. He also advised me that I should send a letter from my doctor to accompany my resignation letter. I discussed the matter further with a few of my closest and most trusted friends, clerical and lay. I discussed it with members of my family. I decided not to discuss this matter with any other priests of the diocese or any of the other bishops lest it would stir up speculation. Furthermore, I could not be certain that Rome would accept my resignation and I wished to avoid the nightmare scenario that would emanate from such a situation, if speculation was already rife about a successor.

At some stage the Nuncio asked me to consider accepting an appointment in a named diocese south of the border. I do not know whether the Nuncio was acting on his own initiative or at the prompting of the Congregation of Bishops in Rome. However, I immediately declined the suggestion. I felt that my health would no longer permit me to give the required level of service to any diocese. I was anxious and determined to get back to a more pastoral type of ministry.

I wrote a letter addressed to Pope John Paul II, dated 13 July 1993, asking him to accept my retirement as Bishop of Derry, detailing the reasons for my request and expressing my wishes to minister in a parish capacity after a period of rest. I pointed out that I had already expressed the wish to retire in my Quinquennial Report of the previous year. I also informed the Holy Father that

> The diocese of Derry now has many blessings, thank God. The laity and priests are generally very good and loyal to the Church. There is a very high level of Mass attendance and Church participation. We have an adequate supply of priests. We have twenty-six seminarians. There is a good level of practice in the diocese. The diocese is financially sound.*

I delivered the letter, by hand, to the Nuncio in Dublin, asking him to forward it to the Holy See.

I went to the bishop's office most mornings during that summer and spent a couple of hours every afternoon working at my speech therapy and physiotherapy. I fulfilled a limited list of public engagements. The Derry County GAA football team enjoyed great success that summer. They won a thrilling semi-final game against Dublin in August and then won the final against Cork in September. I managed to attend both games in Croke Park and greatly enjoyed them. My doctor and friend, Peter Fallon, accompanied me to both

* Derry Diocesan Archive.

matches, so there was assistance at hand! It made for an exciting and very happy and enjoyable summer. Towards the end of the summer, after six months when I was not allowed to drive, I was permitted to drive my car again. I often drove out of the city and went for a walk on a beach in Donegal or in the countryside around the city in the afternoon. I began to find time to relax and to feel much better and stronger. The weeks went by and there was still no response from Rome. I began to get really concerned that my request was about to be turned down.

I was aware that the Northern Ireland peace process was proceeding apace in the background and closely followed developments. I allowed my home to be the location of one meeting between Sinn Féin representatives and a Northern Ireland Office minister. I believed that it was important that new people in leadership and new approaches should emerge in the both Church and state here in the North. People like me carried too much baggage from the past. It was time for fresh faces and fresh minds, a time for people like me to move off the stage.

Then, on 20 October, I received the much awaited and longed-for letter from the Nuncio, dated 19 October 1993. It consisted of three short sentences:

> I wish to inform you that the Holy Father has accepted your resignation and has appointed you Apostolic Administrator with the faculties of Diocesan Administrator.
>
> The relative news will be published in the *Osservatore Romano* on October 26th (Tuesday) at 12 noon.
>
> With the expression of my esteem, I remain. Etc.[*]

The Vatican does not do flowery personal letters. My appointment was announced in a few sentences. Twenty years later, my resignation was accepted in a similar number of sentences. Perhaps that is the best way to do such things. I was privileged and honoured to be appointed and I was even more privileged and honoured to have my resignation accepted twenty years later. I very reluctantly agreed to serve as Apostolic Administrator for a further six months. Bishop

[*]   Derry Diocesan Archive.

Francis Lagan, as always, was most helpful and supportive in this and effectively carried out that responsibility. I have to confess that I no longer had the energy or appetite for any kind of diocesan responsibility.

I made the first public announcement of my resignation at morning Mass in St Eugene's Cathedral at the regular 10 a.m. parish Mass on Tuesday, 26 October. Word had somehow leaked out the previous evening in the media and the *Derry Journal* that morning led with the story that I was about to step down. I greeted the congregation afterwards at the door of the cathedral and there were many fond farewells and copious tears. There followed hundreds of letters and messages of good wishes. People are very kind.

But in the very days after I knew that my resignation had been accepted, the people of the North were again blighted by obscene terrorist actions. On Saturday, 23 October 1993, ten people lost their lives in the bombing of a fish shop on the Shankill Road in Belfast. This caused huge revulsion and anger. This appalling bombing was carried out by members of the Provisional IRA.

Then, a few days after my resignation was publicly announced, the terrorism struck nearer home. On the evening of Saturday, 30 October, members of the UFF attacked the Rising Sun bar in Greysteel, a few miles outside Derry. They murdered seven people by gunfire. It was another dreadful and abhorrent act.

Once again, I visited all the wakes of the Greysteel dead and nearly all of the funerals in both Catholic and Protestant churches. I was accompanied on all of these visits and at the funerals by Bishop Francis Lagan. The grief and shock were devastating. For the previous three months, the North West had been relatively quiet and people had begun to hope that, perhaps, the violence was abating. As well as grief and shock, there was a huge sense of disbelief that we should be visited again by such horror.*

The heartbreak of those terrible days in October 1993 brought many people back to the awful days and weeks in the seventies. Most of us had felt that a corner had been turned, but now murder, destruction and funerals seemed to be back at the top of the agenda

* See Chapter 14.

and demanding everyone's attention. It was one of the most discouraging of times. The growing confidence and sense of security that people were experiencing was undermined. There was fear and mistrust in the community once again.

But the darkest hour ...

CHAPTER 21

The Saville Inquiry

The events of Bloody Sunday, 30 January 1972, have always loomed large in my life. The outrageously partial Widgery Report published a few months later compounded the anger in the wake of events of that day.

For twenty years after Bloody Sunday, the awful succession of atrocities that took place caused the events of that notorious day to take a somewhat lower place on the scale of public attention. There was a commemoration each year but, apart from that, Bloody Sunday had become a relatively distant memory in the consciousness of the general public whilst primary attention was focused on the latest atrocity. Each week brought its own bloody day or days, each month brought its own horror. Around 1992, the twentieth anniversary, the events of Bloody Sunday gradually became more prominent in public attention. Some members of the families of the victims got together with others and began to campaign for a new inquiry into the events of that day. The cases of the Birmingham Six and the Guildford Four had brought renewed public attention to cases of historic injustice and the possibilities of redress being sought through a legal process. The scaling back of paramilitary activities also had its influence. There were several notable television documentaries, mainly from British channels, and some influential books and newspaper articles. Particularly important was the publication of Don Mullan's book, *Eyewitness Bloody Sunday*,[*] in 1997. This was a collection of eyewitness contemporaneous accounts of the events of Bloody Sunday that had been gathered by NICRA (Northern Ireland Civil Rights Association) and lain unnoticed for twenty-five years. All of these served to focus

[*] *Eyewitness Bloody Sunday*, edited by Don Mullan (Wolfhound Press, Dublin, 1997).

more and more attention on the subject in places where it mattered. It is interesting that throughout the conflict in the North, the increasing impact of the printed word and the growing influence of the serious television documentary became more and more evident. The pen, allied to the television camera, was indeed proving mightier than the sword.

Perhaps the most powerful single factor in keeping the Bloody Sunday murders in the forefront of public attention was the work and determination and commitment of the families of the dead and injured. They carried on a brilliant and imaginative campaign for a public inquiry in the mid- and late 1990s, which caused the media, the politicians, opinion formers, writers and the general public to sit up and take notice. Whilst I had always respected them, I came to have huge admiration for the Bloody Sunday families. They ensured that justice would be done to their loved ones. They were very astute politically and were incredibly media savvy.

The ceasefires and the gradual evolution and quickening pace of the peace process and the fact that Bloody Sunday was a festering sore in the background were added influences in persuading the British Prime Minister, Tony Blair, to make a response and announce a Judicial Inquiry in early 1998.

In a statement to the House of Commons on 29 January 1998, the Prime Minister (The Rt Hon Tony Blair MP) said that the timescale within which Lord Widgery produced his report meant that he was not able to consider all the evidence that might have been available. He added that since that report much new material had come to light about the events of the day. In those circumstances, he announced:

'We believe that the weight of material now available is such that the events require re-examination. We believe that the only course that will lead to public confidence in the results of any further investigation is to set up a full-scale judicial inquiry into Bloody Sunday'.

The Prime Minister made clear that the Inquiry should be allowed the time necessary to cover thoroughly and completely all the evidence now available. The collection, analysis, hearing and consideration of all the evidence (which is voluminous) have necessarily required a substantial period of time.*

The Tribunal originally consisted of Lord Saville of Newdigate, an Englishman, Sir Edward Somers, a New Zealander, and William Hoyt, a Canadian. Subsequently, because of ill health, Edward Somers was replaced by John Toohey, an Australian. Lord Saville acted as Chairman throughout the Inquiry.

Nobody I knew had ever heard of any of the Tribunal members. However, everyone I knew welcomed the announcement of the Inquiry. People were not sure quite what to expect. Memories of Widgery were still a raw sore in the Derry psyche. But in the atmosphere and ambience of the peace talks approaching agreement, the prevailing mood in Derry was more positive than in the past. People had a feeling that this Inquiry would be different and were prepared to give it a fair wind.

Lord Saville came to Derry shortly after the announcement of the Inquiry and introduced himself at a press conference in the Guildhall. He made a very good impression.

Gradually over the following months, more and more details about the Inquiry emerged. There were several sessions devoted to legal and technical matters. It was determined, to the great satisfaction of many, that the Main Hall of the Guildhall would be the venue for the hearings. The Guildhall is Derry's Town Hall, spectacularly located right at the heart of the city between Derry's Walls and the River Foyle. The Main Hall had been the setting for many of the key events of the political, civic and cultural life of the city for most of the twentieth century. Feis Doire Colmcille took place there annually at Easter and many young Derry musicians and singers nervously made their first public performance there. The hall has very good acoustics and was the setting for many orchestral concerts over the decades. Above the Main Hall the Guildhall clock chimes out the hours over the city. Beneath the Main Hall is the Council Chamber where the Derry City Council

---

* *Report of the Bloody Sunday Inquiry* (Stationery Office, London), vol. 1, p. 15. The Report can be read in full at http://report.bloody-sunday-inquiry.org/

holds it meetings. The Main Hall in Derry Guildhall was a worthy and dramatic setting for such an important event. Interestingly, Brian Friel's 1973 play *The Freedom of the City*, loosely based on the events of Bloody Sunday, was set in the Guildhall.

The first oral hearing of the Inquiry took place on Monday, 27 March 2000. The hearings began with an opening statement of Counsel to the Inquiry, Sir Christopher Clarke QC. The 100 seats in the public galleries of the Guildhall were filled and the proceedings were transmitted live via closed circuit television to viewers in the 900-seat Rialto Theatre about half a mile away. In the intervening two years since Tony Blair had announced the setting up the Tribunal nearly 1,500 civilians, clergy, media, soldiers, members of the RUC, politicians and government officials had been interviewed by the Inquiry lawyers. A large proportion of these would subsequently be called to give evidence at the hearings. The Inquiry had also commissioned a number of expert reports on aspects of Bloody Sunday. As part of this preparation, I was interviewed at considerable length by Eversheds Solicitors on behalf of the Inquiry in my own solicitor's office on 19 April 1999. I submitted largely the same statement as that given to NICRA* in the weeks after Bloody Sunday and subsequently at the Widgery Tribunal in early 1972. My original NICRA statement was a contemporary, comprehensive and truthful report of all that I knew about the events of that day. In the intervening years, I heard or read nothing that changed my views. The Inquiry did a huge amount of research, studying every statement, press interview, radio or television interview that had been made in the years since 1972. Inconsistencies were highlighted and rigorously challenged.

Christopher Clarke's opening statement went on for several weeks. His statement was incredibly detailed and it was obvious that this was not going to be a cursory Inquiry. After the opening statement had been completed, the hearing of witnesses began. The rows of ranked QCs and lawyers the full length of the Guildhall were a hugely impressive and daunting sight – it was sheer theatre. Some of the most prominent lawyers in these islands took part in the Inquiry. Michael Mansfield and other QCs who took part in the Birmingham Six case were there. The IT on display was remarkable. There were

---

*   Northern Ireland Civil Rights Association.

monitors everywhere. From anywhere in the hall one could view and read the original copy of a statement or other document or any particular paragraph being discussed with the witness or by the Inquiry. They were able to show photographs and play audio and television clips. Witnesses were confronted with long-forgotten interviews and comments made many years ago to some long-retired interviewer. These were recalled. Every recorded word that a witness had written or spoken in the years since 1972 was open to scrutiny. There was no hiding place. There was even a virtual reality recreation of the Bogside area as it was in January 1972. This was remarkably accurate and defined sight lines. It was quite uncanny to see the old streets brought back to life. In contrast, Widgery had a plywood model of the area.

I knew that I was to be called to give evidence to the Inquiry within a few months so I went to the public gallery on quite a few occasions to gain an understanding of the working of the Inquiry, to get 'a feel' for it. Although I knew that I had always told the truth and the full truth about what I had witnessed on that day, I was concerned and nervous about the prospect of giving evidence and having that evidence tested in such a daunting setting. Since the stroke I was frail emotionally – my voice at times became slurred when I was under stress – I hoped that I could stand up to the rigours of giving evidence in that setting. I was reassured by the fact that the Inquiry was not a trial – it was inquisitorial rather than adversarial.

Eventually my day came – Day 75 of the Hearings – Tuesday, 6 February 2001. In the preceding days, I carefully went over my statement and evidence to the Inquiry and reflected on the events of Bloody Sunday as I recalled them. That morning I spent some time in prayer and celebrated Mass at home. Then my solicitor, Paul Hasson, drove me to the Guildhall. There were a lot of cameras and television crews at the entrance. However, once I got inside, officials of the Inquiry took me to a quiet antechamber and advised me on the Inquiry procedures. When I was eventually called, I went into the witness box and took the oath. Lord Saville greeted me courteously. I looked around. The public gallery was crowded. The section for the families of those killed and injured was packed. It was comforting yet challenging to see all the familiar faces. The array of lawyers was formidable. Christopher Clarke took me through my statement in great detail. Lord Saville asked for elaboration on several points. After the initial tension, I became more relaxed. There was a break for lunch, when I was asked to remain in a private room and instructed not to communicate with anyone apart from my solicitor. In the afternoon, I concluded my evidence and then was cross-examined by lawyers for the Army and the soldiers, and was also questioned by some of the lawyers representing the families.

I had great anxiety about being asked the name of the civilian gunman that I had seen whilst attending Jackie Duddy in the courtyard of the Rossville Flats. He became known by the Tribunal as 'Father Daly's gunman'. He came in for a lot of attention during the hearings. In all the years since Bloody Sunday and even up to the time of writing, I never knew or sought to know his identity. I am sure that I could have found out, had I tried. Many people seemed to know who he was. However, I did not want to know his name. I was worried lest I be asked to give his name by one of the Inquiry lawyers. It would seem strange if I had to admit that I did not know his identity. Fortunately, in the event, I was not asked to identify him. I was relieved. Subsequently, this individual apparently appeared as a witness at the Inquiry; as far as I know, he was given the pseudonym OIRA4. I still do not know his real name!

I was in the witness box until mid-afternoon. I was greatly relieved when Lord Saville told me that I could leave. I have to say that I was treated exceedingly well and fairly. I was exhausted when the end came, but I was happy that I was given the opportunity to testify to what I had seen and heard on that day. When I reached the bottom of the Guildhall stairs, I was greeted and embraced by Kay Duddy, Jackie's sister. She had with her the handkerchief* that I had used on Bloody Sunday. It was the first time that I seen it and touched it in all those years. After all the tension of the day, it was

---

* The handkerchief had been sent back from Altnagelvin Hospital to the Duddy family with Jackie's clothes some time after Bloody Sunday. Ever since, it had been kept by the Duddy family. A few years ago, Kay Duddy presented the handkerchief to the Museum of Free Derry in the Bogside, where it is still displayed.

almost too much to bear emotionally, and I had to fight the tears. There was a large media presence, reporters, photographers and cameramen at the Guildhall entrance. But they did not impose too much pressure on me.

I went home and went into my oratory and spent some time there alone. I prayed and hoped that the new Inquiry would lay things to rest and consign the events of Bloody Sunday to history. I was more confident about this after the day's experiences. I was very impressed by Saville himself. He struck me as a person who sought the truth sincerely and earnestly. He was clearly impartial. There was no comparison between this Inquiry and that chaired by Widgery all those years ago.

I followed the Inquiry hearings throughout the process. I sat in the public gallery of the Guildhall from time to time, and avidly followed the daily hearings on the internet. On the direction of the Court of Appeal, the Inquiry moved to Central Hall, Westminster, in London, to hear the evidence of the soldiers and other witnesses. I did not attend any of the London hearings. I found the evidence of the soldiers particularly interesting and, in some cases, distressing and often questionable. I was less than impressed by the evidence of some of those who had served as officers. Members of the families attended every hearing both in London and in Derry. The hearings went on in London for more than a year and then returned to the Guildhall. The hearings eventually concluded in January 2005. A total of 922 people had been called to give oral evidence.

Lord Saville and his colleagues went off to consider all the evidence they had heard and to prepare their report. I was confident that Lord Saville and his team would arrive at a conclusion that reflected the truth about the events of that day and vindicate the innocence of the victims. The evidence had been overwhelming. I felt confident that the Inquiry would find out precisely what had happened, but I was not so confident that it would discover precisely why it happened.

Five-and-a-half years later, on 15 June 2010, the Report of the Bloody Sunday Inquiry was published. This was an historic and unforgettable occasion.

Once again the setting was the Guildhall. I was invited to go there to join the families at 1 p.m. in rooms on the ground floor.

There was great tension in those rooms in the Guildhall. There was quiet optimism. The Report was to be published at 3.30 p.m. after David Cameron, the Prime Minister, had spoken in the House of Commons. Some representatives of the families and some lawyers had been briefed on the document in a sterile area. They were kept away from the rest of us until shortly after 3 p.m. when we were all brought upstairs into the Main Hall, where the hearings had taken place years earlier. Some time during the next fifteen minutes we were each given a Summary of the Report. A cursory glance through the document made it clear that the innocent had been vindicated. The Army, especially the upper echelons, appeared to have got off relatively lightly. But it was not a day for equivocation. It was a day for generosity. The tension was immediately relieved, the anticipation ended; lawyers briefed us on some of the details of the findings and there was unbounded joy and embraces of relief all round the Hall. We could hear the crowds outside in the Guildhall Square – expectant thousands were gathered there including media crews from all over the world with their cameras mounted on the Derry Walls and every other vantage point. There was an atmosphere of simmering excitement that broke into delirious cheering when one of the relatives gave a 'thumbs up' sign through an opening in the stained glass windows above the assembled thousands in the Square.

Then David Cameron spoke in the House of Commons. He made a quite magnificent, magnanimous and gracious speech. In a memorable phrase, he stated that the Bloody Sunday killings were 'unjustified and unjustifiable'. It was remarkable to hear a crowded hall filled with relatives of those killed on Bloody Sunday cheer a British Tory Prime Minister to the echo – another truly unforgettable moment in a remarkable day.

When the Prime Minister's speech ended, those inside the Guildhall were permitted to leave and join the joyous thousands in the Square. There followed a series of speeches from the families – these speeches were brief, dignified and to the point. There was no gloating or vindictiveness; merely unbridled joy that, at last after nearly forty years, the truth had emerged and justice was done. The weather accurately reflected the general mood – it was a gloriously sunny warm summer day.

During the next few hours, I did countless media interviews. I had expected considerable media interest but I was amazed at the intense worldwide interest in the Report. Many of the best-known television presenters and interviewers in these islands were there and presented programmes live into their networks. I had asked a senior journalist and friend, Martin Cowley, to act as my liaison person with the media and he did wonderful work on my behalf and offered wise counsel.

The Guildhall Square, as always, was a superb setting for such a joyful and historic event – the sunshine, the crowds brightly dressed, colourful and so happy. It was such a contrast to the dark winter days of Civil Rights protests in the same Square in late 1968 and early 1969, in the days of black-and-white television, anger and fear, CS gas and batons and sit-down protests on wet cobblestones. That now seemed to be so long ago and so far away.

It was good to have lived to witness that unforgettable day, Tuesday, 15 June 2010.

CHAPTER 21

Father Chesney and the
Claudy Bombing

Two months after the Bloody Sunday Report was published, another investigation published its findings. The Northern Ireland Police Ombudsman's Report into the Claudy bombing was published on 24 August 2010. The Claudy bombing occurred on Monday, 31 July 1972, six months after Bloody Sunday. The Ombudsman had spent several years investigating this matter. The full Report can be read on the website of the Northern Ireland Police Ombudsman.*

The bombing of Claudy was a vile act, a terrorist act of abhorrent murder that killed nine innocent people and injured numerous others. Three car bombs that exploded without warning devastated the life of a peaceful village community. The families of the Claudy atrocity are still waiting for justice to be done and the whole truth to be told about the evil that was inflicted on their community.

I was in Derry on the day of the Claudy bombing. 31 July 1972 was a difficult day in Derry. It was the occasion of Operation Motorman, when the British Army entered Derry in force to remove all the barricades in the Bogside and Creggan. I remember seeing a huge tank rumbling past below my bedroom window in the early hours of the morning. It was followed by a column of armoured vehicles. Two young people were shot dead by the Army in Derry on that day. I heard about the Claudy bombing on the news that evening and I remember being shocked and baffled by it.

1972 was a dreadful year; each atrocity was superseded by yet another somewhere else. Many people temporarily left the more sensitive areas of Derry and evacuated to areas in County Donegal and other parts of the Republic. There were shootings and bomb-

* http://www.policeombudsman.org/

ings almost every day. Each of us strove to survive in all the daily mayhem and chaos around us.

Sometime in late 1972, I heard a rumour that a priest of the Derry diocese, Father James Chesney, was somehow directly or indirectly involved in the Claudy bombing. I had known that he was publicly sympathetic to the Provisional IRA, but I did not take these claims very seriously at the time. Because of my involvement in Bloody Sunday, there were also rumours about me being allegedly involved in some way with the IRA. It was a time of all kinds of wild speculation that had more to do with fantasy and suspicion and bigotry than with truth or fact. I cannot recall paying those rumours any more than cursory attention. I could not believe or even imagine that any priest could be involved in such an evil action. I was, perhaps, preoccupied with the terrible things that were happening around me every day to people in my own parish.

After I became Bishop of Derry in March 1974, I went through a process of meeting priests who had had difficulties of one kind or another. Being aware of the rumours and allegations about Father Chesney, I asked him to come to see me so that matters could be clarified. He was then a curate in Malin Head in County Donegal. He had had coronary surgery, major surgery at that time. He was not in robust health. James Chesney had been a classmate of mine in St Columb's College; he was sent to Maynooth to study for the priesthood; I was sent to Rome. After ordination, I spent most of my time in Derry City; he served in various parishes in Tyrone, Donegal and County Derry. Our paths seldom crossed. He was not a close friend and our political views were different. Prior to his surgery he had the reputation of being a flamboyant individual, with the political views described above. He did not particularly like me or anyone in authority; he had expressed that dislike to other priests.

Father Chesney came to see me at my house in Derry some time in May/June 1974. I was accompanied at the meeting by my Vicar General, Monsignor Bernard Kielt. We interviewed him at considerable length. I talked to him about the stories and rumours of his involvement with the IRA and with Claudy. He denied strenuously that he was involved in any way in the Claudy bombing. He admitted to strong Republican sympathies. At this distance I cannot remember the detail of the conversation. Monsignor Kielt, an older, more astute and wiser man than I, led the questioning and pressed him on the matters at issue. I remember that, at the end of the interview, we were both satisfied that he was not involved in Claudy. We advised him to keep his political views to himself, especially at such a volatile time. I did not receive a single complaint from anyone about his words or actions from then until he died.

I did see one anonymous report concerning him in the late spring or early summer of 1977. It was a sheet photocopied from a page of *Combat*, a Loyalist publication and sent anonymously to me. It mentioned Father Chesney; it featured a poor photograph of him, a description of his car and claimed that he was the leader of the IRA in South Derry and was involved in the Claudy bombing. I subsequently brought this matter to his attention. He was alarmed about it. He revealed that he was terrified for some time that he would be murdered by one or other of the Loyalist paramilitary groups because of the rumours in circulation about him. He thought that he was too near the border and asked if he could be moved to an appointment further from the border. There was nowhere in the Derry diocese further from the border than Malin! Some weeks later, I spoke to the Bishop of Elphin, Bishop Dominic Conway, a friend, and asked him if he could find a position for him within his diocese. Bishop Conway agreed. In September 1977 Father Chesney was appointed to Highwood, which is twenty-two miles from Sligo and nine miles from Roscommon. His health was deteriorating and he never really settled there and he appealed to me to give him another appointment back in the diocese in the summer of 1978. He was appointed as chaplain to Nazareth House, Fahan, in September 1978. He also assisted in the parish of Fahan and became very active in raising funds to build a large youth club building in the parish. This building is still there, and, as far as I remember, bears a plaque in his memory. He died suddenly in the cottage where he lived in Fahan on 9 March 1980. He was 47 years old.

His funeral Mass took place in the parish church in Fahan. I was unable to be present as I was attending the spring meeting of the Irish Episcopal Conference in Maynooth. There was no Republican presence at the Mass. He was buried in his home parish in the family grave in Glen, Maghera. Just before the burial, a local family friend approached the priests attending and said that Father Chesney's Republican friends would like to pay him a tribute. He was told that this would not be acceptable. He did not press the issue. Apart from this family friend, there was no known or recognisable Republican presence at the burial, although there was quite a significant Army and RUC presence in the immediate area. One month later, I celebrated the Month's Mind Mass for Father Chesney in Fahan.

I am sure that if Father Chesney had been involved to the extent that is now alleged, there would have been a very significant Republican presence at both the Mass and burial. If he had been a significant figure in the Provisional IRA, the withholding of permission 'to pay him a tribute' would have been contemptuously brushed aside, as it was in many other funeral situations at that time. Had he been the IRA leader that he was purported to be, I am certain that that organisation would have reaped a huge propaganda harvest after his death. They would have milked it for all it was worth internationally – a Northern Irish Catholic diocesan priest who was an active member. He would have been commemorated as a Republican icon. He died in the period immediately preceding the hunger strikes, a very sensitive time, when that organisation desperately needed such headline figures. There would be at least one Sinn Féin cumann named after him, commemorations at his grave, anniversary demonstrations, a mythology built up around him – he would be part of the IRA iconography like Bobby Sands or similar figures – celebrated and quoted. Ironically, he only seems to be recognised since his death by Loyalist paramilitaries and some individuals in the media who depend on leaks from the old discredited RUC Special Branch officers who repeatedly get their facts wrong.

In the latter months of 2006 there was media speculation regarding the imminent publication of a report by the Police Ombudsman, Mrs Nuala O'Loan, into the Claudy bombing in 1972 and the suggested involvement of Father Chesney. I was very surprised that the Ombudsman had not contacted me during the course of her investigation. I wished to add my evidence and recollection of events. I contacted the Police Ombudsman. She responded immediately and she came to meet me at my home on Wednesday, 1 November 2006.

She was accompanied by one of her officers. I gave her a lengthy interview and provided her with copies of every document relating to Father Chesney in the Derry diocesan archive.

I do not know whether Father Chesney was involved in the Claudy bombing or not. I tend to believe that he was not involved. He certainly was a Republican sympathiser and expressed his sympathies openly. I admit that there was a certain amount of intelligence about his involvement, but intelligence is not evidence. What I am certain about is that, if there was such intelligence, he should have been arrested and questioned. The RUC had many opportunities to arrest him between 1972 and his death in 1980. His location was a matter of public record and even after he moved to Donegal, he visited his mother in Maghera regularly and had to pass through permanent security checkpoints to do so. He was not in hiding.

It has been suggested that the RUC was reluctant to deal with Father Chesney because he was a priest, and because of the potential uproar his arrest would cause. I do not accept this suggestion. Such reluctance was not in evidence when I was arrested in the late 1960s and charged and convicted of running Bingo! I appeared in Bishop Street Court in Derry and was convicted, but subsequently won an appeal against the conviction. During the Troubles, priests were arrested, charged and convicted of offences related to paramilitary organisations in Ireland and England. There was certainly no cosy relationship between the Church and the RUC. I am confident that had there been substantial evidence against Father Chesney, he would have been arrested and charged like anyone else. If there was such evidence, it is disgraceful that he was not arrested and questioned.

Father Chesney's name was never at any time mentioned to me by anyone in the NIO, either before or after his death. I met every Secretary of State who served in Northern Ireland in my nineteen years of office, most of them on several occasions. I met many senior NIO officials, RUC officers and Army officers during those years, many of those meetings being on a one-to-one basis when confidential and sensitive issues were discussed. The issue of Father Chesney was never raised.

On 20 December 2002, details of a meeting in December 1972

between Cardinal William Conway and William Whitelaw, Secretary of State, were revealed by a senior RUC officer, Assistant Chief Constable Kincaid; it was alleged that Chesney was discussed at this meeting; 'the Cardinal knew that the priest was behaving improperly' and mentioned transferring the priest to Donegal.

It was the first time that I had ever heard this. I was utterly shocked by the implications of it. Some years later, in 2009 I think, it emerged that Cardinal Conway had kept diaries. In 2010, I saw Cardinal Conway's diaries and they confirmed that the December 1972 meeting had taken place. There was a cryptic entry in his diary and another entry in early February 1973 that confirmed that my predecessor had been informed about 'C', almost certainly Father Chesney. There was no elaboration of what the 'improper behaviour' was. There was no mention of Claudy.

I would be astounded if the Secretary of State, the RUC and Cardinal Conway brushed under the carpet an issue that involved nine murders. I cannot conceive that anyone accused of involvement in nine murders could be described merely as 'behaving improperly'. However, I would not be surprised at a discussion, at that time, between the Secretary of State and a bishop or cardinal about the alleged political sympathies or activities of a priest and what could be done to curtail his activities. South Derry was a tinderbox at that time and a priest publicly and frequently espousing republicanism would have caused many people to be uncomfortable. If, in the unlikely event that the authorities wanted to spirit a mass murderer away, sending him a few miles up the road to Donegal would not have seemed to me to be a solution. Contemporary wisdom would have suggested that many IRA personnel were based in Donegal and many of their operations were launched from there at that time. If he had been asked to go to Manchuria or Paraguay, for example, my suspicions would have been really aroused. Sending a suspected active IRA member to Donegal in the early 1970s would be tantamount to sending a suspected Taliban member to Afghanistan today. It simply does not make sense.

Shortly before the revelation of the Conway/Whitelaw meeting by Mr Kincaid, a letter suddenly appeared that implicated Father Chesney. It was allegedly written by a 'Fr Liam' in September 2002.

He claimed to be priest in England. I do not believe that this letter was written by a priest. In fact, I do not believe that it was written by a person who is familiar with our faith. The style is completely wrong. There are several errors of fact in it. Father Chesney was not in Malin Head in 1972. Father Chesney was always known as 'Jim' not 'John' and there are other obvious mistakes. I believe that the letter was a fake and a clumsy effort to reopen the case.

I have never come across any credible evidence that would substantiate the allegation that Father Chesney was involved in the Claudy bombing. Dodgy intelligence and an obviously bogus letter are not the grounds on which to base such serious charges. I have given the matter much thought, particularly in recent years. I have always felt that there is some missing element in the Claudy investigation. It just does not add up. Perhaps some informer is being protected. Perhaps there is some other factor. I do not know.

I was deeply disappointed in the quality of journalism displayed in the reporting of this story in 2010.

The bombing of Claudy was a despicable crime. I have huge sympathy for the families of the Claudy victims and all the victims of the Northern conflict. Much of my life has been spent ministering to such people. Just recently, in 2010, I spent much time with a man who survived the Claudy bombing.

In the aftermath of the huge publicity and wild speculation aroused by the Police Ombudsman's Report, I wrote the following article that was published in several newspapers in September 2010. The article addresses several issues brought up in the Ombudsman's Report and subsequent media coverage and summarises my feelings at that time. I was appalled at the approach of some sections of the media and their condemnation of a man against whom there is no substantial evidence. This article states and draws together my current views on this distressing issue:

> I retired from public life seventeen years ago but recently have felt obliged to come out of retirement temporarily to deal with media demands arising out of the Saville Report and, now, the Police Ombudsman's Report on the Claudy bombings.
>
> As a curate and bishop in Derry during some of the worst

episodes of the 'Troubles', I got to know many journalists who came to report on many sensitive issues.

I see a less challenging style of journalism at work now. Maybe it is just that many of the reporters have no experience of the exacting pressures that their professional predecessors faced as they foraged for truth here in the 1970s.

Journalists then soared above the pressures of spin from government and combatants on all sides. They had exacting standards as they scrutinised and recorded controversial events.

They asked awkward questions. Papers and broadcast networks took independent lines on stories. They did not sheepishly follow Establishment or State.

In contrast, I find media coverage of the Claudy Report very disquieting. Media have not questioned key aspects of the Ombudsman's Report in relation to allegations that Father James Chesney was a senior IRA figure directly linked to the bombings.

Everyone takes the same unquestioning line and competes to write the most lurid headline. The once sacrosanct presumption of innocence has been dispensed with and replaced with a presumption of guilt.

I am not at all convinced that Father Chesney was involved in the Claudy bombings. I may be mistaken, but I do not think so. I was a contemporary of his at school. I did not know him very well but knew him reasonably well; and certainly better than most of the current commentators. He denied his involvement to me on two occasions, in 1974 and 1977.

Personal involvement in several major miscarriage of justice cases, for example the Birmingham Six, has bred in me constructive scepticism. I have seen convictions based on signed admissions and forensic evidence completely overturned years later.

Father Chesney was never arrested, questioned, charged or convicted. He cannot answer for himself. He has been dead thirty years.

The Report aired suspicions about him that were based solely on intelligence reports. But intelligence and evidence are completely different things. Why was the Ombudsman unable to find evidence against him after years of investigation? He found only these 'intelligence reports', and 1972-type RUC intelligence at that.

In the 1970s there was widespread scepticism about RUC Special Branch intelligence. Hundreds were interned on such intelligence.

Now, media portray as fact unsubstantiated claims emanating from agencies whose history is anything but clean. Where have all the campaigners for justice gone?

The Claudy dead and wounded and their relatives deserve both truth and justice. They were victims of evil acts of violence. They were also cruelly deceived by senior RUC figures and the Northern Ireland Secretary in the failure to ensure that the bombing was thoroughly investigated.

If police suspected Father Chesney in the atrocity, they should have arrested him rather than closing the case, thus allowing all the perpetrators to go free.

Can anyone believe that just because 'Man A', whom the RUC suspected of involvement in major horrendous terrorist crime, gave another major suspect (Father Chesney) in the same crime as an alibi, that police could allow them both walk free?

How did security forces became so coy whenever Father Chesney came on their radar – even when they alleged that a dog detected explosives in his car?

That was not my experience in South Derry then, when I was often terrified and humiliated by the treatment and delays I experienced at security force checkpoints as I returned from Confirmations and other pastoral duties late at night.

Other aspects of the Report are strange. For example, an NIO note of 6 December 1972 attributes to Cardinal Conway an uncorroborated description of Father Chesney as being 'a very bad man' – a very mild commentary on someone alleged to be a mass murderer.

I knew Cardinal Conway quite well during 1974–7. That was not a phrase he would use. It appears to me it was Northern Ireland Secretary William Whitelaw's version of what the cardinal did or did not say.

Does anyone sincerely believe that if Cardinal Conway and my predecessor Bishop Farren believed a mass murderer was in the Church's ranks they would have permitted him to continue in the active priesthood?

I cannot believe they would have omitted to tell me when I was appointed as Bishop of Derry in 1974 if they had for a moment believed one of the priests in my future diocese was a mass murderer.

Mass murder cannot be compared with any other sin or crime. It is the foulest and most obscene of deeds. I witnessed mass murder at first hand in 1972. I am more aware than most of how appalling and grotesque it is and the enormity of it.

It is a huge insult to suggest I would knowingly allow someone whom I knew to be a mass murderer to serve as a priest in my diocese.

I do not accept theories – voiced by several people in the aftermath of the Report – about priests being endangered and a possible subsequent fall-out in society if Father Chesney had been arrested.

Two priests were murdered by the British Army in Belfast just months earlier that year and there wasn't exactly community uproar. Did anyone believe the mere arrest of an obscure priest in County Derry would worsen the already chaotic N. Ireland climate? Northern Ireland was a war zone in 1972. Some 500 people were killed.

I do not accept the Ombudsman's suggestion to reporters that Father Chesney continued his Republican activities when he was in Donegal. As bishop at that time, I was aware of his previous espousal of views, and he knew I was having him observed. There was a never a complaint about him.

I believe it possible that the RUC wanted Father Chesney out of South Derry because of his publicly proclaimed Republican sympathies and a fear of the influence these might exert on young people in the area.

The IRA was seeking recruits and Father Chesney's public views were seen, perhaps rightly, as dangerous. Police wanted him out of a potential powder keg and used William

Whitelaw to persuade Cardinal Conway into facilitating this.

Of course it would have been preferable if the cardinal had told Whitelaw 'to get lost' and to arrest Father Chesney if there was evidence. I can reach that conclusion in the comparatively peaceful climate of today. Thank God I was not in the cardinal's position in the mayhem of 1972.

It is worth bearing in mind that, despite what many media reports suggest, the Ombudsman's Report does not claim that the Church was involved in collusion.

Perhaps Father Chesney's conduct did spark suspicion that he was involved with the IRA. The pertinent questions must be, however; was he or was he not a member of the IRA and, if so, was he involved in the Claudy bombing?

I don't know. The Ombudsman's report and the subsequent media reporting do not offer any evidence to help answer these questions.

Claudy has at last received its legitimate and long overdue recognition as one of Northern Ireland's most despicable acts of terror.

I will continue to pray 'the truth will out'. The families, the community and Father Chesney's relatives need to hear it.

I hope the Claudy families launch a campaign that achieves justice and truth. I hope that clergy will continue to offer pastoral and spiritual support. I am pleased to hear that the Bloody Sunday families, with all their years of expertise, have offered to assist the Claudy families.

I hope journalists will assist them, too.

I now plan to return once more to private life. I hope that justice will finally be done to the dead of Claudy as well as the dead of Bloody Sunday.*

The only thing that is certain about the Claudy atrocity is that it was the work of more than one individual. There were three car bombs and at least one getaway vehicle. I believe that the concentration on one individual who is dead for more than thirty years has been an impediment to the investigation.

*   Derry Diocesan Archive.

The Claudy families and victims deserve better. The searing pain generated by the events of that morning all those years ago is still deeply felt.

I leave Father Chesney to the merciful and just judgment of the Lord. I challenge the real perpetrators to come forward and admit their guilt before it is too late, because, one day, they too will face judgment.

CHAPTER 23

Hospice Ministry

In the years since I retired, I have written two books, one a memoir of my life as a priest mentioned earlier and one an historical index to the clergy of the Derry diocese.* The latter was written jointly with Father Kieran Devlin and a second edition was published in 2009. I have also written a booklet on Hospice ministry† and articles for various publications and newspapers.

During the first ten years of retirement, with the encouragement of my successor, Bishop Séamus Hegarty, I set up the Derry Diocesan Archive and catalogued all the items in the archive on a database. Bishop Séamus has always been very kind to me. There are more than 60,000 documents on the database. Sadly, the archive holds only a very limited and sparse range of documents with an origin before 1939 when Neil Farren became Bishop of Derry. I was greatly saddened by this. I started the work about two years after my retirement when I began to feel somewhat stronger. I was motivated in this work by the fact that I was constantly frustrated searching for older diocesan documents during my term as bishop. There was no formal archive, just a few antique wooden filing cabinets and old tea chests stuffed with unsorted and very dusty documents. But it has all been worthwhile. There is now a reasonably accessible archive with documents from Bishop Farren's episcopate and my own episcopate. There are particularly interesting collections of documents from the Second World War period in Derry, the post-war development of education in the North and a fairly comprehensive collection of letters and documents and

---

*   Edward Daly and Kieran Devlin, *The Clergy of the Diocese of Derry – An Index* (Four Courts Press, Dublin, 1997; 2nd ed., 2009).
†   Edward Daly, *Do Not Let Your Hearts be Troubled* (Veritas, Dublin, 2004).

newspaper clippings relating to the Troubles in Derry from 1968 onwards. There is a large collection of letters to and from people in prison during that period.

The assembly and organisation of the diocesan archive and the experience of writing this book caused me to regret the failure to take more copious notes and contemporaneous records of events during my life as bishop. The memory, and particularly the precise recollection of things, fade and become confused with the passing of the years.

However, the primary focus of my attention since 1994 has been my ministry in the Foyle Hospice, ministering to the terminally ill and their families and friends. It has been an immense privilege to engage in this apostolate, to spend the last weeks and days and hours of life with such people. It keeps one fully concentrated on the really important things in life. I work there as a volunteer.

It has been a wonderful experience to be part of a caring team that is largely female. I spent almost forty years, the first part of my priesthood, with mostly male colleagues. Hospice ministry provided a complete change of working environment and it has been most instructive and enlightening.

I came to have a whole new understanding of the precious and sacred nature of every human life. I came to have a new appreciation of the importance and value of religious faith. I have met and spent time with people of all denominations and none. I have listened to the life stories of many patients, stories of difficulties and challenges and successes – stories often of emigration in search of work and opportunity. I met a patient on the day after the publication of the Saville Report who told me quietly that he had been a member of the Parachute Regiment in 1972! He was not in Derry on Bloody Sunday but he was a soldier in the regiment at that time serving abroad. He was very critical of what his colleagues did on that day and expressed regret for it. Subsequently, we had lengthy chats together and became very good friends. He died a few months ago. I met others who were involved in paramilitary groups – people who had lost relatives during the conflict and others who were relatively unaffected by the conflict.

Most patients, however, are those who have had a relatively normal life, bringing up a family and coping with the challenges with which life confronted them. Patients are at various stages in their journey of faith. Some have been committed to the practice of their faith for all of their lives. There are some who have drifted away for one reason or another. Some have been understandably alienated and angered by the stance of the Church on issues during the Troubles or on sexual issues, or they have experienced difficulties in their marriages or relationships. Some have told me that they were critical of me and what I said at times in the past. We made our peace. Everyone is accepted as they are, but, with the exception of very few, all are interested in practising or reactivating the practice of their faith. I have been almost fifty years in Derry and had the opportunity to come know a lot of people in the city and surrounding area. A lot of people know me. So there is usually little need for introduction and that is a great advantage.

Every patient is treated with dignity and respect. They are made to feel welcome and feel secure. The Hospice movement is, to my mind, one of the great movements of our time. The Irish Sisters of Charity and Dame Cicely Saunders pioneered the modern hospice movement. It is an essentially Christian movement. Hospice care and palliative care are relatively recent phenomena. The Foyle Hospice where I work is largely funded by the local community with a disgracefully low grant from the statutory authorities. The community in Derry and the North West is hugely supportive.

It is a great gift to have time to talk with and to pray with people and to listen to them – to be finally rid of the commitment to rush off to the next meeting or the next engagement. I have experienced a whole new dimension of pastoral ministry since I retired. For the first time in my life, there has been adequate time to read and time to think and reflect and time to pray. I have the privilege each day to bring the Eucharist to the Catholic patients. I have come to have a new appreciation of the Sacrament of the Sick, the Anointing of the Sick. I experienced the comfort that that sacrament brings when I was a patient myself and was sick and weak. As mentioned earlier, it brought me great strength. I am now privileged to administer that sacrament to so many others. There are so many beautiful passages in the Bible suitable for reading to the sick. Reading the scriptures aloud at a bedside to someone is a great privilege and brings out the significance of the teaching to both reader and listener.

I celebrate Mass in the Hospice every Sunday morning. The Mass is celebrated with patients and their families, and with members of the staff and others who come along to mark anniversaries and birthdays of former patients. People of other faiths and denominations often attend. Everyone is made welcome. We have an excellent small choir. On many Sundays, it is challenging to preach in that situation, especially during November when the readings at Mass can be very dark. The congregation is very attentive and patients often discuss aspects of the homily during the following week. Very often, people are aware that they may be partaking in worship for the last time. It gives the celebration of Mass an added dimension.

A remarkable local GP, Dr Tom McGinley, a man of great vision and foresight, founded the Foyle Hospice. The Home Care nurses began their work in the mid-1980s, the In-Patient Unit was opened in 1991 and the Day Care Unit was opened about ten years later. Tom is still involved. He pioneered Hospice Care in the North West. I am filled with admiration for him and his work.

Hospice ministry has made it possible for me to accompany hundreds of people up to and across the final threshold of earthly life in recent years. I have endeavoured to comfort and to pray with them and with their families around the deathbed. On such occasions, one comes to a new realisation and appreciation of the real value of faith, and prayer and the sacraments and the great comfort and tranquility that they can bring.

I consider that my previous forty years in the priesthood, as curate and bishop, prepared me for hospice ministry. It is a ministry that makes considerable emotional and spiritual demands, but it is a hugely fulfilling ministry. I am so grateful that the Lord steered me in that direction.

CHAPTER 24

The Other Conflict

Not all the conflicts I experienced were those from without. There were also conflicts and challenges experienced within myself and within the Church.

I look back as an old man who loves the Catholic Church and loves the priesthood and I look forward as one who cares deeply for the Church and I cannot help but feel profoundly concerned about the ever-decreasing number of priests serving in our diocese and elsewhere. I think of St Paul's Epistle to the Romans, where he writes 'they will not believe in him unless they have heard of him, and they will not hear of him unless they get a preacher' (Rom 10:14).

I attended a priest's funeral Mass earlier this year in a small rural community in County Derry. The deceased priest had been active in the priesthood for more than sixty years. The church was packed to overflowing on a miserable rainy weekday morning. Hundreds of people were there – men, women, children, young and old – representative of every age group. The congregation was most attentive. There was a delightful children's choir – the liturgy was uplifting, prayerful and beautiful. I gazed at the priests who were in attendance – most of them were, like me, grey-haired senior citizens – few were under forty years of age. I worried fearfully about the provenance of priests in the future to serve that parish community and other vibrant faith communities like that. I wondered why there were not more people coming forward for the priesthood from such communities in recent years as was the case in the past?

In every Catholic community, the priest is and has always been there; he is there on the good days and on the bad days; he is there at the community celebrations, sharing the happiness; he is there after every tragedy, big or small, he is there comforting his people, sharing the sadness – day or night – whether it is an earthquake, flooding, a road traffic accident, or a murder – wherever in the world; he lives among the people; he is there to celebrate Mass with them, to minister to them, to do his best to bind up hearts that are broken; being with his people as a sacramental and prayerful support and to stand with them, as a point of reference; the media often seek out the local priest in the aftermath of tragedy and focus on the funeral rites, the burial, the memorial service. How much longer will there be a priest there? Will a deacon or some part-time lay minister have the time or presence or knowledge of his people to fulfil those roles in the future?

If things continue as they are, a lot of parish communities will not have a priest in a few years time, and those that they have will be older, weary and greatly over-worked. It is not that I do not trust in the Lord of the harvest or His word. It is more that I do not trust in human beings.

I remember reading an article in a magazine somewhere recently in which the writer commented that whenever commitment to the priesthood or to the Church is mentioned, sexual morality, for some strange reason, seems to be the touchstone and overriding criterion. I ask myself, more and more, why celibacy should be the great sacred and unyielding arbiter, the paradigm of diocesan priesthood. Why not prayerfulness, conviction in the faith, knowledge of the faith, ability to communicate in the modern age, honesty, integrity, humility, a commitment to social justice, a work ethic, respect for others, compassion and caring? Surely many of these qualities are at least as important in a diocesan priest as celibacy – yet celibacy seems to be perceived as the predominant obligation, the *sine qua non*. Celibacy is an obligation that has caused many wonderful potential candidates to turn away from a vocation, and other fine men to resign their priesthood at great loss to the Church. The quality of some of those whom we have lost to the priesthood has always been a cause of great sadness for me. Some of the most heartbreaking moments during my years as bishop were when priests came to me saying they could no longer live a celibate life and wished to resign from the active priesthood.

I see and meet men who would potentially be fine priests – but the rule of celibacy causes or has caused them to consider other vocations. One of the finest lay men whom I have ever met, a man who served this country with huge distinction, once seriously contemplated the priesthood and decided to go in another direction solely because of the rule of celibacy. I am sure that he is merely one of many.

I ask, in all charity, is it not time for our Church to make a vocation to the priesthood possible and accessible for more men? Something needs to done and done urgently and I hope that senior members of the clergy and laity make their views more forcefully known, views that are often expressed privately but seldom publicly. The introduction of non-celibates into the priesthood would certainly not cure all our problems, but it should serve to ease them. Admission of married men to the priesthood could well create new problems and issues. However, under the guidance of the Holy Spirit, major decisions must be made. Vocations have not dried up. The faith has not dried up. The hope that is in Christ has not dried up. It is there, still in our midst. But preachers must be harvested to serve in this new millennium, priests drawn from our diocese to serve in our diocese. There is certainly an important and enduring place for celibate priesthood. But I believe that there should also be a place in the modern Catholic Church for a married priesthood and for men who do not wish to commit themselves to celibacy.

I retired as bishop in 1993, and it was shortly after that that the revelations of child sexual abuse by clergy and religious and the dreadfully inadequate response of too many of those in authority became a huge public issue in Ireland and elsewhere. I have to confess that I scarcely ever heard the term 'child sexual abuse' in relation to clergy until the late 1980s. I can only recall very few occasions when there was reference to it at meetings of the Irish Episcopal Conference during my time as a member. I cannot remember it being the subject of a major or protracted debate. I have not attended a meeting of the Conference since I retired. Since then, this has rightly become a hugely important and emotive issue.

I am deeply ashamed and profoundly shocked that there have been so many instances of child sexual abuse perpetrated by clergy and religious here in Ireland and worldwide. I have been heartbroken and appalled that colleagues in the priesthood could engage in such horrible criminal acts against the most vulnerable. It has brought about much soul searching. I am perplexed by it. It is a betrayal of the Christ whom these abusers purported to serve.

I have experienced at first hand the intense and furious anger of some victims and survivors and got some little understanding or sense of the long-term damage and suffering that child abuse can cause. I have offered my apologies and asked their forgiveness. The victims of such evil crimes have my sincere sympathy.

I have always been immensely proud of my calling and this has magnified the hurt caused by the revelations of recent years. Priests and bishops were and are in a unique position of trust. That trust has been seriously damaged. Priests and bishops must now redouble their efforts to regain and earn that trust and respect.

There has been a huge amount of discussion in the IEC on this problem during the years since I retired. Protection of the most vulnerable is now at the top of the agenda. The understanding of this issue and the response to it have evolved significantly since my time in office. As I have not been a participant in these discussions, I feel I cannot usefully comment further.

It has been an agonising time for the victims and I hope and pray that they receive the peace and justice that they so richly deserve.

Despite all its difficulties and human failings I still love the Catholic Church and the Catholic faith. I love the people, women and men, in parishes and I have great respect and affection for my fellow priests and bishops who serve them. I think that it is a wonderful community of fragile and sometimes broken people, saints and sinners, endeavouring and sometimes struggling to live the type of life that Jesus Christ taught and exemplified; a group of pilgrims on a journey. Our Christian faith gives us something to live for; a set of values to follow and sacraments that offer us grace and spiritual nourishment. At its best the Church is beautiful and inspiring. I am so grateful to God for my faith. It is the most precious gift I have. I could not live without it.

I still love the priesthood after all these years. It is a most meaningful way of life that gives me purpose and direction. It is a life of service, the service of preaching God's word, serving the people placed in one's pastoral care, administering God's sacraments, and carrying out the mandate that Christ first spoke about when he stood up and read that passage from Isaiah in the synagogue in Nazareth two thousand years ago. 'The spirit of the Lord has been given to me, for he has anointed me. He has sent me to bring the good news to the poor, to proclaim liberty to captives and to the blind new sight, to set the downtrodden free' (Luke 4:18).

The ministry of the diocesan priest is varied and challenging. It can be such an interesting, stimulating and fulfilling life. I consider myself greatly blessed to have been called to such ministry. In the later years of life, as one becomes more keenly aware of one's mortality, there comes a new appreciation of prayer and reflection and the comfort they bring and a new understanding of the gift of priesthood. Communication with the Lord takes on a new priority. It gives one new hope. The Church never stands still and has undergone much change over the centuries. There will be more change in the centuries ahead. Only Jesus and His teaching are constant.

CHAPTER 25

Final Thoughts

During my life I have been very fortunate to meet or speak with wonderful writers and storytellers. Communicators and the art of communication have always fascinated me.

I have a great love of Brian Friel's work. Many of his plays are superb and imaginative studies of communication and the difficulties of communication between different individuals, generations and groups. The language is magnificent. Brian lived a few hundred yards from me in Marlborough Street in Derry in the 1960s when he began his writing career. My rural background enables me to feel very much at home with his work. The location and background music seem so familiar. I can identify with the population of Ballybeg.

Another wonderful writer whom I have met in more recent years is the Liverpudlian, Jimmy McGovern. I met him when he was writing the script for the film *Sunday* (released in 2002), about the events of Bloody Sunday. I had admired his work in television drama for many years previously. He is the writer who created *Cracker* and many other highly successful and edgy television dramas. He sought truth and stressed the importance of conveying that. I spent many hours with him being interviewed when he was preparing the film script for *Sunday*. I greatly enjoyed the experience. Every statement was analysed and challenged. Eight years before the Saville Inquiry published its report, Jimmy McGovern told the story of Bloody Sunday on film with uncanny accuracy.

I have memories, too, of the late Leon Uris in the early 1970s, a different kind of writer, a writer of blockbusters. He spent three or four days walking around the Bogside with me when he was researching in preparation for his novel *Trinity*. He was a Jewish

American and had already written the bestselling novel *Exodus*. He was a most interesting individual, who equated the activists in the Bogside with the Zionists in Israel a few decades earlier.

Peter Taylor of BBC *Panorama*, in more recent years, made some fine and very courageous programmes and wrote books about various issues relating to the North, works that I greatly admired and appreciated. I met him on his first visit to the North, in Rossville Street in the Bogside, on the morning after Bloody Sunday. We have remained firm friends ever since then.

Historians, researchers, newspaper editors, academics, countless journalists, television and radio producers, students writing dissertations or theses, all passed through my life at one time or another – people like the brilliant *Sunday Times* Insight Team in the 1970s, Robert Fisk and Mary Holland, cartoonists like Paul Conrad* of the *Los Angeles Times*, all of them were interested in various aspects of the conflict here. I was fortunate to meet many excellent writers, seekers of the truth and perceptive observers of the scene.

So it is with a considerable amount of trepidation and sense of inadequacy that I have approached this attempt to write down my own recollections and my views on various issues, my observations on the various conflicts in my life in a turbulent time. I have largely depended on personal memory and checked this against archives and contemporary records. In the main, I have confined myself to writing about events and issues in which I had personal involvement or experience. It is a very subjective view of a tumultuous period in the life of the North and the life of the Catholic Church here in Derry and internationally. Not every reader will agree with me and what I have written. Not everyone will agree with my analysis or my views.

I believe that it is important to remember and to record the past precisely as one has experienced it. However, it is even more important to learn from the past and to strive to ensure that the dreadful cruelties and the sufferings of those decades will never again be repeated in our country.

---

* Paul won three Pulitzer Prizes. He died in 2010. In the early 1970s, I met him on a couple of occasions in Los Angeles and he gave me two autographed copies of his cartoons on the Northern Ireland situation. They occupy a prominent place in my study.

The experience of ministry in the Foyle Hospice in recent years has had a profound influence on me. Again and again, I have listened to hundreds of people as they shared and confided their memories and stories as they approached the end of life. I have come to a new appreciation of the importance of personal memory and the communication of those memories to others. Everyone has his or her unique story to tell.

This is my story.

Over the last fifty years, there have been good times and bad, but they have, at all times, been both challenging and fulfilling. I have travelled from the mayhem and savagery of the streets of the 1970s to the gentle, quiet and calm environment that I now experience. I have been privileged to meet so many people who edified me or horrified me, caused me to be uplifted or caused me to despair, people who interested me or entertained me and people who taught me so much about faith and life, people who showed me kindness and tolerance. I am deeply grateful to my sisters and my late brother, Tom. They have always stood by me. I am hugely indebted to my housekeeper, Betty Doherty. She has supported me and cared for me and tolerated me in sickness and in health for more than twenty years. She has been extraordinarily kind.

I am keenly aware of my own multitude of weaknesses and inadequacies, my impatience and my impetuosity. I give thanks to God today for his forgiveness, goodness and mercy to me over the past fifty years. God has been so generous to me. I ask forgiveness of those whom I have hurt by word, deed or omission. I thank my many friends in the laity, clergy and episcopate who have been so good and supportive to me.

I just hope that more people can have the opportunity to enjoy the sheer fulfilment of a similar experience of diocesan priesthood in the Catholic Church.

Index